D1274407

Building Neural Networks

Building Neural Networks

David M. Skapura

Brightware Corporation
and
Adjunct Faculty, School of Natural and Applied Sciences
University of Houston at Clear Lake

ACM Press
New York, New York

Addison-Wesley Publishing Company
Reading, Massachusetts • Menlo Park, California • New York
Don Mills, Ontario • Wokingham, England • Amsterdam • Bonn
Sydney • Singapore • Tokyo • Madrid • San Juan • Milan • Paris

Excerpt from STAR TREK © 1995 by Paramount Pictures.
All rights reserved. Reprinted with permission.

Quotation from Arthur C. Clarke excerpted from *Profiles of the Future and Inquiry Into the Limits of the Possible,* published in 1962 by Harper and Row Publishers, copyright 1962 by Arthur C. Clarke. Used with permission of the Scovil Chichak Galen Literary Agency Inc.

Sponsoring Editor: Peter S. Gordon
Associate Editor: Helen M. Goldstein
Production Supervisor: Nancy Fenton
Cover Designer: Diana C. Coe
Senior Manufacturing Supervisor: Roy E. Logan
Composition: Windfall Software (Paul C. Anagnostopoulos, Jacqueline Scarlott), using ZzTEX
Project Manager: Diane B. Freed

This book is published as part of ACM Press Books—a collaboration between the Association for Computing Machinery and Addison-Wesley Publishing Company. ACM is the oldest and largest educational and scientific society in the information technology field. Through its high-quality publications and services, ACM is a major force in advancing the skills and knowledge of IT professionals throughout the world. For further information about ACM, contact:

ACM Member Services
1515 Broadway, 17th Floor
New York, NY 10036-5701
Phone: 1-212-626-0500
Fax: 1-212-944-1318
E-mail: ACMHELP@ACM.org

ACM European Service Center
Avenue Marcel Thiry 204
1200 Brussels, Belgium
Phone: 32-2-774-9602
Fax: 32-2-774-9690
E-mail: ACM_Europe@ACM.org

Library of Congress Cataloging-in-Publication Data

Skapura, David M.
   Building neural networks / David M. Skapura.
      p.   cm.
   Includes bibliographical references and index.
   ISBN 0-201-53921-7
   1. Neural networks (Computer science)   I. Title.
QA76.87.S615   1996
006.3—dc20   94-39062
                                                   CIP

Many of the designations used by manufacturers and sellers to distinguish their products are claimed as trademarks. Where those designations appear in this book, and Addison-Wesley was aware of a trademark claim, the designations have been printed in initial caps or all caps.

Access the latest information about Addison-Wesley books from our Internet gopher site or from our World Wide Web page:
   gopher aw.com
   http://www.aw.com/

1 2 3 4 5 6 7 8 9 10–MA–99 98 97 96 95

P R E F A C E

The need for a book such as this one became apparent to me as a result of teaching neural-network theory to computer science graduate students at the University of Houston–Clear Lake and of advising practicing programmers. As part of that ongoing experience, I found that most people were able to grasp the concepts underlying the operation of the different networks in fairly short order, but when I asked them to *apply* the networks they had learned about toward solving a problem of their own choice, most of them had a great deal of difficulty constructing the application. The reason for this difficulty, I discovered, was that the network theory alone offered the student very little insight into what kind of applications the network could address, or how to go about formatting the application data for use by the network.

I then began a search for a book that would complement the theoretical presentation of neural-network operation with material describing the application of the networks to real-world problems. To my dismay, I could not find one that adequately described the process of building neural-network applications. It seems that those of us who earn our livelihood investigating neural networks and developing applications that utilize the technology have taken for granted the development process for new applications. We read about a network architecture or learning algorithm, and almost without consciously thinking about it, we see ways to apply the network to some problem we have not yet solved.

However, for the student or practitioner who does not yet have the benefit of experience working with connectionist models, the process of constructing an application is typically the most confusing part of utilizing a neural network. Even after a semester or two of studying the theory, most students do not fully comprehend the potential of a network, nor do they completely understand the limitations of each of the network models. For the working professional, who may not have time to attend formal classes in the theory underlying neural networks, the problem is even more profound.

Thus, anyone interested in learning about the practical applications of neural-network technology is faced with a quandary: The theory governing the operation of neural networks can be learned by studying any of the currently available textbooks, yet learning to successfully apply the technology is usually a trial-and-error process. It is to the resolution of this quandary that I have dedicated this book. My own experience teaching neural networks indicates that people learn best when shown numerous examples of how other people have applied the technology. If they can relate how a similar problem was solved using a neural network, the approach for the problem at hand becomes self-evident. The key, then, is to give readers plenty of examples, each in sufficient detail so that the student can assimilate the information and use the accumulated experience of others to create his or her own applications.

For this reason, I have written this book as a survey of many different neural-network applications as described in the literature. While researchers on the cutting edge of neural-network technology will likely find the examples described in this book simplistic, I have nevertheless deliberately restricted the applications to those that are easily understandable and recreatable by the novice practitioner. In almost every case, I have also elaborated on the details of the applications as they were originally described. I have done so in an attempt to illustrate why the original authors selected the network they did, to show how the application data were collected and formatted for the network, and to describe the interpretation of the output of the network. In some cases, I have described possible alternative approaches to the same application, to allow the reader to compare and contrast the different approaches.

This book is organized to allow the reader to examine application *areas*, without regard to specific network architectures or learning algorithms. I feel that this is probably the best method for allowing readers to compare the operation of the different network architectures, although it does force a certain amount of overlap in the content of the book. Hopefully, it will also convey an understanding of why certain networks are better suited to certain kinds of problems than others. To accommodate the wide variety of readers I anticipate for this book, I have divided the text into nine chapters; an introductory chapter to establish the principles of neural information processing, a review chapter in which I summarize the operation of the most popular neural network processing models, a chapter dedicated to the practical issues of application design, and six topic-oriented chapters. I have attempted to organize the book into a sequence where the information presented becomes progressively more difficult. However, each of the last six chapters is devoted to a specific topic that is relatively independent of the other five topic chapters. Thus, an instructor can tailor the material to suit the needs of a specific class. Entire chapters may be skipped without fear of missing background information on which later chapters depend.

For readers who may be unfamiliar with the different application areas described by the chapter titles, I offer the following chapter synopses:

- Chapter 1 is an introduction to information processing using neural networks. This chapter is intended to provide the reader with the information necessary to appreciate the operation of the various neural-network models. Beginning neural-network practitioners should read this chapter without fail, because much of the background for the remainder of the text is established here.

- Chapter 2 provides a review of the most popular neural network models, with an emphasis on the practical aspects of the technology. In this chapter, I have also attempted to show how the various models compare with each other, because many times the success of an application can be determined based on the selection of an appropriate neural-network model.

- Chapter 3 describes the process of engineering a neural-network application. In this chapter, I have provided a detailed overview of the critical issues of data formatting, network training, and performance evaluation. This chapter concludes with a detailed example of a practical neural-network application. Readers already comfortable with neural-network theory, but not the practical issues of application development, should therefore begin their studies here.

- Chapter 4 begins the discussion of real applications of the technology. In this chapter, I focus on networks that perform simple pattern matching, storage, and recall. Networks that exhibit these characteristics are typically used for applications where the input patterns (those that are presented after training) are noisy or incomplete.

- Chapter 5 contains a survey of business- and finance-related applications, where neural networks have been used for a variety of purposes, from forecasting stocks and bonds future values to performing credit risk assessment.

- Chapter 6 presents a survey of applications where the neural network is used to classify the input pattern presented to the network into one of several useful categories. Also covered in this chapter are the concepts of static and dynamic categorization, with example applications of each type.

- Chapter 7 describes applications of the technology where a neural network is used to extract meaningful information from image data to identify (and in some cases classify) familiar objects in the images. Most of the applications described in this chapter also illustrate how multiple networks can be linked together to perform different aspects of the image-recognition process.

- Chapter 8 focuses on applications where the neural network is used to control a mechanical process, with special attention paid to issues in robotic control. Also contained in this chapter is a brief review of process-control theory, for readers that may not be familiar with the traditional methods of system control.

- Chapter 9 describes a new type of neural network, combining the pattern-matching abilities of neural networks with the inexact reasoning power of fuzzy logic. After a brief introduction to the concepts underlying the operation of fuzzy-logic systems, this chapter describes the implementation of networks that may portend the future of neural-network technology.

I expect that the readers of this book will be primarily practicing engineers in industry who are interested in exploring the practical aspects of this exciting technology, or upper-level undergraduate or first year graduate students in an engineering or computer science discipline. Because of the emphasis on practical applications, this book can be used as part of a self-study program. In that regard, a strong background in mathematics is not essential to gain the maximum benefit from this book, although a good understanding of vector and matrix mathematics should be considered essential when dealing with neural networks.

Readers who are already familiar with the general concepts underlying neural-network theory can expect to use this book as a guide to developing successful applications of the technology. Readers with little or no understanding of neural networks should seriously consider augmenting the review material contained in Chapter 2 with a more theoretical text book. I highly recommend *Neural Networks: Algorithms, Applications, and Programming Techniques,* which I co-authored with Dr. James Freeman in 1991, because many of the ideas contained in this book originated, in part, from applications built by my students using our original text.

Because the emphasis of this book is on the practical application of neural-network technology, I have included a number of application-oriented exercises interspersed throughout the text. These exercises are designed to encourage the reader to consider the different aspects of the neural network that contribute to the successful solution of a problem in the application being described, or to reinforce the understanding of a technique used to model the application data for use by the network. In some cases, the solution to the exercises can only be found through a correct understanding of the operation of the network. For these problems, I have included an appendix to the book that describes the solution and how it can be found. In other cases, the solution is a matter of individual creativity, and a single *correct* solution does not exist. I must therefore rely on the class instructor to determine the correctness (or perhaps more correctly, the *appropriateness*) of the student's solution to these exercises.

For those readers interested in the application of neural networks, but not necessarily in the implementation of the code needed to simulate them, Addison-Wesley has graciously agreed to provide the reader with access to source code, written in C, needed to simulate most of the networks described in this book. Readers may obtain the source code for programs in this book at `http://www.aw.com/cseng/`. The reader need only download the code (and, for example problems, the application data files), compile it using any of the C compilers available commercially, and execute the program. The availability of these simulators provides another learning tool for the student, in that many of the applications described in the text can be recreated, verified, and tested by the reader, simply by providing the network simulator with the appropriate application data file. The network simulators also allow readers to quickly begin creating and testing applications of their own design by allowing them to concentrate on the appropriateness of the network solution, without having to concern themselves with the correctness of the simulator code.

Finally, there are many measures of success in the publishing industry. Many people judge the success of a book on the number of sales it produces. Others have a more qualitative assessment of success—such as how well the material is presented, or how closely the subject matter maps to a particular curriculum.

Personally, I will consider this book a success if my readers come away from this book with a new insight into how neural-network applications can be successfully developed. I hope that my enthusiasm for the technology carries over to you, and that some day I will get the chance to read about the successful applications created by my readers.

ACKNOWLEDGMENTS

This book exists because of the selfless efforts of many people—far too many to name here. The many students who acted as unwitting guinea pigs when exercises were tried in class, or those students who worked out the solutions to the in-class problem sessions contributed more to the quality of this text than they will ever know. However, there are a few people whose efforts went far beyond the call of duty, and I would like to formally thank those individuals for their help and cooperation.

First of all, there are a few of my students whose work was so superlative that their class projects or thesis work was incorporated as one of the applications in this text. Jean-Baptiste Enombo developed the concept and the working proto-type for the prostate cancer recognition application described in Chapter 6 as his masters thesis research project. Pratibha Rao Boloor and Libin Wu developed the computer diagnostic application described in Chapter 4 as their in-class project, and Ms. Boloor went on to incorporate the core of that application as part of her masters thesis research project.

Next, I owe a great debt to Dr. James Freeman, quite possibly one that I will never be able to repay. In many ways, Jim's efforts as mentor, counsel, friend, and critic contributed significantly to the quality of this text. He taught me almost everything I know about neural network technology, and, in ways he will probably never recognize, he pushed me to be better than I thought I was. It was through my collaboration with him on our first book that I recognized that I really could write professionally, and that I had something to contribute technically.

Then there are the people responsible for the actual publication of this book: Peter Gordon and Helen Goldstein, both with Addison-Wesley, decided to take a chance on an obscure author, and allowed me to solo on this project; Diane Freed, whose attention to detail makes reading this finished book easy, acted as publica-tion manager during the production efforts on the project; Nancy Fenton, with Addison-Wesley, managed the coordination of several different tasks (e.g., the cover design and the manuscript revisions); Paul C. Anagnostopoulos oversaw the composition of the book, and Jacqui Scarlott generated the page makeup from my original LaTeX source files and artwork; my copyeditor, Kathy McQueen, who no doubt tired of my use of the word "data" instead of "datum," converted my prose into proper English; and Diana C. Coe, who produced the outstanding cover art from my disorganized concept. Thank you all.

Finally, to Darlene, Danielle, and Devin, my wife and children, and my parents, Michael and Dorothy Skapura, I only hope that you know how much your love, support, and patience has meant to me while this book was being written. Words alone can never completely express my gratitude.

D. M. S.
Houston, Texas

C O N T E N T S

CHAPTER

Foundations

Any sufficiently advanced technology is indistinguishable from magic.

—Arthur C. Clarke

The publication of the three-volume set titled *Parallel Distributed Processing (PDP)* [6] in 1986 marked the beginning of the renaissance in neural-network technology. Originally a field that predated the digital computer by a decade, and one that received an enormous amount of attention in the 1960s, neural-network research dwindled to almost nothing after the publication of *Perceptrons* [5] in 1969 by Professors Marvin Minsky and Seymour Papert of the Massachusetts Institute of Technology (MIT). In their dissertation, Minsky and Papert analyzed the operation of the simple two-layer perceptron in great detail. Their analysis revealed many fundamental limitations of the two-layer, linear-threshold perceptron, and they further suggested that these limitations would naturally carry over into the more complex multilayer perceptron architectures.

In Volume I of *PDP*, Stanford University's David Rumelhart and his colleagues popularized a mathematically sound technique (originally described by Paul Werbos [7]) showing that multilayer perceptrons could indeed overcome the limitations Minsky and Papert had found with the two-layer perceptron. Moreover, they popularized the notion that there were other, perhaps more viable network architectures that could be successfully used to address complex pattern-recognition applications. The renewed interest in neural networks generated by the publication of *PDP* convinced government and independent research organizations to begin again their investigations into the potential of the connectionist networks. Subsequently, many research papers and textbooks were published describing a multitude of variations on the basic connectionist ideas popularized in *PDP*. Conferences were organized, and, by 1989, there were at least two professional societies chartered to act as a forum for neural-network researchers.

By 1991, neural networks had received such an enormous amount of attention that even people outside the research and development (R&D) community understood the significance of computers that could *learn* new things without having to be explicitly reprogrammed. As proof of this popular recognition, consider the fact that the main character in the most popular motion picture of 1991 spoke a line of dialogue indicating that his

"CPU is a neural net processor—a learning computer"

—and almost everyone who saw the film understood the technological significance of that comment. Currently, the character called "Data" in *Star Trek: The Next Generation* is portrayed as an android with the ability to learn via his "neural net" circuitry.

Yet, with all of the attention that neural networks have received in the last decade, there are still only a handful of commercially successful applications of the technology. Many people have heard of neural networks, yet relatively few, computer professionals and laypersons alike, have any concept of what they are or how to successfully apply them. Even university students, after having studied the theory of the technology for a semester or two, usually fail miserably in their first (several) attempts to build a neural-network application.

Why, then, are people so enthralled with neural-network technology? One of the primary reasons why neural networks are exciting is because the technology offers the promise of computer systems that can dynamically adapt to new situations. In every other form of programming, all the actions to be performed by the computing system, and the data structures that define the world model for the computer, must be explicitly and procedurally declared by a human programmer prior to execution on the computer. The programmer is therefore ultimately responsible for every aspect of the application. If something does not work as expected (or desired), it is the human programmer that must make the necessary changes to the application.

In contrast, neural networks only require that an application developer specify the appropriate network learning algorithm, define an interpretation for the *signals* that will be propagated through the network, and provide a set of application-specific data patterns that collectively represent the desired behavior of the network. The details of how an input pattern is transformed into an appropriate output pattern are determined by the network itself, which provides an information-processing architecture that is, by its nature, adaptive. The network *learns* the application data patterns by modifying a set of *weight* values contained in its internal structure. With each alteration, the knowledge contained by the network is modified. In some networks, a weight modification represents an increase in knowledge; in others, it represents a modification of the entire knowledge base. In either case, the ability to adapt to better accommodate new circumstances is what makes neural-network technology so intriguing.

Unfortunately, this approach to information processing is so radically different from the mainstream approach to computer programming that relatively few people understand the concepts underlying the operation of the neural-network paradigms that have thus far been defined. Even fewer have a deep understanding of the operation of the networks, a knowledge that must be considered essential if we are to create successful applications of the technology, and transition it into widespread, commercial use.

In subsequent chapters, we will review several of the most popular algorithms that govern the operation of the different network paradigms. We shall also explore how neural networks have been successfully applied to a variety of real-world problems. However, before we plunge into the details of the networks and their applications, let us first review some of the reasons why we should consider the use of neural networks as an information-processing technology, and how we might go about successfully building neural networks.

1.1 MOTIVATION

Computers are everywhere. It is now virtually impossible to function in modern society without interacting, in some manner, with a computer-controlled system. Computers perform most of our banking and financial transactions, they control the performance of most of our automobiles, they even control the operation of many of our household appliances. Computer technology is so pervasive that we have come to accept computers as an integral part of our everyday lives, perhaps without even realizing the extent of our dependence on them.

Why have computers had such a profound effect on our lives? From a practical perspective, the answer to this question lies in the old "biggest bang for the buck" adage. Modern computer technology is inexpensive, reliable, and, from our human perspective, extremely fast. Today, for example, an 8-bit microcontroller containing 16,384 bytes of memory (16 KB), that can execute upwards of half a million instructions every second, can be had for less than $5 each (in quantity). Given such a low cost for so much general-purpose capability, it should be no surprise to anyone that computers are now integrated into almost every new electronic control system devised.

However, for all the performance offered by these modern, electronic wonders, there remain many types of automation problems that conventional computer systems simply cannot address. These problems can be classified in several different ways; some are referred to as **nonpolynomial** (NP) problems, because the amount of time needed to solve such a problem, when implemented on a sequential processor, increases at a rate that cannot be expressed as a polynomial function of the size of the problem. Others are called **intractable,** meaning that the problems, by their nature, are extremely difficult to cast in terms of the conventional, Von-Neumann computer architecture. Examples of such problems include weather forecasting; vision and image interpretation; speaker-independent, connected-speech understanding; and cursive, handwritten character recognition.

It is interesting to note that, with the possible exception of weather forecasting, all of the example application areas cited are things that people do extremely well. So well, in fact, that, most of the time, we perform these *difficult* tasks without even being consciously aware that we are solving the problems. Moreover, we

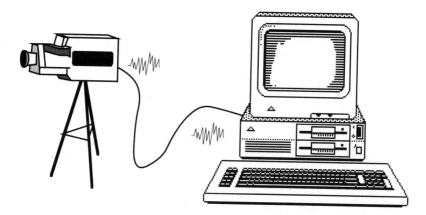

Figure 1.1   This diagram illustrates the use of video equipment to capture images for processing by a computer. Visible light is captured by the video camera, which converts the image into an analog, electrical signal that is transmitted to the video-acquisition subsystem. This *raster* signal is then subjected to an analog-to-digital conversion process that translates each resolvable point in the image into a binary number that indicates the luminescence (and color mapping, if appropriate) of the pixel. The matrix of digitized pixels is finally transferred to the computer for further processing.

solve these problems through the use of chemical-based switching components—*neurons*—that turn on and off at a maximum rate of about 1,000 times per second. Computers, however, are composed of electronic devices that can switch in excess of a *billion* times per second. So, why is it that people can instantaneously solve these difficult problems if computers that operate a million times faster cannot?

The answer to this question probably lies in the architectural differences between the human brain and the computer. The brain, while limited to operations measured in milliseconds, appears to be able to process a vast amount of information *in parallel*, while a computer, though much faster, usually processes all of its information sequentially. To put these differences in perspective, consider the process a serial computer must perform to simulate human vision.

Because a computer has no peripheral devices that can sense information in the visible spectrum of electromagnetic radiation, we can synthesize the operation of the human eyes through the use of video equipment. Visible light can be acquired by a video camera, digitized into a binary form, and arranged into a matrix of dots (also known as *picture elements,* or simply *pixels*) that a computer can process. Figure 1.1 illustrates just such an arrangement.

However, when the computer processes the digitized image information, it must, by the inherent structure of the machine, access the image data one pixel at a time. In order to make any sense of the image data, the computer must execute a program that somehow attempts to correlate the state of each pixel to the state of many surrounding pixels. The specific algorithm employed to analyze the image data, while not necessarily the same as the one we propose here, begins by scanning the entire image for edges, or areas of high contrast. Having found all discernible edges, the next step might be to eliminate those edges that do not abide by certain real-world constraints. Then, after all of the objects in the image have been outlined, the computer must attempt to *fill in* the objects by determining texture or simply identifying which objects might be opaque, which are translucent, and which are transparent. Finally, after the entire image has been processed, the computer can then attempt to classify the objects in the image to categories that are meaningful to the vision application.

Compare that process with how a neural network might process the same image. As depicted in Figure 1.2, a network composed of several layers of simple, analog processing elements receives the entire image in parallel at the input layer, after the image has been collected from the image-acquisition subsystem.[1] The image data are then distributed to other layers of processing elements by transmitting the information, again in parallel, through a set of *weighted connections* that modulate the image pattern. The receiving elements integrate the modulated input pattern, and respond with a single output signal that indicates the magnitude of the input stimulation received by each unit. The output from each unit on the layer is then propagated forward to the next layer in the same manner. This process repeats, layer by layer, until the final layer in the network has produced an output. Ultimately, it is this output layer that the vision-application program will interpret as the identification of the objects contained in the image data.

Note that, unlike the sequential approach we described for the conventional computer, a neural network can exploit the parallelism inherent in the video image. By its very nature, the amount of time needed to completely analyze all of the pixels in an image pattern is equivalent to the amount of time needed by a single processing element to generate an output from a steady-state input pattern, multiplied by the number of layers in the network. The time required to process an image does not vary with the number of objects in the image, nor does it change as a result of fluctuations in the ambient lighting. Rather, it is predetermined by the size and physical implementation of the network. Because our emphasis in this text is the practical implementation of applications based on these networks, let us now turn our attention to the computations performed by the network, to better understand how to go about successfully implementing our applications.

---

1. Neurobiology tells us that biological neural systems operate primarily in the frequency domain, with neural cells being stimulated by repetitive activation of neighboring cells. Our models, however, operate primarily (although not exclusively) as spatial-pattern classifiers, with patterns being represented by signal amplitude.

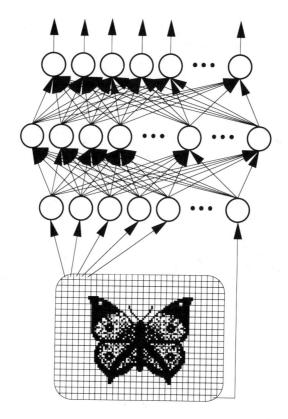

Figure 1.2 This diagram illustrates how a layered neural-network structure could be used to process a video-image pattern. In this diagram, each node in the network represents a single processing element, and each arc represents a weighted connection. In this example, each pixel from the display image is interpreted as an input signal to one processing element on the input layer. Signals from the input layer are then propagated to all the elements on the subsequent layer through the weighted connections between the elements. The arrowhead on each arc is used to indicate the normal direction of information flow through the network.

1.2   NEURAL-NETWORK FUNDAMENTALS

In general, a neural network is a collection of simple, analog signal processors, connected through links called **interconnects,** or simply **connections.** Schematically, a neural network is represented in the form of a directed graph, where the nodes represent the processing elements, the arcs represent the modulating connections, and arrowheads on the arcs indicate the normal direction of signal flow. As shown in Figure 1.3, the processing elements are usually grouped together into a layered structure known as a **slab,** or **layer,** where each processing element on

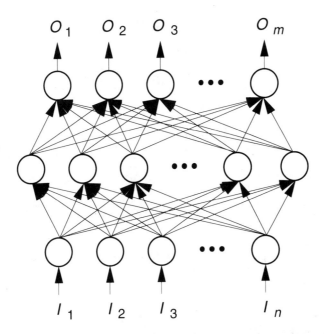

Figure 1.3 The general structure of a layered, feed-forward neural network is shown. In this diagram, the signals representing the input pattern vector are applied to the input connections on the bottom layer. Similarly, output signals from the network are transmitted to the outside world through the connections from the top layer. For clarity, we will henceforth omit the input and output connections to the network, because these connections do not alter the signals applied to them.

each layer performs an analog integration of its inputs to determine its **activation** value.

Processing begins with the entire network in a quiescent state. An external pattern, comprised of a set of signals to be processed by the network, is then applied to the input layer, where each signal stimulates one of the processing elements on the input layer. Each processing element on the input layer generates a single output signal, with a magnitude that is a function of the total stimulation received by the unit. Collectively, the outputs produced by all of the processing elements on the layer are then passed on as the input pattern to the subsequent layer of processing elements. This process is repeated, until the final layer of processing elements has produced an output for the current input-pattern vector.

While there are many variations on this general neural network processing model, it is easy to see that the macroscopic behavior of the network is determined by the microscopic behavior of the individual processing elements. For that reason, let us now focus our attention on the operation of the processing element.

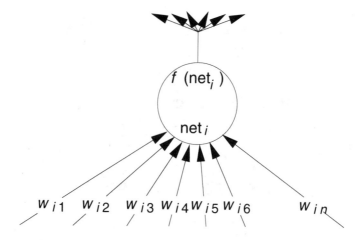

Figure 1.4   A typical processing element is shown. Notice that each input connection to the unit has a *weighting value* associated with it, and that the unit produces a single output that is transmitted to many other processing elements.

1.3   SINGLE NEURON COMPUTATIONS

Figure 1.4 illustrates the "typical" model of a neural-network processing element (also known interchangeably as a *node,* or *unit*). At its input, the unit behaves like an analog integrator, where *modulated* input signals are combined to form an aggregate input signal to the unit. An important aspect of our typical unit is the notion that both the magnitude and the polarity of the input signals contribute to the net input received by a network unit. In this manner, we provide a mechanism whereby input signals can have a relatively large or small, excitatory or inhibitory effect on the unit.

In some neural-network paradigms, like the early McCulloch-Pitts [4] model, units are defined such that a single inhibitory input signal is sufficient to squelch the output from the unit, independent of the total excitatory input. Because most of the current neural-network models forego that approach, we will focus our attention on units that combine their inputs in direct proportion to the stimulation signal driving the connection.

In a truly analog system, each unit would operate continuously on its inputs. However, in order to facilitate the simulation of these networks on a digital computer system, we shall model the behavior of the unit as though it operates in discrete time. As we have already indicated, each unit receives input stimulation from a variety of other units, with the notable exception of the input layer, which receives inputs from only one source. In either case, the computation performed by the unit to determine its input stimulation is almost always the same: The signal driving each connection is modulated (multiplied) by the weighting value of the connection, and each modulated input is then integrated (algebraically summed) by the unit to produce the stimulation signal to the unit.

The calculations needed to perform the input computation described above for each unit i in the network at time t are given by the equation

$$\text{net}_i(t) = \sum_{j=1}^{n} w_{ij}(t)o_j(t) \tag{1.1}$$

where the term $\text{net}_i(t)$ represents the net input signal to the ith unit in the network, $o_j(t)$ represents the output from the jth unit in the network, the term $w_{ij}(t)$ represents the weighting value associated with the connection that runs *from* the jth unit *to* the ith unit, and the value n represents the number of other units connected to the input of the ith unit.

Using this model, we can see the similarity between the input computation performed by the network unit and a vector *inner-product* computation. Specifically, if we consider the set of input signals to a unit as a vector, $\mathbf{o}$, having dimension n, and we consider the input connection weight values to the unit i as another vector, $\mathbf{w}_i$, also of dimension n, then the input calculation performed by the unit is analogous to the equation

$$\text{net}_i = \mathbf{o} \cdot \mathbf{w}_i \tag{1.2}$$

$$= \|\mathbf{o}\| \, \|\mathbf{w}_i\| \, \cos(\theta) \tag{1.3}$$

where θ represents the angle between the two vectors in n-dimensional Euclidian space.

At this point in our discussion, it is useful to recall the mathematical implications of the inner product. As shown in Figure 1.5, the inner product between two vectors in n-dimensional hyperspace is a measure of the *projection* of one vector onto the other. In many of the neural-network applications we will discuss in subsequent chapters, we will find this vector analogy useful in understanding the behavior of the network. We shall therefore consider patterns of signal activity within a network as *pattern vectors,* and connection weight values to individual units as *weight vectors.*

1.3.1 Neuron Activation

Referring again to Figure 1.4, the next step after determining the input stimulation received by the unit is to convert the input value to an **activation value** (or simply, **activation**). The activation of a unit is analogous to the degree of excitation of the unit. The stronger the activation, the more likely the unit is to excite (or inhibit) other units in the network. Typically, a unit determines its activation directly from its input stimulation, according to the general equation

$$a_i(t) = F_i(a_i(t-1), \text{net}_i(t)) \tag{1.4}$$

This formulation allows us to account for the fact that the activation of the unit is always an explicit function of the net input to the unit at the current time

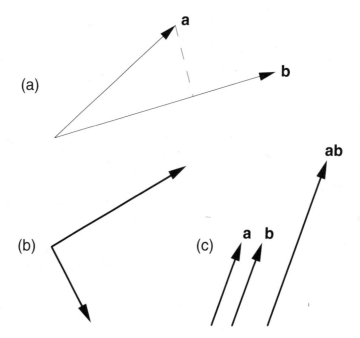

Figure 1.5   The projection of one vector onto another is shown. (a) The projection of vector **a** onto **b** in n-space. (b) Orthogonal vectors have an inner product equal to zero, meaning that no part of one vector projects onto the other. (c) Parallel vectors produce an inner product that equals the product of the magnitude of the two vectors.

$(\text{net}_i(t))$, while also allowing us to account for the fact that it may also depend on the activation of the unit at the previous time step, as denoted by the $a_i(t-1)$ term.

In most cases, the activation of the unit is equivalent to the current input; that is,

$$a_i(t) = \text{net}_i(t) \tag{1.5}$$

1.3.2   Activation Functions

Once the activation of the unit is known, the unit produces an output signal that is related to its activation by a transfer function known as the **activation function.** Expressed mathematically,

$$o_i(t) = f_i(a_i(t)) \tag{1.6}$$

$$= f_i(\text{net}_i(t)) \tag{1.7}$$

where Eq. (1.7) is a more intuitive formulation of Eq. (1.6), but is only valid when Eq. (1.5) holds.

The specific form of the activation function used by a unit is dependent on several factors, including

- The type of network containing the unit.
- The function being performed by the unit.
- The external interpretation of the output of the network.

The networks that form the basis of the applications we will study in all subsequent chapters share many general characteristics, yet each is also unique in terms of how it behaves with respect to certain kinds of applications. Because our objective in this chapter is to establish a strong foundation for the applications-oriented studies we will pursue in later chapters, we shall begin by focusing on the basics of neural-network operation.

Because of the important role played by activation functions in the various neural-network paradigms, we shall now describe the details of the most popular (and versatile) activation functions.

1.3.2.1   The Linear Unit

The linear unit is a very straightforward processing element—basically, the sum of everything that comes in to the unit is what goes out. Expressed mathematically

$$f_i^l(\text{net}_i(t)) = \text{net}_i(t) \tag{1.8}$$

where the superscript l is used here to indicate the linear activation function.

Units exhibiting this kind of response play several important roles in neural-network applications, including use as

- Fan-out units, where a single input signal must be distributed unaltered to many other processing elements. The application of such a device can be seen in the input layer of the general network structure described earlier in this chapter.
- A linear combiner, where many input signals must be integrated in a coherent manner. Applications of this device include linear pattern interpolation and pattern multiplexing.
- An analog output device, where the signal produced by the unit is to be interpreted by either another network unit or by the outside world as a continuously variable indicator.

Because of its versatility, the linear function is one of the most often used neural-network activation functions. We will see many applications of the linear unit in subsequent chapters, where these units are used in all three of the capacities described above.

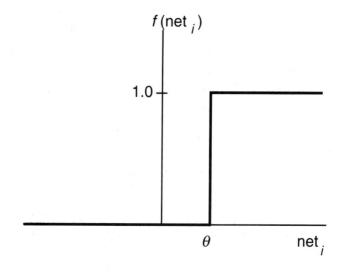

Figure 1.6   The response of a binary-threshold unit is shown. In this diagram, the output from the unit can be in one of two possible states. The transition region, which is shown here as the vertical line between the two states, is depicted only to indicate the transition point between states.

1.3.2.2   Binary-Threshold Units

A binary-threshold unit, as its name implies, is a unit that has two stable states—essentially active or inactive. The activation function used to impart this behavior to a unit is given by the equation

$$f_i^{bt}(\text{net}_i(t)) = \begin{cases} 1 & \text{if net}_i(t) > \theta \\ 0 & \text{otherwise} \end{cases} \tag{1.9}$$

where the term θ is used here to represent the point of transition between the two states. In many neural-network paradigms, θ is set to zero, in which case the unit becomes a polarity detector. If the input activation is positive (greater than zero) the unit *fires*, and produces an active output. In any other case, the output from the unit is inhibited (set to zero), indicating the absence of sufficient stimulation in the input to overcome the threshold. In Figure 1.6, we have graphed the response of this activation function with respect to the input stimulation received by the ith unit.

Neural-network units that exhibit this behavior are typically used to detect the presence (or absence) of *features* in the input pattern presented to the unit. For example, consider the binary-threshold unit illustrated in Figure 1.7. Looking at the weighting values associated with each of the input connections, you can see that the unit will only respond with a positive output when input signals two and four are active *simultaneously,* while input signal three is not active. We can

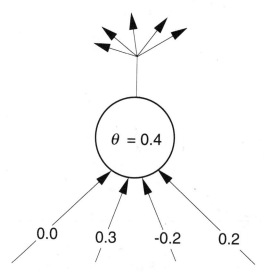

Figure 1.7 This diagram illustrates how a binary-threshold unit can act as a feature detector. The operation of the unit is described in the text.

therefore interpret a positive response from this unit as an indication that features two and four are present in the input pattern, while feature three is absent.

1.3.2.3 Sigmoidal Units

Sigmoidal units operate in a manner similar to the binary-threshold units described in the previous section. Like the binary-threshold units, sigmoidal units produce an output signal that has two stable states and a transition region. The difference between sigmoidal and binary-threshold units is that sigmoidal units are mathematically *continuous,* and therefore differentiable. There are many functions that can be used to model a sigmoidal response curve: The two most commonly used formulations are given by the equations

$$f_i^s(\text{net}_i(t)) = \frac{1}{1 + e^{-(\text{net}_i(t) - \theta)/\tau}} \tag{1.10}$$

and

$$f_i^{s*}(\text{net}_i(t)) = \frac{1}{2}(1 + \tanh(\lambda \text{net}_i(t)) \tag{1.11}$$

Eq. (1.10) is the most general formulation for the sigmoidal function, because we can control both the point of transition and the shape of the curve by varying the values of θ and τ. It also has the benefit of being computationally less expensive than the formulation of Eq. (1.11). However, Eq. (1.11) also allows us

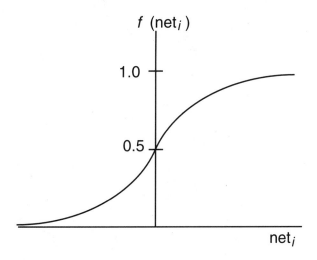

Figure 1.8   The response of a sigmoidal unit is shown. Notice the smooth S shape of the curve. The continuous response exhibited by this activation function makes it a natural choice for networks that employ the use of derivatives to minimize error.

to control the shape of the curve by varying the independent gain parameter, λ. This function is used in some specialized networks where the gain required must be determined empirically for the application.

In either case, the response of a unit that utilizes the sigmoidal activation function is illustrated in Figure 1.8. Notice the similarity between the sigmoidal function and the binary-threshold function shown earlier in Figure 1.6:

- Both activation functions have two regions where significant variations in input do not drastically alter the output produced by the unit.

- The width of the transition region in both functions is negligible when compared to the width of the stable regions.

- In both functions, the transition region tends to exist around zero activation, although it can be shifted left or right by modifying the value of θ in Eq. (1.10).

As in the case of the binary-threshold unit, sigmoidal nodes are typically used as feature detectors and for purposes of pattern classification. In these applications, the output from a sigmoidal unit is interpreted in the same manner as an output from the binary-threshold unit: An active output is interpreted as an indication of the presence of a specific combination of features in the input pattern, while an inactive output usually indicates the absence of those features.

However, do not make the mistake of assuming that a sigmoidal unit is merely a differentiable form of a binary-threshold unit. The continuous nature of the sigmoidal function also creates a situation that can cause confusion about what the unit is actually classifying. To illustrate this point, recall our previous

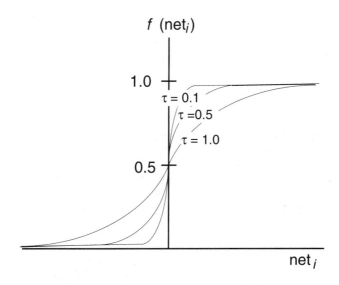

Figure 1.9 The graph of the sigmoid function for different values of τ is shown. Notice that as τ approaches zero, the sigmoid becomes deterministic, because there is no stochastic element to the function value.

discussion of the binary-threshold unit, where we indicated that there were two valid states for the output signal: an active and inactive state that we could interpret as an indication of the presence or absence of some set of features in the input pattern. With the sigmoidal activation function, we are allowing a third possible state for the output of a unit—an undefined state somewhere between active and inactive.

To clarify this concept, consider again the response curve illustrated in Figure 1.8. Notice that because the sigmoidal function is continuous, a unit that uses the sigmoid-activation function can generate any real output value between its minimum (0.0) and maximum (1.0) limits. Because our objective is to classify the input into one of two valid states, we shall interpret an output from the sigmoidal unit that has a value greater than 0.8 as an active output, while we consider an output value less than 0.2 as an inactive output. Output values that fall between 0.2 and 0.8 will be considered *in transition.*

Now, consider the output produced by the sigmoidal unit when the entire input pattern is inactive (numerically zero). Zero stimulation, modulated by any weighting value, produces zero activation. Yet, zero activation to a sigmoidal unit produces an output of 0.5, halfway between our valid output states. This kind of response is counterintuitive, because most of the time we would expect the absence of *all* features in the input to result in an inactive output from the unit.

As we mentioned earlier, we can change the effect of the transition region on the behavior of the sigmoidal unit by changing the value of τ. Figure 1.9 shows the effect of τ on the sigmoidal function.

We will explore the ramifications of this behavior further in Chapter 2, when we begin our discussions of network paradigms. For now, we shall continue our analysis of activation functions with a discussion of competitive units.

1.3.2.4 Competitive Units

The **outstar** [3] is a dynamical unit that, in most network simulations, behaves like a unique form of the binary-threshold unit. Like the binary-threshold unit, it typically has only two stable states[2]—active (which we represent numerically with a value of one) and inactive (indicated by a value of zero). When active, the outstar transmits a *memory pattern,* described by the weight values stored in the output connections from the unit, to the subsequent layer of units. Similarly, when inactive, the outstar contributes nothing to the next layer.

By itself, the behavior of the outstar is interesting, but it is not very useful. A unit that can produce memory patterns has little practical value unless we can somehow incorporate the ability to selectively activate multiple outstars. We accomplish this selectivity by combining the outstar function with another neural device called, appropriately enough, the **instar.** The instar complements the outstar, in that instars are excited only by specific input patterns. Moreover, units on a layer of instars can *compete* among themselves whenever a new input pattern is present. The competition can be thought of as a selection process. By associating a specific outstar with each instar, and then allowing each instar to excite its corresponding outstar only upon winning the competition, we will have constructed a network capable of storing, and selectively recalling, output memory patterns that are associated with specific input patterns.

As you can probably tell from this discussion, the process of determining the winner of the competition occurs locally during the input-activation calculation. If we were concerned with designing truly analog neural networks, the design of the network would have to account for the competition among units as part of the activation of each competitive unit. For the purpose of describing applications,[3] however, we can account for any conceptual differences between competitive instars and the general unit through the implementation of the activation function of the outstar. Also, rather than trying to continue distinguishing the function of the instars and the associated outstars, we will henceforth simplify our discussion by referring to the combined function as a *competitive unit.*

The general form of the activation function used by the competitive unit is given by the equation

$$f_i^c(\text{net}_i(t)) = \begin{cases} 1 & \text{if net}_i(t) = \max\{\text{net}_j(t)\}, \ 1 \le j \le n \\ 0 & \text{otherwise} \end{cases} \qquad (1.12)$$

---

2. Being a dynamical unit, the behavior of the outstar is governed by a difference equation that describes not only the continuously variable output from the unit but the dynamic learning law as well. We have simplified the discussion of the unit here to illustrate its practical value as a memory device once training has been completed.

3. Applications that will be, at least initially, *simulated* on digital computers.

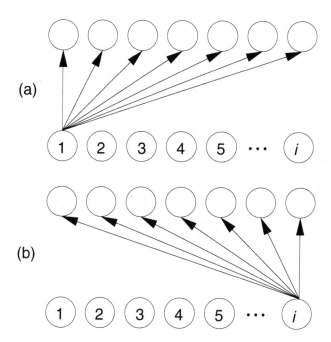

Figure 1.10   The process of accessing memory patterns is shown. (a) Unit 1 wins the competition, and sends its memory pattern to the output layer. (b) When unit i wins the competition, the output from the network becomes the memory pattern stored in the connections between unit i and the output layer.

Inspection of Eq. (1.12) tells us that, for all n units on a competitive layer, only competitive unit i (the one with the largest activation, and therefore the winner of the competition) will fire, while all the other units on the layer will remain inactive. By itself, this behavior means that for any input pattern applied to a layer of competitive units, one unit[4] will dominate the others and it alone will generate an active output.

To see how this behavior might be used to perform a useful function, consider the network structure depicted in Figure 1.10. As illustrated in the diagram, we have allowed a layer of competitive units to feed a layer of linear units. Now recall the operation of a linear unit: The output produced by the unit is the sum of all the modulated inputs it receives. If only one competitive unit activates for any input pattern applied to the layer, the linear units are each receiving only one active input signal—the one connected to the winning unit on the layer of competitive units—while receiving no activation from any of the other competitive

---

4. Usually, but not always, a different unit for each different input pattern.

units. Thus, the layer of linear units has become a **pattern multiplexer,** producing an output pattern that is *exactly* equal to the pattern stored in the connection weights between the linear layer and the winning competitive unit.

Viewed from this perspective, the connections between the competitive layer and the linear layer become a **pattern memory,** each connection storing one component of one pattern. Using this kind of network structure, with a layer of n competitive units feeding a layer of m linear units, we have the ability to store and recall n, m-dimensional pattern memories, each one accessed by activating one and only one of the competitive units. In several of the applications we will discuss in subsequent chapters, this type of pattern storage is critical to the successful operation of the network.

There is, however, another interesting facet to the operation of the competitive unit; namely, **linear interpolation.** Suppose we were to modify the activation function of the competitive unit to allow two or more units to win the competition and generate an output. Suppose, further, that we modified the activation function for competitive units to make the output from each winning unit proportional to the activation of the unit with respect to the activation received by all winning units.

Specifically, let

$$\mathbf{X} = \{X_i | X_i \in \mathrm{R}, \, 1 \le i \le n\}$$

and

$$\mathbf{Y} = \{Y_i | Y_i = \max\{\mathbf{X} - \mathbf{Y}\}, \, 1 \le i \le w, \, w \le n\}$$

where we will interpret $\mathbf{X}$ as the set of activations in the competitive layer of n units, and $\mathbf{Y}$ as the subset of $\mathbf{X}$ containing the largest w values from $\mathbf{X}$. These equations, while somewhat confusing in their form, are actually quite simple in their function: We are simply recursively extracting the largest w values from $\mathbf{X}$ and placing them in subset $\mathbf{Y}$ by first eliminating the values already extracted from $\mathbf{X}$, then finding the largest value in what remains, and adding that value to the subset $\mathbf{Y}$.

Thus, to achieve the desired interpolation response from the competitive layer, we merely change the activation function of the competitive units to

$$f_i^i(\mathrm{net}_i(t)) = \begin{cases} \frac{\mathrm{net}_i(t)}{\mathrm{net}_{\Sigma w}(t)} & \text{if } \mathrm{net}_i(t) \in \mathbf{Y} \\ 0 & \text{otherwise} \end{cases} \tag{1.13}$$

where

$$\mathrm{net}_{\Sigma w}(t) = \sum_{j=1}^{W} Y_j$$

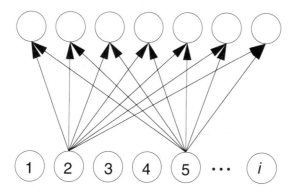

Figure 1.11 Interpolation by competitive units is shown. In this example, units 2 and 5 have won the competition with almost identical activations. The linear units act as pattern integrators, combining the two pattern vectors being sent from the competitive layer into a linear interpolation between the patterns.

To illustrate how the interpolation function works, consider the two-layer network structure illustrated in Figure 1.11. Here, as in Figure 1.10, the layer of linear units acts as a pattern integrator. The difference in this example is that now there are multiple competitive units sending pattern memories to the output. Moreover, each pattern memory is being attenuated by an output signal that has been diminished by an activation relative to the total activation from all other winning units.

In this example, the output produced by the linear units will be a linear interpolation among the patterns stored in the connection weights that run from the winning competitive units to the linear units. If the pattern memories stored in the network represent a continuous mathematical function, the integration of the patterns represents a linear interpolation among the memory patterns.

We can also view the pattern interpolation as a vector average. As shown in Figure 1.12, the linear units combine the pattern vectors sent from the competitive layer into a resultant vector that represents the average pattern from the competitive units. This kind of behavior is very useful when performing best-approximation applications, where it is desirable to produce an output pattern that is interpolated between the r output patterns associated with the r input patterns that most closely match the current input pattern.

1.3.2.5 Gaussian Units

Units that employ a Gaussian activation function are used primarily in applications where it is desirable to *classify* input patterns into one of several predefined classes. Like the other network units that we have already investigated, Gaussian

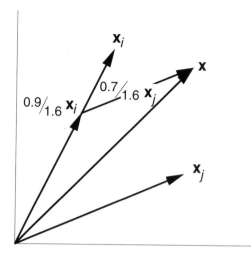

Figure 1.12   The interpolation process among pattern vectors is shown. In this diagram, vectors $\mathbf{x}_i$ and $\mathbf{x}_j$ represent the two pattern vectors stored in the output connections from winning outstars i and j. If unit i wins the competition with a total activation of 0.9, and unit j finished second with an activation of 0.7, the resultant vector $\mathbf{x}$ is

$$\left(\frac{0.9}{0.9 + 0.7} \right) \mathbf{x}_i + \left(\frac{0.7}{0.9 + 0.7} \right) \mathbf{x}_j$$

units convert their input activation into an output signal by applying an activation function to the input. Unlike the other types of units that we have studied, Gaussian units are not necessarily output limited.

Let us now consider the form of a typical Gaussian activation function

$$f_i^g(\text{net}_i) = e^{\frac{\text{net}_i - 1}{\sigma^2}} \tag{1.14}$$

where, as before, net_i represents the net input to the unit, and the term σ is a smoothing parameter. The form of this function is shown in Figure 1.13 for values of net_i in the range between -1 and 1.

We can observe from the graph of the Gaussian activation function that there is a very narrow range of input values that will allow the unit to generate an active output. In this case, any input value from approximately 0.5 to $-\infty$ will be quickly squelched, while inputs above 0.5 will cause the unit to quickly saturate. In this manner, the Gaussian unit acts like a filter, allowing only input patterns that produce activations within a very narrow range to pass, while effectively cancelling all other inputs.

Consider the behavior of this unit in a neural network. Because each unit on a layer is typically excited by a number of connections coming from another layer,

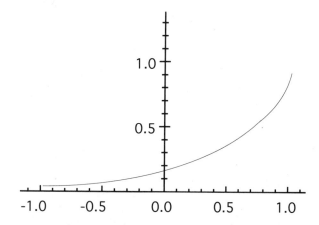

Figure 1.13   This graph shows the form of a Gaussian activation function. Because this is an exponential function, the output is limited only by the value of the input. Units that employ this activation function must therefore be designed to ensure that their input value never exceeds one.

the pattern contained in the input connections to the unit act as a **tuner.** When the layer feeding the Gaussian unit produces an output pattern that matches the pattern contained in the input connections to the Gaussian (in an inner-product sense), the Gaussian detects the match and generates a signal indicating that the match occurred. Conversely, when the output pattern from the layer feeding the Gaussian is significantly different from the pattern contained in the input connection weights, the Gaussian produces no output, indicating the input was not successfully matched.

1.4   NETWORK COMPUTATIONS

In the previous section, we saw how each unit in the network behaves. Now, let us turn our attention to the *macroscopic* behavior of a network consisting of these processing elements. In the brief summary that follows, we shall see how, collectively, a network can perform computations that are beyond the capability of any single processing element.

As an illustration of network computation, consider the network shown in Figure 1.14. For the sake of clarity, we shall assume that prior to any pattern presentation, the network is quiescent. Further, we assume that each processing element in this example network operates according to the following two-step algorithm:

1.   When an input signal is present, the ith unit computes its activation, $a_i(t)$, using Eqs. (1.1) and (1.5). Specifically,

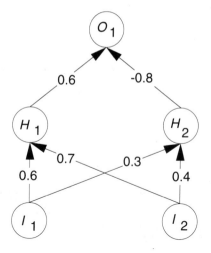

Figure 1.14   This diagram shows how a neural network can be made to perform complex pattern transformations. The details of this process are described in the text.

$$a_i(t) = \text{net}_i(t) = \sum_{j=1}^{n} w_{ij}(t)o_j(t) \qquad \textbf{(1.15)}$$

2.   When the activation, $a_i(t)$, is known, the unit produces an output according to the activation function

$$f_i(a_i(t)) = \begin{cases} 1 & \text{if } a_i(t) \geq 0.5 \\ 0 & \text{otherwise} \end{cases}$$

If we examine the configuration of the network based on the weighting values of the connections, we now observe several interesting facts about the behavior of the network. For example,

- If the input signals are assumed to be binary (0 or 1 only), the units on the input layer act as noise filters for the input signals. Only input signals that are above the 0.5 threshold point are admitted. Signals below the threshold point are eliminated.

- The middle, or hidden, layer of units act as *feature detectors,* activating only in response to certain conditions at the output of the input layer. In this example, unit H_1 detects the condition that *either* input unit is active, while unit H_2 responds only when *both* input units are active simultaneously.

- The output layer, which, in this case, consists of only one unit, is performing a logical conjunction between the features detected by the hidden-layer units.

Based on these observations, we can express the output of the network in this example as a Boolean function of the input signals to the network. Namely,

$$o(t) = (a(t-2) + b(t-2)) \cdot \overline{(a(t-2) \cdot b(t-2))}$$
$$= a(t-2) \oplus b(t-2)$$

where the notation $o(t)$ is used to represent the output signal from unit o at time t. Similarly, $a(t-2)$ and $b(t-2)$ are used to represent the input signals to the network, a and b two time steps earlier. Assuming that we interpret the input and output signals from this network as binary patterns, we can see that the network is performing a logical *exclusive-or* (XOR) operation on its inputs.

Perhaps more importantly, this example illustrates how we can use a neural network to perform complex functions *in parallel*. In the XOR network of Figure 1.14, the hidden-layer units are acting as feature detectors. If each processing element in the network is, in fact, a discrete processor, we can see that the two units on the hidden layer are operating on the same data[5] at the same time. Hence, the amount of time required to detect two features in the input pattern is equivalent to the amount of time it takes *one* of the units to compute its activation and generate an output.

We can extend this notion of parallelism indefinitely. For example, imagine another network designed to perform a function similar to, but significantly more complex than the XOR function. Suppose the input pattern vector in this new application contains 10,000 input elements, rather than just two. By understanding the process of pattern **propagation** through the simple XOR network, we can surmise that a larger network could operate fundamentally the same way. The only difference between these two example networks is in the complexity of their respective tasks: Rather than detecting the occurrence of only two features in the input pattern, the larger network can detect *thousands* of features in the input pattern. Moreover, if each processing element on each layer operates in parallel with every other unit on the same layer, the time required to detect all pertinent features in any pattern is reduced to the propagation time of just *one* unit.

1.5   NETWORK SIMULATION

If we were to construct networks of analog processors that had variable interconnection weights to communicate information among themselves, the amount of time needed to completely propagate patterns through the network would be very short—essentially unit time. In fact, several such devices exist. Some use optical methods for implementing the interconnections, while others use conventional electronic schemes. No matter which approach is taken, though, such implementations are almost always application specific. By committing the interconnection scheme to silicon (or to volume holograms), the structure of the network itself becomes fixed. Often, such a restriction is not an issue once an application has been completed. In the early stages of application design, however, when the network

---

5. The output pattern vector from the input layer of nodes.

is learning the desired behavior, it is almost always necessary to modify (or completely redesign) a network to achieve better results. Thus, in the early stages of application development, it is preferable to have a *soft* network architecture, one that can be changed rapidly in both network size and learning method.

This desire for flexibility can be accommodated by network *simulators*—programs that run on conventional computers that cause the computer to mimic the behavior of the simple, analog processors that comprise the network. In software, the network structure is modeled in memory, allowing easy alteration. The network paradigm—the algorithm that governs the operation of the processing elements within the network and, ultimately, the behavior of the network itself—is simply a computer program that is performed repetitiously.

As an illustration of how a software simulator works, consider the generic neural-network structure depicted in Figure 1.15, and the algorithm needed to simulate that network structure on a conventional computer:

```
Locate the input layer structure in memory.
Copy the input pattern into the output of the input layer.
For each layer from the first non-input layer to the output,
   For each unit on the current layer,
      Set the accumulated input value for this unit to zero.
      For each input connection to this unit,
         Compute the modulated input across this connection.
         Add the modulated input to the accumulated input.
      End loop.
      Convert the accumulated input to its corresponding output.
      Store the output value for the unit in the layer structure.
   End loop.
End loop.
Return the output values from the top-most layer structure.
```

A software simulator for a neural network allows an application developer to rapidly construct different neural networks, and test the behavior of each network on specific problems. However, there are also two significant issues that must be addressed when relying on software for simulating these networks. These issues are

- *Memory consumption.* Each connection in the network is usually modeled as one or more floating-point numbers in the simulation program. At ten bytes of memory per 80 bit floating-point number, and as many as three floating-point variables that must be allocated per connection in the network, the amount of memory needed to construct a neural-network simulation grows geometrically with the number of processing elements in the network.

- *Simulation time.* The input to each processing element in the network is normally computed by performing a floating-point multiply and a floating-point addition for each input connection attached to the unit. Given the combinatorial relationship between connections and processing elements, the amount

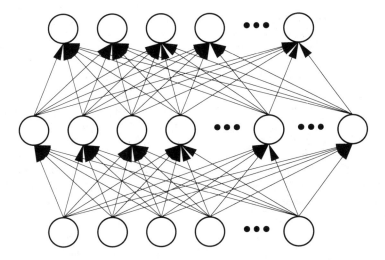

Figure 1.15   The structure of a multilayer, feed-forward network is illustrated. Notice that the number of connections needed to construct this network grows geometrically with the number of processing elements in the network. To simulate this structure on a computer, each connection weight must be stored in computer memory, as must the output signal produced by each processing element in the network. The algorithm that must be executed by a computer to simulate the signal flow through the network is described in the text.

of computer time needed to simulate even rather small networks (networks containing fewer than 10,000 connections) can rapidly overwhelm the host processor.

While these issues present a problem for simulating large neural networks, they are usually not insurmountable—one merely finds a higher-performance computer on which to run the simulator if the network grows too large. Moreover, from an application-development perspective, the flexibility attainable through the use of software usually more than compensates for the problem of finding a host computer with enough power and online memory to simulate the network.

When an application is completed to the point where no additional "tweaks" need to be made to the network, the network can be deployed in either its software form or by migrating the network to one of the previously mentioned neural-network devices. As a software implementation, the network has the advantage of being transportable between compatible machines. However, if simulation time is important in the application, and the network is fairly large, a dedicated neural-network device, which has the dual benefits of being much faster than software and lower cost (in large quantities), should be considered.

1.6 FOUNDATIONS SUMMARY

In this chapter, we have presented an overview of what neural networks are and how they work. We have discussed a little of how neural networks can help us solve "difficult" computer automation problems, and shown how the architecture of the network lends itself naturally to problems that are inherently parallel. We have seen how the microscopic operation of the individual processing elements in the network influence the operation of the entire network. We have also explored some of the practical issues associated with the development of neural-network applications, including the issues associated with simulation of the network. We have touched on the concepts of data representation and shown how different types of neural-network units can be used to implement those representations. In short, we now have a solid understanding of the fundamentals of neural networks.

The only fundamental issues we have not addressed in this chapter are those related to the algorithms governing the operation of the various network models. In the next chapter, we shall overcome this deficiency by reviewing several of the most popular network paradigms, in order to provide the background ·to determine the kinds of problems for which each network paradigm is best suited.

SUGGESTED READINGS

There are now many excellent books available describing the many different aspects of neural networks. The PDP set [6] continues to be the "bible" of neural-network technology. It contains an excellent description of several different neural-network paradigms, and in the process shows how the study of biological intelligence has led to the development of these neural models. It is also an excellent resource for the novice practitioner, with software to simulate several of the network models described in the text provided in Volume III of the series.

Researchers interested in a comprehensive presentation of the most common neural-network paradigms, from the perspective of an application developer, are referred to *Neural Networks: Algorithms, Applications, and Programming Techniques* [2] by James A. Freeman and David M. Skapura. Another excellent text describing the theoretical operation of neural networks is Jacek Zurada's *Introduction to Artificial Neural Systems* [8]. Finally, for those readers interested in exploring the subtle details of neural-network operation, and understanding the behavior of the different networks from a mathematical point of view, James A. Freeman's *Simulating Neural Networks with Mathematica* [1] is an outstanding work that also provides easy-to-use source code for interactively experimenting with neural networks from within the Mathematica environment.

BIBLIOGRAPHY

1. James A. Freeman. *Simulating Neural Networks with Mathematica.* Addison-Wesley, Reading, MA, 1993.

2. James A. Freeman and David M. Skapura. *Neural Networks: Algorithms, Applications, and Programming Techniques.* Addison-Wesley, Reading, MA, 1991.

3. Stephen Grossberg. *Studies of Mind and Brain.* Reidel Publishing Company, Boston, MA, pp. 79–88, 1988.

4. Warren S. McCulloch and Walter Pitts. A logical calculus of the ideas immanent in nervous activity. *Bulletin of Mathematical Biophysics,* 5:115–133, 1943.

5. Marvin L. Minsky and Seymour J. Papert. *Perceptrons, Expanded Edition.* MIT Press, Cambridge, MA, 1988.

6. David Rumelhart, James McClelland, and the PDP Research Group. *Parallel Distributed Processing, Vols. I–III.* MIT Press, Cambridge, MA, 1986.

7. Paul J. Werbos. *Beyond Regression: New Tools for Prediction and Analysis in the Behavioral Sciences.* PhD thesis, Harvard University, November 1974.

8. Jacek Zurada. *Introduction to Artificial Neural Systems.* West, St. Paul, MN, 1992.

C H A P T E R

Paradigms

I'm attempting to build a mnemonic memory device using stone knives and bear skins.

— *Mr. Spock in* Star Trek: City on the Edge of Forever

In Chapter 1, we described the process of propagating pattern vectors through a general network structure. Throughout that discussion, we assumed that the networks had been previously configured with the appropriate connection-weight values to make the network perform the desired input-to-output pattern transformation. Now that we understand the process of propagating information through a neural network, the next logical question is *How do we configure these networks with the appropriate connection weights for a given application?*

In most cases, the answer is—*we* do not. It is the *network* that finds the appropriate set of connection-weight values to solve the problem.[1] In so doing, the network is said to be *learning* to reproduce the desired transformation.

In this chapter, we shall present an overview of several of the most common neural-network architectures and learning mechanisms. The material covered in this chapter is by no means comprehensive; readers interested in a more formal treatment of the theory underlying these networks are referred to the books described in the Suggested Readings section at the end of this chapter. Instead, our intent here is to summarize the learning methods employed by the most popular network models in order to convey an understanding of the types of problems each network is best suited to solve.

2.1 THE BACKPROPAGATION NETWORK

The backpropagation network (BPN), which is also sometimes referred to as a multilayer perceptron (MLP), is currently the most general-purpose, and (not

---

1. The Multidirectional Associative Memory and Hopfield Memory being the notable exceptions.

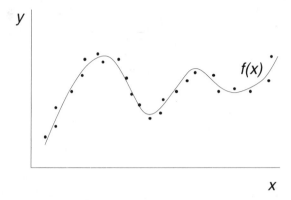

Figure 2.1   This diagram illustrates the process of minimizing the error of a function through a set of empirical data points. In this graph, the horizontal axis represents the independent variable, x, while the vertical axis represents the dependent variable, y. The curve plotted through the graph represents the value of a function $f(x)$, such that the distance between the value of y for any x and the computed value of $f(x)$ is minimal.

coincidentally) commonly used neural-network paradigm. The BPN achieves its generality because of the *gradient-descent* technique used to train the network.

Gradient descent is analogous to an error-minimization process. *Error minimization,* as the term implies, is an attempt to fit a closed-form solution to a set of empirical data points, such that the solution deviates from the exact value by a minimal amount. Figure 2.1 illustrates the error-minimization concept.

The BPN learns to generate a **mapping** from the input pattern space to the output pattern space by minimizing the error between the actual output produced by the network and the desired output across a set of pattern *vector pairs,* or **exemplars.** The learning process begins with the presentation of an input pattern to the BPN. That input pattern is propagated through the entire network, until an output pattern is produced. The BPN then makes use of what is called the *generalized delta rule* to determine the error for the current pattern contributed by every unit in the network. Finally, each unit modifies its input connection weights slightly in a direction that reduces its error signal, and the process is repeated for the next pattern.

As shown in Figure 2.2, the BPN is a *layered, feed-forward* network, comprised of one input layer, one or more middle, or *hidden,* layers and one output layer. Processing elements are usually connected only between layers, and then only to layers immediately above or below any given layer. The number of processing elements on each layer will differ from application to application, as will the number of hidden layers. Usually, however, there is only one hidden layer, because the availability of such a layer is sufficient to allow the BPN to form intermediate representations of the training inputs, which, in turn, allow the net-

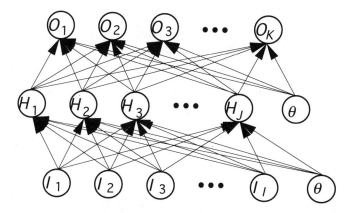

Figure 2.2 The typical structure of the BPN is shown. In this diagram, we illustrate the use of a *bias* unit on each layer. The bias unit is a processing element with an output that is always active (1). In such an architecture, the connection weight between the bias unit and each unit on the subsequent layer forms an activation that must be overcome by the remainder of the inputs to each unit—thereby preconditioning the activation of each unit.

work to reproduce the set of desired output patterns for all of the training vector pairs.

2.1.1 Learning in the BPN

A BPN application begins by creating a BPN structure with a pseudorandom internal configuration. The network is initially randomized to avoid imposing any of our own prejudices about an application on the network. Next, we collect a set of training patterns that are representative of the application we will ask the BPN to learn. These training patterns can be thought of as a set of ordered vector pairs $\{(\mathbf{x}_1, \mathbf{y}_1), (\mathbf{x}_2, \mathbf{y}_2), \ldots, (\mathbf{x}_P, \mathbf{y}_P)\}$ where each $\mathbf{x}_i$ represents an input pattern vector and each $\mathbf{y}_i$ represents the output pattern vector associated with the input vector $\mathbf{x}_i$.

The process of training the network then proceeds according to the following algorithm, which is derived as a natural result of finding the gradient of the error surface (in *weight-space*) of the actual output produced by the network with respect to the desired result:

1. Select the first training vector pair from the set of training vector pairs. Call this the vector pair $(\mathbf{x}, \mathbf{y})$.

2. Use the input vector, $\mathbf{x}$, as the output from the input layer of processing elements.

3. Using Eq. (1.1), compute the activation to each unit on the subsequent layer.

4. Apply the appropriate activation function, which we denote as $f(\text{net}^h)$ for the hidden layer and as $f(\text{net}^o)$ for the output layer, to each unit on the

subsequent layer. Here, *appropriate* refers to the one activation function that is best suited to the function to be performed by this layer of units. The selection of this function will vary by layer and application.

5. Repeat steps 3 and 4 for each layer in the network.

6. Compute the error, δ^o_{pk}, for this pattern p across all K output layer units by using the formula:

$$\delta^o_{pk} = (y_k - o_k) f'(\text{net}^o_k) \qquad (2.1)$$

7. Compute the error, δ^h_{pj}, for all J hidden layer units by using the recursive formula

$$\delta^h_{pj} = f'(\text{net}^h_j) \sum_{k=1}^{K} \delta^o_{pk} w_{kj} \qquad (2.2)$$

8. Update the connection-weight values to the hidden layer by using the equation

$$w_{ji}(t+1) = w_{ji}(t) + \eta \delta^h_{pj} x_i \qquad (2.3)$$

where η is a small value used to limit the amount of change allowed to any connection during a single-pattern training cycle.

9. Update the connection-weight values to the output layer by using the equation

$$w_{kj}(t+1) = w_{kj}(t) + \eta \delta^o_{pk} f(\text{net}^h_j) \qquad (2.4)$$

10. Repeat steps 2 through 9 for all vector pairs in the training set. Call this one training *epoch*.

11. Repeat steps 1 through 10 for as many epochs as it takes to reduce the sum-squared error to a minimal value. The calculation of the sum-squared error is performed for the output-layer units only, across all P training patterns, according to the formula

$$E = \sum_{p=1}^{P} \sum_{k=1}^{K} (\delta^o_{pk})^2 \qquad (2.5)$$

Examination of the algorithm just described reveals that the BPN is learning to recognize features in the input patterns, and convert the detection of those features into the desired output pattern, by slowly altering the network connection weights to minimize the error across all of the training patterns. We can see this

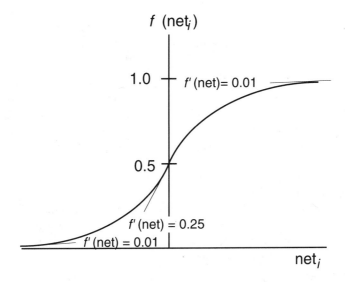

Figure 2.3   The sigmoidal activation function, showing how the magnitude of its derivative changes with the amount of saturation, is illustrated.

behavior in the form of the equations that define the error signal at each layer: In this case, Eq. (2.1) determines the error signal, δ^o_{pk}, for the output layer and Eq. (2.2) computes the error signal, δ^h_{pj}, for the hidden layer. We shall first examine Eq. (2.1).

   In computing a value for δ^o_{pk}, we are first taking the difference between the actual output produced by each unit (o_k) and the desired output from the unit (y_k). That much is intuitive; error *should* include some measure of the difference between the actual and the desired results. However, the role of the derivative of the activation function is somewhat mysterious. Other than the fact that the derivative is required as part of the differentiation of the sum-squared pattern error with respect to the activation of the unit, it also controls the amount of change allowed at this unit, and, through Eq. (2.2), to units that provide input to this unit.

   To illustrate this concept, consider the sigmoidal activation function, as graphed in Figure 2.3. Here, we can see that the derivative of the sigmoid has its largest value (slope) in the transition region. Once the unit has been saturated, either positively or negatively, the derivative of the sigmoid is almost zero. Hence, by Eq. (2.1), the derivative is used to control when units are allowed to make relatively large changes to their input connections, because it governs the magnitude of the error signal at each output unit. Output units that are saturated are very slow to change, while output units that have inputs that have not yet saturated them can be strongly influenced by an error signal.

Exercise 2.1: Determine the effect of the linear activation function on learning in a BPN. Will linear units train more rapidly, or more slowly, than sigmoidal units? ∎

With respect to hidden-layer units, Eq. (2.2) says that the error signal to a hidden unit, δ^{h}_{pj}, is the product of the derivative of the activation function of the unit and the weighted sum of the errors at units to which the particular hidden unit contributed. We have already seen how the derivative plays a role in determining error; let us now consider the role played by the weighted sum-of-errors in the computation of the hidden-layer error.

We must first note that, unlike for the output-layer units, we have no *a priori* knowledge about what state hidden-layer units should be in to produce the correct output from the network. Therefore, an error measure with respect to a desired value has no meaning for a hidden-layer unit. However, we *do* know what the error at each output-layer unit is, and we also know that the actual output from the network is a function of the input stimulation received from the top-most layer of hidden units. We can therefore infer[2] a relationship between the error measure at the first hidden layer and the contribution (through the connection weight) of each hidden unit to the error at the output layer.

Finally, if we combine the error computation with the weight update equation for the hidden layer, we see that only connections to *active* input units are allowed to be modified significantly. The net effect of the entire process, as we have illustrated in Figure 2.4, is to reduce the negative effect from active inputs while increasing the positive effect of units that lead to lower error signals. Thus, the units in a BPN layer tend to organize themselves in ways that allow them to recognize features in an input pattern that leads toward the correct output, while ignoring features that tend to misclassify the pattern.

Exercise 2.2: In all practical applications of the BPN, the hidden layer units use the sigmoidal activation function, never a linear function. Why is this true? ∎

2.1.2 BPN Training Issues

In spite of its generality, there are a few issues that any good application developer must consider when training the BPN. The first is the role that the hidden layer plays when the network is learning. In most cases, the hidden layer is learning an **internal representation** of the input patterns that will enable it to perform a **nonlinear mapping** from the input space to the output space. For that reason, the sigmoid function described in Chapter 1 is employed almost exclusively as the activation function for a BPN hidden layer.

Exercise 2.3: Consider the operation of a three-layer BPN that uses the linear activation function for the hidden layer units. Such a network will be unable to

---

2. And mathematically derive.

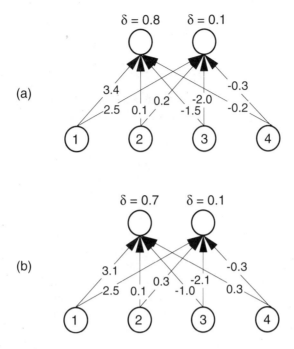

Figure 2.4   The process of changing connection weights to reduce error values is shown. (a) The initial state of this simple, two-layer network shows input 1 actively contributing to a large and small error, unit 2 passively contributing to the errors, unit 3 contributing to a reduction in the errors, and unit 4 passively contributing to a reduction in the errors. (b) After applying Eq. (2.18), the connection weights have been modified to reduce the error and reinforce the correct state from the active units, while only minimal changes occur to the connections from the passive units.

learn training sets that contain exemplars that are linear combinations of other exemplars, unless the output patterns associated with each are also linear combinations. Why? ∎

The second most common problem encountered by a novice when training a BPN is the issue of dealing with binary outputs when training a BPN with sigmoidal output units. Specifically, the application designer should ensure that the network is trained to produce output values of {0.1, 0.9} instead of the desired response values of {0, 1}. Also, we should interpret output values generated by a sigmoidal unit in the BPN in excess of 0.8 as active (1) and values less than 0.2 as inactive (0) after training has been completed.

The reason for these constraints can be seen with a simple analysis of the equations governing the behavior of the BPN. In Chapter 1, we described the function used to compute the sigmoidal response to an arbitrary input value, which we repeat here for reference.[3]

$$f(\text{net}_k) = \frac{1}{1 + e^{-\text{net}_k}} \tag{2.6}$$

As we discussed earlier in this section, the derivative of the sigmoid function with respect to the input to the unit is needed to compute the error signal at the kth output unit. Specifically,

$$f'(\text{net}_k) = \frac{\partial f(\text{net}_k)}{\partial \text{net}_k} \tag{2.7}$$

$$= o_k(1 - o_k), \tag{2.8}$$

where the term o_k is used to represent the output signal from the kth output unit. Inspection of Eq. (2.7) tells us that the derivative of the sigmoid will approach zero as the output from the sigmoidal unit saturates.

Considering then Eq. (2.1), which governs the computation of the error signal at the output layer on the BPN, we can see that sigmoidal units that have saturated always have a very small error signal, even if the actual output (o_k) is *opposite* the desired output (y_k). Thus, saturated sigmoidal units in a BPN adapt very slowly.

We can decrease the training time for such a network by simply limiting the target value for output patterns to $\{0.1, 0.9\}$, thus preventing saturation and allowing the output units to continue to adapt. Likewise, we can improve the network's ability to classify new input patterns after training has been completed by allowing a margin of error around the actual output. We can interpret output signals in excess of 0.8 as "close enough" to the target value of 0.9 in sigmoidal units, because the output value 0.8 is just above the knee of the sigmoidal curve, as shown in Figure 2.5.

2.1.3   BPN Production Mode

Once the BPN has successfully learned to replicate all the training output vectors given any of the input patterns, learning stops, and the connection-weight values are frozen. To access the information stored in a trained network, we select an input pattern vector typical of the patterns in the training set, and repeat steps 2 through 5 of the learning algorithm. Essentially, we simply propagate the new input pattern through to the output. If the input were identically equal to one of the training input patterns, the BPN will produce the output pattern that was associated with that input pattern during training, within some small margin of error. If the input pattern is slightly different from any of the training input patterns, the

---

3. We have simplified the analysis here by assuming an instantaneous pattern, p, is being propagated through the network.

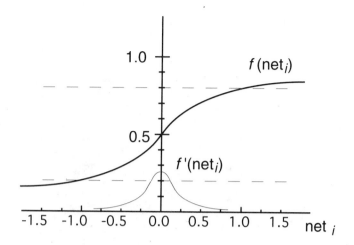

Figure 2.5   This graph shows the relationship between the sigmoidal activation function and its derivative. Notice that the transition region of the sigmoid is centered at zero, with the highest rate of change between output values of 0.2 and 0.8. This is why we tend to classify outputs from a sigmoidal unit below 0.2 as zero and values above 0.8 as one.

BPN will respond with an output pattern that resembles one of the training outputs, to a degree that the number of features in the current input pattern match the features the BPN learned to recognize during training.

When is this kind of behavior desirable? Practically speaking, the BPN is most useful when you have an application that requires a *generalization* of the input training patterns into different classifications, or categories. For example, consider the problem of converting written text into phonemes for speech synthesis. In 1986, Dr. Terrence Sejnowski and his associates showed how a MLP network could be trained to categorize a sliding window of seven alphabet characters into a single phoneme in discrete time using an explicit training set containing 2,000 words.[4] They further showed that the same BPN, after training, could be used to process words the network had never seen before [9]. This application, like many of the other applications discussed at length in this book, succeeds because of the ability of the BPN to identify features in input patterns and produce meaningful outputs based on the detection (or observed absence) of those features in a new pattern.

2.1.4   BPN Variants

As we mentioned earlier, the BPN is perhaps the most commonly used neural-network model, due to its generality. There are, however, numerous variations

---

4. The NETtalk application mentioned here is described in detail in Chapter 6.

Output Pattern

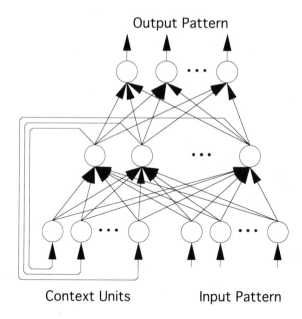

Context Units   Input Pattern

Figure 2.6   The structure of the Elman network is shown. The operation of the network is described in the text. *Source:* Simulating Neural Networks with Mathematica [3]. *Copyright ©1994, Addison-Wesley. Used with permission.*

on the standard BPN model, each offering a slightly different, if not better, processing model for information storage. While space precludes us from a detailed description of each of these variations, we shall now briefly summarize several popular BPN variants, describing the strengths and weaknesses of each model from an application perspective. Readers interested in an in-depth description of the operation of the following networks are referred to *Simulating Neural Networks with Mathematica* [3].

2.1.4.1   The Elman Network

The Elman network is essentially a standard, three-layer BPN, except that a number of **context units** are added to the input layer. As shown in Figure 2.6, the context units do nothing more than duplicate the activity of the hidden layer, at the previous time step, at the input of the network. This variation allows the Elman network to deal with what we shall refer to as **conflicting patterns** in the next chapter.

For our purposes here, we shall consider pattern conflicts to be simply a one-to-many mapping; that is, multiple outputs generated from a single input pattern. Such a condition will confound a standard BPN. The Elman network, however, deals with such a situation by augmenting the input pattern with the condition of hidden layer at the previous time step. Thus, the feedback units are essentially

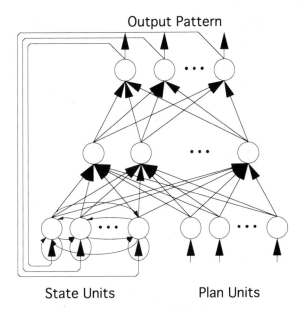

Figure 2.7   The architecture of the Jordan network is shown. Notice that the feedback in this network is not only from the output layer to the state units on the input layer but also between the state units themselves. The operation of the network is described in the text. *Source:* Simulating Neural Networks with Mathematica [3]. *Copyright ©1994, Addison-Wesley. Used with permission.*

establishing a *context* for the current input, allowing the network to discriminate between "identical" input patterns that occur at different times.

2.1.4.2   The Jordan Network

The Jordan network is essentially a modified Elman network, in that both networks extend the input pattern with feedback to distinguish between similar input patterns. However, as shown in Figure 2.7, the Jordan network obtains its feedback from the output layer, instead of the hidden layer. Also, unlike the Elman network or the BPN, the Jordan network provides interconnections between **state units** on the input layer.

The Jordan network is designed to learn sequences of patterns, in that the feedback from the output layer not only serves to set the context for the input pattern but also establishes the output of the network at the previous time step as part of the input. In this manner, the Jordan network is quite useful in applications where the pattern vectors that must be learned are related to each other in a specific time sequence.

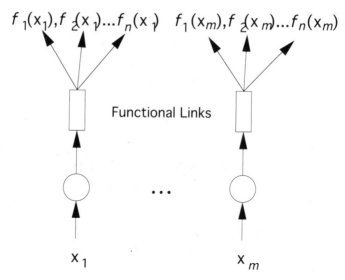

Figure 2.8   The input layer of the FLN is shown. In this diagram, each element of the input pattern, **x,** passes through a functional link before it is distributed to the next layer in the network. In this model, all n components of the modified input are received by each unit on the subsequent layer. In effect, this version of the FLN increases the dimension of the input pattern by a factor of n, which increases the likelihood of having unique patterns at the hidden layer, thereby allowing the FLN to more easily discriminate between similar exemplars. *Source:* Simulating Neural Networks with Mathematica [3]. *Copyright ©1994, Addison-Wesley. Used with permission.*

2.1.4.3   The Functional-Link Network

The functional-link network (FLN) is almost identical in form and operation to the BPN. The only difference between the two paradigms is in the operation of the input layer. In the BPN, and most of its derivative networks, the input pattern is distributed unaltered through the input layer. In effect, the input layer in the BPN is nothing more than a **fan-out** layer. In the FLN model, the operation of the input layer is modified to include a **functional link,** which allows the input layer to modify the input pattern before distributing it to the hidden layer of the network. Figure 2.8 shows the conceptual model of the input layer in the FLN paradigm.

There are two types of modifications that the functional links can perform in the FLN architecture: the **functional-expansion model,** which produces multiple data elements from a single input through the application of a set of predefined functions, and the **tensor model,** which multiplies certain components of the input pattern together. The primary benefit to the FLN is that the number of processing units needed to learn the application is significantly reduced over the equivalent BPN model. In fact, it is often possible for an FLN to learn an

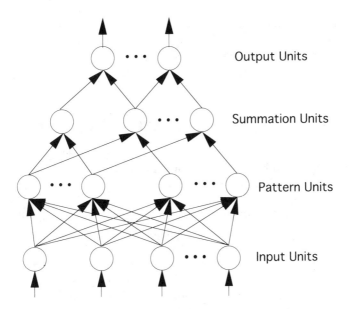

Figure 2.9 A typical PNN architecture is shown. In this network, the number of pattern units always equals the number of exemplars in the training set, while the number of summation units equals the number of groups into which the input pattern can be classified. Notice the selectivity of the connections between the pattern layer and the summation layer. The operation of the network is described in the text. *Source: Simulating Neural Networks with Mathematica [3]. Copyright ©1994, Addison-Wesley. Used with permission.*

application without a hidden layer, which is needed to encode intermediate representations in the BPN.

2.1.4.4 The Probabilistic Neural Network

The probabilistic neural network (PNN) is related to the BPN primarily in structure. As shown in Figure 2.9, the structure of the PNN is a layered, feed-forward network, just like the BPN. The primary difference between the PNN and the BPN is in the operation of the units in the network. In the PNN, we implement a Bayesian decision strategy for classifying input vectors. This behavior is provided by using a Gaussian activation function on the pattern layer, combined with the operation of the summation units. The pattern units operate by computing the inner product of the input pattern vector and weight vector to each unit, just as in the BPN. Here, however, we must ensure that the input vector has been normalized prior to presentation to the network.

In essence, the network operates by summing the outputs from all pattern units, which, because of the Gaussian activation function, serve to classify the input patterns into classes. Thus, the PNN is actually computing the *a posteriori* probability distribution function for a single class, evaluated at the point defined by the input pattern. This behavior is useful in classification applications, where we want to estimate the likelihood that a new pattern is a member of any of our predefined classes.

2.2   THE COUNTERPROPAGATION NETWORK

The counterpropagation network (CPN), as originally defined by Robert Hecht-Nielsen [7] is a network that learns a **bidirectional mapping** in hyperdimensional space; in other words, it learns both a forwardmapping (from n-space to m-space) and, if it exists, the inverse mapping (from m-space back to n-space) for a set of pattern vectors. Interestingly, the complete CPN learns both of these mappings *simultaneously.* In most practical applications, however, we are only concerned with the forward-mapping operation. We will therefore restrict our discussion of the CPN to the forward mapping half of the network, and henceforth use the term *CPN* to refer to the feed-forward half of the complete network.

The architecture of the CPN is illustrated in Figure 2.10. Notice that, unlike the general neural-network architecture we have already seen, the CPN has *exactly* three layers: an input layer composed of a number of (primarily) fan-out units; one hidden layer, containing a set of competitive units; and a linear-output layer. In the discussion that follows, we shall deliberately ignore the dimension of all three layers in the network, because the number of units needed will vary from application to application. What will not vary is the learning process used by the CPN to store pattern vectors, which we shall now describe.

2.2.1   The CPN Learning Process

Initially, a CPN constructed to perform a specific application will know nothing about the application: The connection weights in the network will be in an initialized state.[5] We start the learning process by collecting a set of exemplars, or training patterns, that collectively define the entire application. Because we want the CPN to perform a vector-mapping function, we define our training patterns to be an ordered set of vector pairs, $\{(\mathbf{x}_1, \mathbf{y}_1), (\mathbf{x}_2, \mathbf{y}_2), \ldots, (\mathbf{x}_p, \mathbf{y}_p)\}$. The CPN then learns to produce $\mathbf{y}_i$ given $\mathbf{x}_i$ by adapting itself according to the following algorithm:

1.   Randomly select any training pair, $(\mathbf{x}_i, \mathbf{y}_i)$, from the training set. Call these vectors the current training vector pair, $(\mathbf{x}, \mathbf{y})$.

2.   Normalize the input vector, **x,** by dividing every component of **x** by the magnitude of the vector, where we compute the magnitude by

---

5. The exact state of the connections *can* be precisely defined at initialization. A good explanation for how the initial connection weights are determined for a CPN can be found in several of the texts listed in the Suggested Readings section of this chapter.

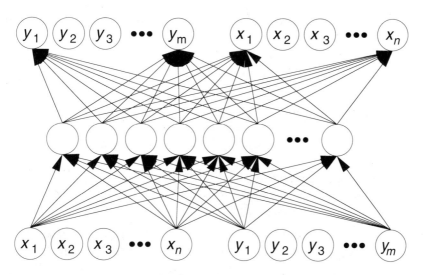

Figure 2.10 The architecture of the CPN is shown. In this diagram, we have unwrapped the five layers of the network to show the signal flow as a feed-forward network. The details of the operation of this network are described in the text. *Source:* Neural Networks: Algorithms, Applications, and Programming Techniques [2]. *Copyright ©1991, Addison-Wesley. Used with permission.*

$$\|x\| = \sqrt{\sum_{j=1}^{n}(x_j)^2} \tag{2.9}$$

3. Using the normalized input vector as the output from the input layer in the CPN, compute the activation to each unit on the competitive hidden layer by using Eq. (1.1).

4. Determine the winning unit on the competitive layer by selecting the unit with the largest activation. Call this unit W.

5. Adjust the connection weights between the winning unit and all n input-layer units according to the equation

$$w_{Wn}(t+1) = w_{Wn}(t) + \alpha(x_n - w_{Wn}(t)) \tag{2.10}$$

where the term α is a small constant used to limit the amount of change to the connections.

6. Repeat steps 1 through 5 until all p input patterns have been processed once.

7. Repeat step 6 until each input pattern is consistently associated with the same competitive unit. Note that some input patterns may be exclusively

associated with one competitive unit, and sometimes several patterns will cause the same unit to win.

8. Select the first vector pair in the training set. Call it the current pattern.

9. Repeat steps 2 through 4 for the current training pattern.

10. Adjust the connection weights between the winning unit and all M output-layer units according to the equation

$$w_{mW}(t + 1) = w_{mW}(t) + \beta(y_m - w_{mW}(t)) \tag{2.11}$$

where the term β is used to limit the amount of change to the output connections.

11. Repeat steps 9 and 10 for each vector pair in the training set.

12. Repeat steps 8 through 11 until the difference between the desired output, y_i, and the weight vector $\mathbf{w}_{mW}$ is reduced to an acceptably small value.[6]

Now that we know the mechanics of learning in the CPN, let us consider the qualitative aspects of the learning algorithm. First, from inspection of the algorithm, we observe that input vectors to the network are normalized prior to propagation to the hidden layer. The reason for the normalization is not intuitive, until you consider the process of computing activation in a competitive unit. Recall that each competitive unit computes an input value, net_i, using a process that is analogous to computing an *inner product* between vectors. We have already ensured that the input vector to the competitive layer, $\mathbf{x}_i$, is normalized. If we further ensure that the input weight vectors to each hidden layer unit, $\mathbf{w}_i$, are normalized,[7] Eq. (1.3) tells us that each competitive unit will receive an input stimulation that exactly corresponds to the cosine of the angle between these two vectors in Euclidian space. Thus, in the CPN, hidden-layer units compete for the right to adapt their connection weights (and later produce an output) based on how closely their input-weight vectors match the current input vector *in direction only*. This process is illustrated in Figure 2.11.

The output connections from the hidden layer in the CPN are adjusted in a manner similar to the adjustment made to the input connections. However, notice that the competitive training occurs first in the algorithm. The reason for this separation is to ensure that all of the input training patterns have successfully been categorized by the competitive units. Once all of the input patterns are correctly classified (by being associated with a particular, competitive unit), training the network to produce the correct output is simply a matter of adjusting the connection weights from the appropriate winning unit such that

---

6. Here, as with most neural-network models, the definition of the term *acceptably small* is application specific, and must be determined by the developer.

7. Input-weight vectors *are* normalized to the competitive layer. The process by which this normalization occurs is a function of the interaction between the initialization of the connection weights and the adaptation process, described by Eq. (2.10).

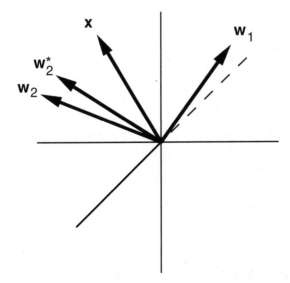

Figure 2.11 The process of matching patterns in Euclidian space is shown. In this diagram, the vector **x** represents the current input to the network, while vectors $\mathbf{w}_1$ and $\mathbf{w}_2$ each represent a weight vector to two competitive units in a CPN. Because all vectors are normalized, unit 2 wins the competition because **x** is *closer* to $\mathbf{w}_2$ in an inner-product sense than it is to $\mathbf{w}_1$. the new value of $\mathbf{w}_2$ is the vector $\mathbf{w}_2^*$, which has been adjusted toward **x**.

- If the winning unit is uniquely associated with a single input pattern, the output pattern associated with that input pattern is *exactly* encoded into the output connections to the linear layer.
- If the winning unit is associated with more than one input pattern, the output pattern encoded into the connections to the linear layer is the *vector average* of the output patterns associated with the inputs categorized by that competitive unit.

2.2.2 CPN Pattern Recall

After all of the training patterns have been successfully encoded in the CPN, learning stops and the network is then used exclusively in its production mode. In this mode, new input patterns are applied to the network, and the CPN is expected to return an appropriate output pattern vector. In the case of the CPN, *appropriate* means that the network should produce the *exact* pattern ($\mathbf{y}_i$) associated with the input pattern ($\mathbf{x}_i$) that most closely resembles the current input pattern.

The process by which the CPN performs this function is through the interaction between the competitive units and the linear-output units; when the CPN is learning, a new input pattern is normalized and propagated to the hidden layer.

The hidden-layer units compete for the right to fire, based on how closely the normalized input pattern matches the pattern vectors stored in the input connections to each competitive unit. The one unit with the strongest activation[8] wins the competition, and it stimulates the memory pattern stored in its output connections. The linear units serve to either *multiplex* the outputs from the competitive outstars or *integrate* the outputs from multiple, winning outstars, depending on the behavioral mode of the network.

Exercise 2.4: Consider the use of a CPN in an application to determine the parity bit of an eight-bit binary input pattern. Is the CPN the best choice for such an application? Justify your answer by relating the behavior of the CPN to the behavior of a BPN trained to perform the same application. ∎

Because of this behavior, the CPN excels in applications that require exact (or interpolated) output patterns from noisy input patterns.

2.3 ADAPTIVE RESONANCE THEORY

The adaptive resonance theory (ART) networks, and most of the networks derived from the basic ART architecture, were developed by Stephen Grossberg, Gail Carpenter, and colleagues at Boston University as part of an attempt to resolve what they called the *stability-plasticity* dilemma [5] common in most neural-network paradigms.

As an example of this dilemma, consider how a BPN is used when constructing a neural-network application. After collecting pattern data about the application domain, the BPN is placed in a learning mode where the training vectors are encoded by the network. Once the network has converged to a solution, training stops and the BPN is used in its production mode to perform the application. If new application data patterns are later acquired, the BPN must be completely retrained using the expanded training set, because attempting to retrain the BPN using only the new patterns will result in the network *forgetting* previously learned patterns.

Exercise 2.5: Why does the BPN forget previously encoded patterns when retrained only on new exemplars? ∎

Grossberg and his colleagues set out to develop a network that could adapt itself to store new information when presented with previously unseen patterns, yet remain stable enough to retain previously learned patterns without corrupting them. Additionally, they wanted to show how a neural network could solve such a problem, and remain *biologically plausible*. The resulting network architectures were called ART1 and ART2. The only real difference between them, aside from

---

8. Which is also the unit that has an input-weight vector most closely aligned in Euclidian direction to the current input vector.

the relative increase in complexity in the structure of the ART2 input layer, is that ART1 is restricted to binary input patterns while ART2 can handle continuously variable inputs.

Before we begin our discussion of the ART networks, however, you should be aware that these networks are fairly complex dynamic systems. Grossberg has developed a set of equations for the networks that simultaneously endow them with the desired behavior and effectively replicate functions observed in biological systems. For our review, however, we shall simplify the discussion by presenting a qualitative overview of the operation of the networks. Readers interested in the theoretical details governing the operation of the ART networks are referred to the Suggested Readings section at the end of this chapter.

2.3.1 ART1 Operation

The ART1 network consists of two layers of processing elements, labeled F_1 and F_2, each fully interconnected with the other. The units in layer F_2 also have lateral inhibiting connections, so that competition can be accommodated. As illustrated in Figure 2.12, ART1 also requires two additional functional elements called the *gain control* and *orienting subsystem*. The purpose of these elements is to guide the network toward an appropriate solution to the pattern-matching problem.

A concept fundamental to the operation of ART1 is the notion of *memory*. In the ART1 network, memory can take two forms: Short-term memory (STM) is the term used by Professor Grossberg to refer to the activation patterns in each layer, while long-term memory (LTM) refers to the information stored in the connections between layers.

With this background in mind, let us now consider how information is processed in the ART1 network. As in the case of the BPN, the network is initially stimulated by the application of some pattern vector from the outside world. Unlike the BPN, where input-layer units are simply fan-out units, ART1 preprocesses the input vector, **i,** to compensate for the bias from the gain control.[9] This processing, which is performed automatically by the activation function of the F_1 layer units, amounts to a prescaling that ensures that the outputs produced by the F_1 units remain binary, even though they also receive input from the gain-control unit.

After preprocessing, the F_1-layer units produce an output vector (**x**) that simultaneously stimulates the F_2-layer units and the orienting subsystem (**r**). At this point, the stimulation on **r** is such that **i** and **x** both cancel each other, effectively inhibiting the reset function produced by **r**. The units on layer F_2 then compute their activation using the by-now familiar sum-of-products calculation described by Eq. (1.14). As with the hidden layer in the CPN, the F_2 layer in the ART1 network is competitive.

---

9. All units in the ART1 network are constructed such that activation can only occur if any two of the three possible inputs are active. This restriction is referred to as the *two-thirds rule*.

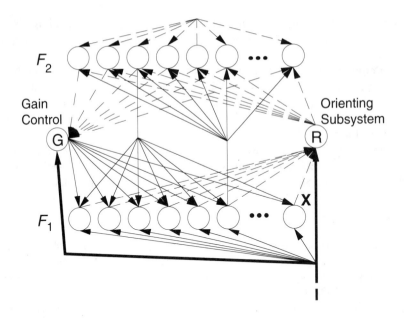

Figure 2.12   An example of an ART1 network structure is shown. In this diagram, solid lines represent excitatory connections and dashed lines represent inhibitory connections. *Source:* A connectionist approach to heuristically pruninglarge search trees [5]. *Copyright ©1990, by David M. Skapura. Used with permission.*

At this point, we should note that the competition performed in the ART1 F_2 layer is slightly different from the competition implemented in the hidden layer in the CPN. Whereas the competitive layer in the CPN used *normalized* pattern vectors, the ART1 F_2 layer uses the full magnitude of the pattern vectors to compute their activations. Hence, we can see that the F_2-layer units are competing with each other using the entire projection[10] of the input pattern on their connection-weight vectors as the basis for their competition.

If we further note that the patterns stored in the **bottom-up** connections that run from layer F_1 to layer F_2 are *memories* of STM patterns seen previously by the F_2-layer units, it then becomes evident that the F_2-layer units are performing a coarse pattern match between the current STM pattern, **x**, and the long-term memories of patterns previously seen. Thus, during each pattern propagation cycle, the F_2-layer units are competing with each other based on the degree of match between the current STM pattern at F_1 and the LTM pattern stored in the bottom-up connection weights to the F_2-layer units.

---

10. As compared to just the direction of the vectors, as in the CPN.

For now, we shall assume that the F_2 unit with the largest activation is the unit that has learned to recognize the specific input pattern vector (although, as we shall see, that is not always the case). That unit is declared the winner, and activity on all other F_2 units is inhibited. We accomplish this by applying the competitive activation function, given by Eq. (1.12), to all F_2-layer units.

Having found a candidate match, the F_2 layer can now be viewed as a competitive layer, in that the winning unit activates a memory pattern stored in its connections back to the F_1 layer. The units on the F_1 layer then begin processing the feedback pattern from F_2, comparing the memory pattern (which we shall call $\mathbf{x}^*$) with the activity pattern, $\mathbf{x}$, generated by F_1. If the two patterns match, the reset signal is again inhibited and the network enters its *resonant* state where the F_2 memory reinforces the input.

If, however, the memory pattern sent back from F_2 does not match the $\mathbf{x}$ template, the new activity pattern on F_1 will cause the orienting subsystem to activate, sending a reset signal back to the F_2 layer. This has the effect of forcing any *currently active* F_2 unit into a long-term inhibition state, thus preventing the unit from again matching the $\mathbf{x}$ template on the next iteration (note that it has no effect on any inactive unit). With all F_2 units off (due to a memory mismatch), the entire process is repeated until a matching pattern is found or all F_2 units are reset, in which case a new F_2 unit is encoded with the pattern to be stored ($\mathbf{x}$).

Notice that in the scenario just described there is no separation between learning and production modes. The ART1 network processes information in the same way any time a new external stimulation is provided. If the external pattern is one that the network has already learned, it will quickly recall and reinforce that pattern. If the input represents a previously unseen pattern, the ART1 network will extend itself to encode that new information by adding a unit to the F_2 layer and encoding the new information in the connections between this new unit and all F_1 layer units. Thus, ART1 behaves like an extensible pattern memory, starting out knowing nothing about the world, and rapidly expanding as it learns about its application environment.

2.3.2   ART2 Operation

Macroscopically, ART2 is virtually identical to the ART1 network in the way it operates. The only real difference between the two networks is in the operation of the F_1 layer. The structure of the F_1 layer in ART2 is composed of seven sublayers, each with units that directly connect to corresponding units on other sublayers. The purpose of these sublayers is to allow the ART2 network to process analog, continuously variable inputs. The network accomplishes this goal by implementing the behavior described by the following equations for each sublayer:

$$w_i = I_i + a u_i \tag{2.12}$$

$$x_i = \frac{w_i}{e + \|w\|} \tag{2.13}$$

$$v_i = f(x_i) + b f(q_i) \tag{2.14}$$

$$u_i = \frac{v_i}{e + \|v\|} \tag{2.15}$$

$$p_i = u_i + \sum_j g(y_j) z_{ij} \tag{2.16}$$

$$q_i = \frac{p_i}{e + \|\mathrm{p}\|} \tag{2.17}$$

$$r_i = \frac{u_i + c p_i}{\|\mathrm{u}\| + \|c \mathrm{p}\|} \tag{2.18}$$

where the term e is used to represent a small constant value to prevent division by zero. While these equations may make the operation of the ART2 F_1 layer clear to the reader with a strong mathematical background, it is equally important that we illustrate the operation of the layer from a practical standpoint, because many readers will likely want to employ the use of the ART2 network for some application.

First, you should note the various feedback paths provided in the structure of the F_1 layer, as shown in Figure 2.13. Specifically, feedback exists between the **u** and **w** sublayers, and between sublayers **q** and **v**. This feedback structure indicates that signals must propagate completely through the F_1 sublayer structure at least twice in order to ensure that the layer is operating as it is intended: once when the input pattern is first applied, while all of the sublayers are quiescent, then again to allow the sublayers that receive feedback to process the feedback signals.

Now let us consider the function of each sublayer in ART2. We shall begin by stepping through the pattern propagation process in the F_1 layer structure as though the network were processing a new input pattern. We therefore assume that the initial state of each sublayer in F_1 is inactive, and that there is no active pattern being propagated downward from layer F_2.

From Eq. (2.12), we can see that each unit on **w** produces an output signal that is, initially, just the input received by the unit from the external source. Sublayer **x** then normalizes the input vector received from **w**, as shown by Eq. (2.13). Next, sublayer **v** performs a **contrast enhancement** on the normalized input vector, effectively filtering out any pattern component that does not significantly affect the direction of the pattern vector. This behavior is shown in Eq. (2.14), where the term $f(x_i)$ performs the filtering function. The contrast-enhanced, normalized pattern is then propagated to sublayer **u**, where it is re-normalized and buffered for presentation to sublayers **p** and **r**.

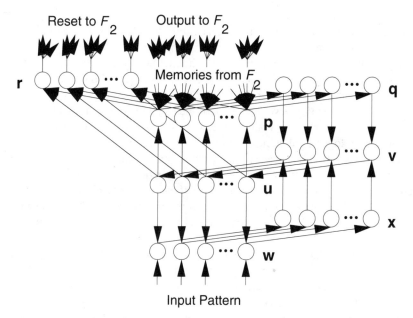

Figure 2.13   This diagram illustrates a typical structure for the ART2 F_1 layer. In this structure, the seven sublayers that comprise the ART2 F_1 layer act to buffer the input pattern (**w**), normalize it (**x**), contrast enhance it with feedback from the output of the layer (**v**), normalize the enhanced input pattern and hold it for comparison with the LTM pattern sent back from F_2 (**u**), buffer the output of the F_1 layer and hold the LTM pattern from F_2 (**p**), and normalize the output pattern prior to feeding it back into the contrast enhancer (**q**). The sublayer **r** replaces the single unit in the orienting subsystem of the ART1 network, allowing the internal pattern at the **u** sublevel to be compared component by component with the LTM pattern sent back from F_2, seen at **p,** which becomes the equivalent of $\mathbf{x}^*$.

Now things start to get interesting. Sublayer **p** buffers the output pattern vector from sublayer **u** for propagation to layer F_2 and sublayer **q**, and simultaneously provides a comparison pattern for sublayer **r**, which controls the reset function for the network. Sublayer **q** then normalizes the output pattern, and buffers it for feedback to sublayer **v**. At this point, all sublayers on F_1 are active. Because the patterns received by sublayer **r** from sublayers **u** and **p** are identical, reset is inhibited. In a real network structure, the output from sublayer **p** would then be propagated forward to layer F_2. Simultaneously, the F_1 layer would itself be changing its state, due to the introduction of the feedback signals.

Because this network is currently implemented in software only, we can simplify the signal propagation process by ignoring the pattern propagation to F_2 until the F_1 layer has stabilized. Thus, we now begin the second pass of signal propagation through the F_1-layer structure. Sublayer **w** produces a new output pattern, based on the feedback it receives from sublayer **u**, which is the contrast-enhanced form of the input. The feedback loop from **u** to **w** then serves to amplify the significant components of the true input pattern, while squelching the components that were filtered out during the first phase of pattern enhancement. Similarly, sublayer **v** receives feedback from sublayer **q**, which serves to enhance the components of the internal pattern that are actually propagated to layer F_2.

We should also observe that, as described by Freeman and Skapura [4], the form of the function $f(q_i)$ controls the contrast enhancement performed by sublayer **v,** with logistic functions (such as the sigmoid, or other rapidly transitioning functions) providing a very sharp pattern enhancement. Likewise, a linear, or other gradual activation function, on sublayer **q** will provide a soft contrast enhancement in the F_1 layer. In any case, after the second phase of pattern enhancement has completed, the output from the **p** sublayer can be propagated to the F_2 layer to stimulate a memory retrieval competition, as we described in the ART1 network.

Once F_2 produces an output, the memory stimulated by the winning F_2 unit is fed back into the F_1 layer for pattern comparison. We can see this behavior in Eq. (2.16), where the function $g(y_j)$ is nothing more than the output from the competitive F_2 layer. Thus, the final output produced by sublayer **p** is the combination of the normalized output vector (which is still buffered as the output from sublayer **u** and the memory stored in the top-down connections between the winning F_2 unit and the F_1 layer.

When F_2 activates its memory pattern, sublayer **r** is provided with two pattern vectors for comparison: the normalized output pattern from the F_1 layer, as represented by the output from sublayer **u**, and the memory stimulated by the propagation of the input pattern to the F_2 layer, as provided by the modified output of the **p** sublayer. If these two patterns compare favorably, reset is inhibited, and the network enters its resonant state. If the two patterns do not compare, the reset signal is activated by the **r** sublayer, and the pattern propagation process starts anew, just as in ART1.

Applications of this network include systems that must perform complex pattern classification and recognition. The ART networks also form the basis of several other networks designed to perform visual pattern recognition: A network to detect boundaries in computer vision applications (the boundary-contour system [5]) and a motion-detection network, also applicable to computer-vision applications [1].

2.4   THE MULTIDIRECTIONAL ASSOCIATIVE MEMORY

All of the networks described to this point share the attribute of *learning* about an application through repetitive exposure to example patterns taken from the application domain. In this section, we shall consider a network paradigm that performs complex, multidimensional pattern transformations after being *initialized* with connection weights that are computed ahead of time for the desired application. To simplify the discussion, we shall first consider the operation of the bidirectional associative memory (BAM), [8] which performs a two-way mapping between pattern spaces. We then extend the discussion to include networks that perform a mapping function among multiple pattern spaces.

2.4.1   The Bidirectional Associative Memory

As in our previous discussions, we begin our examination of the BAM with a description of the type of function we desire the network to perform. The BAM is designed to perform a simultaneous mapping between two vector spaces, which we will refer to as $\mathbf{x}$ and $\mathbf{y}$. Specifically, let our training[11] data consist of a set of L ordered vector pairs, $\{(\mathbf{x}_1, \mathbf{y}_1), (\mathbf{x}_2, \mathbf{y}_2), \ldots, (\mathbf{x}_L, \mathbf{y}_L)\}$, with $\mathbf{x}_i \in R^n$, and $\mathbf{y}_i \in R^m$. Then, we can describe the desired behavior for the BAM in the following manner: Given any pattern vector from the training set, $\mathbf{x}_i$, the BAM will produce the corresponding $\mathbf{y}_i$ as output and, conversely, will produce the appropriate $\mathbf{x}_i$ from its associated $\mathbf{y}_i$.

If we make the further restriction that all $\mathbf{x}_i$ vectors form an orthonormal set, we can construct an **interpolative associative memory** by defining the weight matrix, $\mathbf{W}$, for the interconnections from the $\mathbf{x}$ layer to the $\mathbf{y}$ layer as

$$\mathbf{W} = \sum_{i=1}^{L} \mathbf{y}_i \mathbf{x}_i^t \qquad (2.19)$$

Similarly, the connection weights from the $\mathbf{y}$ layer back to the $\mathbf{x}$ layer are simply the transpose of $\mathbf{W}$.

In this context, an interpolative associative memory is a device that performs a mapping, Φ, from $\mathbf{x}$ to $\mathbf{y}$ such that $\Phi(\mathbf{x}_i) = \mathbf{y}_i$ if $\mathbf{x}_i$ is a member of the training set, and, if presented with an arbitrary $\mathbf{x}$, $\Phi(\mathbf{x}) = \mathbf{y}_i$ if $\mathbf{x}$ is *closer*[12] to $\mathbf{x}_i$ than it is to any other $\mathbf{x}_j$, $j = 1, 2, \ldots, L$.

The network architecture needed to perform this type of function is shown in Figure 2.14. Here, as with the ART networks, the BAM consists of two layers of units, with the output from each layer fully interconnected with the units on the other layer. Activation patterns, $\mathbf{x}$ and $\mathbf{y}$, are accessed through the external connections to the network.

By combining the standard computation for the activation of units given by Eq. (1.4) with an activation function for units in the BAM given by

$$f(a_i(t)) = \begin{cases} +1 & a_i(t) > 0 \\ a_i(t-1) & a_i(t) = 0 \\ -1 & a_i(t) < 0 \end{cases} \qquad (2.20)$$

---

11. The word *training* is used here only to indicate that the application data embody the desired mapping. As mentioned previously, no iterative *learning* occurs in this network.

12. The concept of *closeness* is relative to how patterns are compared by the network. In the BAM, closeness is measured in terms of Hamming distance.

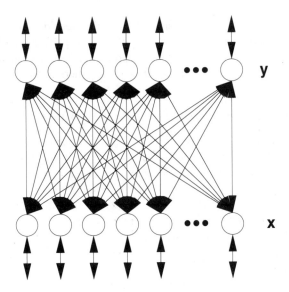

Figure 2.14   This diagram illustrates the structure of the BAM. Notice that the connections between layers are shown as bidirectional connections, indicating that the units on each layer communicate directly with all units on the other layer.

we will have constructed a processing model that behaves like the interpolative associative memory, described previously. To illustrate the operation of the network, consider the following algorithm:

1. After initialization of the weight matrices, apply an initial input vector to either (or both) the **x** and **y** layers in the BAM. Use a -1 to represent the inactive state, and a $+1$ to indicate the active state of the units.

2. Propagate the input pattern to the other layer (or, in the case when both inputs are present, select either **x** or **y** as the initial source) using Eq. (1.1).

3. Compute the new activation pattern at the destination layer by applying Eq. (2.20).

4. Propagate the new activation pattern back to the source layer, again using Eq. (1.1).

5. Update the activation on the first layer by applying Eq. (2.20).

6. Repeat steps 2 through 5 until the activation patterns stop changing in both layers.

In my earlier text [4], we provide a detailed mathematical analysis of the operation of the BAM, and show why it will always converge to a stable configuration. Without going into that level of detail here, we can conceptualize the operation of the BAM by drawing an analogy between the iteration of activation patterns between layers in the network, and the process of minimizing an energy (or **Lyapunov**) function in a dynamical system. Using this analogy, we can describe the configuration of the network (given by the connection-weight matrix) as an *energy landscape*. The initial state of the system, specified by the input pattern vector(s), describes a point on the energy landscape. If the input vector(s) match one (or both) of the training vectors, the starting point is one of the energy minima. If, however, the input vector(s) differ from the patterns in the training set, the starting point is a point of higher potential on the energy landscape.

Successively iterating the new pattern between layers lowers the energy in the system, and, eventually, the network settles into a state where the activation in each layer of units represents either the best match input pattern and its associated output, or the complement of those patterns. Because the connection weights in the BAM remain unchanged after initialization, we can now see that pattern matching and associative memory recall is accomplished in the BAM by minimizing the Lyapunov function defined by its connection-weight matrix, starting from a point on the energy landscape determined by the input pattern vector.

2.4.2   Extending the BAM

Using the BAM architecture as a starting point, Masifuma Hagiwara [6] of Keio University described a straightforward method for extending that architecture into a multidirectional associative memory (MAM). Figure 2.15 depicts several possible configurations of such a network, with the interconnection-weight matrices defined between each combination of two layers in the same manner as they were defined for the BAM.

The algorithm for accessing the information stored in such a network is the same as for the BAM, with the addition of the extra steps necessary to account for all of the layers in the MAM. One benefit of extending the architecture to allow MAM mappings is to improve the performance of such a system in the face of noisy input patterns. In the BAM, for example, it is possible to settle in a minimum energy state that recalls the *complement* of the training patterns. That possibility is reduced by the addition of the extra layers, because each additional layer provides a feedback mechanism to every other layer. Figure 2.16 illustrates this performance enhancement by comparing the ability of a BAM and a three-way MAM to accept a noisy input and convert it into the appropriate pattern.

2.5   THE HOPFIELD MEMORY

A **recurrent network** is one in which **feedback** connections are implemented between layers. In its simplest form, a recurrent network has feedback connections only from the output layer directly back to the input layer. The BAM is an example of such a network. However, there are multilayer recurrent-network models that allow feedback between all layers; that is, a hidden layer will provide feedback to the input layer, and the output will provide feedback to the hidden layer. The common denominator in all multilayer recurrent networks is the function of

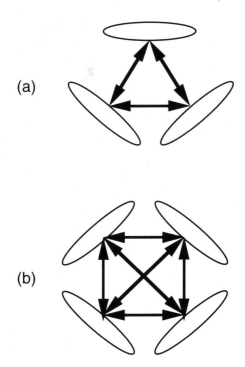

Figure 2.15 Several possible configurations for the MAM are shown. In each case, the connection-weight matrix between layers is defined in exactly the same manner as the connection-weight matrix was defined for the BAM. (a) A three-way associative memory. (b) A four-way associative memory.

the feedback connections—they are used as a *state indicator,* endowing the network with the ability to anticipate its next state from its current state. Figure 2.17 illustrates the general form of a multilayer recurrent network.

The Hopfield memory (named for its inventor, Professor John Hopfield) is a unique implementation of a recurrent network. Unlike the BAM and multilayer networks that we have already studied, the Hopfield memory is constructed with only a single layer of units. In this arrangement, each unit receives a direct input signal from an external source, and feedback from every other unit in the network. A typical Hopfield network is illustrated in Figure 2.18.

Inspection of the architecture of the Hopfield memory suggests the behavior of such a network: An external pattern is provided as an initial input, which the network then iterates (in discrete time) until it stabilizes in a particular state. At each time step, the activation of each Hopfield unit is dependent on the initial input and the feedback received from all other units.

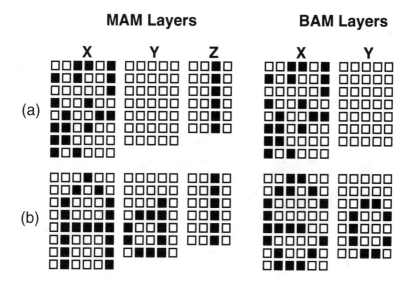

Figure 2.16   The ability of a MAM and a BAM to recall patterns stored in their internal connection-weight matrices is shown. (a) The initial input, shown as the activation pattern on layer **x**, is intended to represent the bit map of the character "A," corrupted with an error probability of 44%. (b) The three-layer MAM settles into a steady-state solution that shows the correct pattern, while the BAM converges into a false recollection state. *Source:* Multi-directional associative memory [6]. *Copyright ©1990, Lawrence Erlbaum Associates, Inc. Used with permission.*

2.5.1   Recurrent Signal Propagation

Before we consider the operation of the Hopfield memory, let us first investigate the process of recurrence in neural networks. We shall begin by looking at the propagation of signals through a single layer, feed-forward network. As illustrated in Figure 2.19, such a network takes an input pattern vector, **i,** and produces an output pattern vector **o** by propagating **i** through its internal connections and transforming the resulting activations through the application of an activation function. The process of computing the output pattern is analogous to a **vector-matrix multiplication**. We can represent the computation performed by this simple network mathematically as

$$\mathbf{o}(t) = \Gamma[\mathbf{Wi}(t)] \tag{2.21}$$

where $\Gamma[\cdot]$ represents the application of the activation function to each component of the vector produced by the vector-matrix multiplication between the input pattern $\mathbf{i}(t)$ and the weight matrix $\mathbf{W}$.

Specifically, let

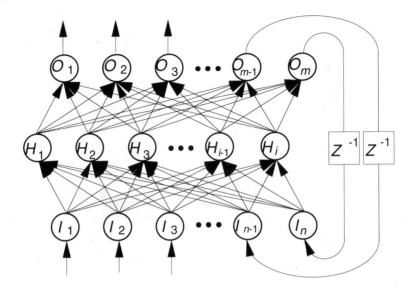

Figure 2.17 This diagram illustrates the architecture of one type of recurrent network. In this diagram, we have borrowed the z^{-1} notation from mathematics to denote a discrete time-step delay. The operation of this network is similar to the operation of the BPN, except that connections from the feedback units in the output layer are provided directly to the respective input units in the network. Notice that feedback connections are matched 1:1 between input and output units, not fully interconnected like the normal units on each layer.

$$\mathbf{W} = \begin{bmatrix} w_{11} & w_{12} & \cdots & w_{1n} \\ w_{21} & w_{22} & \cdots & w_{2n} \\ \vdots & \vdots & \cdots & \vdots \\ w_{m1} & w_{m2} & \cdots & w_{mn} \end{bmatrix} \tag{2.22}$$

Now, given an input vector $\mathbf{i}(t)$, the function performed by the operator $\Gamma[\cdot]$ is described by a vector-matrix multiply, followed by the application of the activation function to each component of the resulting activation vector.

Equation (2.21) describes the general process of computing an output from an input performed by a layer of network units. However, because we are now dealing with recurrence, we must consider the operation of the network in discrete time. At every time step, t, the input received by a unit is the combination of the original input vector, $\mathbf{i}(t)$, and the output produced by the layer at an earlier time, as seen through the feedback connections to the unit, $\mathbf{o}(t-1)\,\mathbf{W}$. For the purpose of simplifying our analysis, we shall consider the delay to be equivalent to a single time step, which is also the amount of time required by each unit to compute an output from the current input. Such a network is depicted in Figure 2.20.

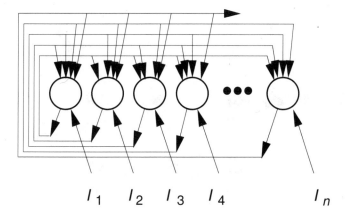

Figure 2.18 The architecture of the Hopfield memory is shown. In this diagram, we have eliminated any feedback connections from each unit to itself. The operation of this network is described in the text. *Source:* Neural Networks: Algorithms, Applications, and Programming Techniques [2]. *Copyright ©1991, Addison-Wesley. Used with permission.*

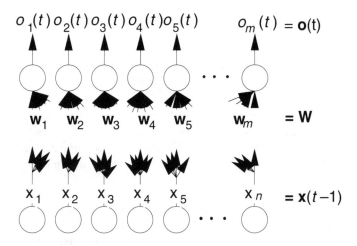

Figure 2.19 A neural-network model illustrating the analogy between network computation and a vector-matrix multiplication. The details of this computation are described in the text.

We assume that, prior to receiving any external input, all units on the layer are quiescent. When the first input pattern arrives at time t_0, the total input received by a unit is restricted to the external input, $i_i(t_0)$, because

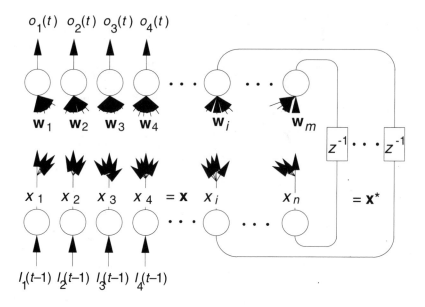

Figure 2.20 A recurrent neural network illustrating the delay required by the feedback from the output is shown. To distinguish between the external input, $\mathbf{i}(t)$, and the net input received by each unit (including the feedback signals), we will refer to the net input as $\mathbf{x}(t)$.

$$\Gamma[x(t_0)] = \Gamma[\mathbf{i}(t_0) + \mathbf{W}\emptyset] \qquad (2.23)$$
$$= \Gamma[\mathbf{i}(t_0)]$$

Using this model, we can describe the processing performed by a recurrent network as a series of **state transitions**. At time t_0, the output from the network is determined only by the input pattern. Feedback from the output is delayed until the next time step. At each subsequent time step, the output from the network is given by

$$\mathbf{o}(t) = \Gamma[\mathbf{W}\mathbf{x}(t-1)] \qquad (2.24)$$

where the input vector is the recurrent function of all previous time steps. The dependence of the network on the initial input becomes evident if we expand Eq. (2.21) to an arbitrary time step t,

$$\mathbf{o}(t_1) = \Gamma[\mathbf{W}\mathbf{x}(t_0)]$$
$$\mathbf{o}(t_2) = \Gamma[\mathbf{W}\Gamma[\mathbf{x}(t_0)]]$$
$$\vdots$$
$$\mathbf{o}(t) = \Gamma[\mathbf{W}\Gamma[\dots\Gamma[\mathbf{W}\mathbf{x}(t_0)]\dots]] \qquad (2.25)$$

where, according to Eq. (2.23), $\mathbf{x}(t_0) = \mathbf{i}(t_0)$.

This processing model summarizes the operations performed in an iterative recurrent-network, such as the Hopfield memory, but obviously is not appropriate for all recurrent-network models. In fact, the Elman and Jordan networks described earlier in this chapter do not operate iteratively at all; rather, these recurrent networks rely on the fact that the feedback units are in a stable state *prior* to any forward pattern propagation. That being said, let us now consider the operation of the Hopfield memory.

2.5.2 Signal Propagation in the Hopfield Memory

To put the operation of the Hopfield memory in practical terms, we should note the similarity between this network and an analog electrical circuit with feedback. As shown in Figure 2.21, the Hopfield memory can be implemented as a series of sigmoidal amplifiers providing feedback to each other through resistive elements. The inputs to the amplifier are not perfect: Each has a resistive-capacitive (RC) component that must be considered. Inspection of the electrical model indicates that every unit in the network receives an input that is the combination of the external input and the feedback signals from all other units, minus the leakage that must occur across the input resistor. Thus, we can write the computation performed by each unit in the Hopfield network at each time step as

$$\Delta u_i = \left(\sum_{j=1}^{n} w_{ij} v_j - \frac{u_i}{\tau} + i_i \right) \Delta t \qquad (2.26)$$

where the term v_j represents the output from the jth unit at the previous time step, and τ is the system time constant.[13]

The Hopfield memory is similar in structure to the single-layer network we examined in the previous section, with only the interconnections between each unit and itself eliminated. Thus, the weight matrix ($\mathbf{W}$) for the Hopfield memory is described by

$$\mathbf{W} = \begin{bmatrix} 0 & w_{12} & \cdots & w_{1n} \\ w_{21} & 0 & \cdots & w_{2n} \\ \vdots & \vdots & \cdots & \vdots \\ w_{m1} & w_{m2} & \cdots & 0 \end{bmatrix} \qquad (2.27)$$

By substituting this new matrix for $\mathbf{W}$ in Eq. (2.23), we can see the similarity between the computation performed by the Hopfield memory, as described in Eq. (2.24), and the computation performed by a general recurrent network. In the Hopfield memory, the activation at each time step for every unit in the network is determined by the external input to the unit (i_i) and the weighted sum of the feedback to the unit from all other units. Moreover, the feedback in the Hopfield memory, and hence the output at any time $t \gg 0$ is a recurrent function of the

---

13. From the analogy to the analog RC electrical circuit indicated earlier.

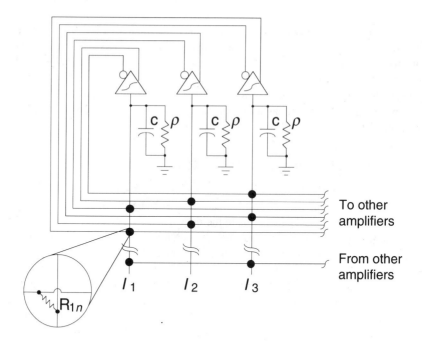

Figure 2.21   The electrical model illustrating the structure of the Hopfield memory is shown. In this diagram, the solid dots represent weighted connections, as shown in detail in the exploded view. Because resistors always have positive values, we instead use inverting amplifiers to model the inhibitory connections. Note that there is no feedback between any unit and itself in this arrangement. *Source:* Neural Networks: Algorithms, Applications, and Programming Techniques [2]. *Copyright © 1991, Addison-Wesley. Used with permission.*

original input. Given this processing model, there are only two outcomes that can be reasonably expected: The network will either oscillate between output states forever, or will eventually settle into a stable pattern that is reinforced by the feedback in the network. Obviously, the desirable situation is to have the network stabilize. But how can we guarantee that it will?

The answer to that question is in the form of the connection-weight matrix. Mathematically, if the weight matrix is symmetric, convergence is guaranteed. The issue, then, becomes one of ensuring that the connection weights in the Hopfield memory are configured appropriately for the specific application.

2.5.3   Connection-Weight Initialization

The Hopfield network, like the BAM and MAM networks described earlier, is initialized to perform a specific application, rather than adapting its connection weights during a learning period. Unlike the BAM and MAM networks, however, the connections in the Hopfield network are initialized to values that numerically describe an energy function that is defined specifically for the application. The classic example of the Hopfield network is the "Traveling Salesperson" (TSP) problem, which is described at length in [13] and [4].

In essence, the connection weights in the Hopfield network are *selectively* set to ensure that only certain units are active at any given time. This is accomplished by setting the feedback connections between each unit and its neighboring units such that an active output from one unit tends to inhibit its neighbors. Because feedback is provided between all units in the network, and all other units, we can guarantee that the weight matrix is symmetrical by simply ensuring that the feedback connection weight between any two units, which we shall arbitrarily refer to as A and B, is the same as the feedback connection between B and A.

Thus, by initializing the network connection weights, instead of allowing the network to find its own weighting values, *we* ensure that the network will converge to a solution. In Chapter 8, we shall investigate an interesting variation on the Hopfield memory, which allows the connection weights to be adapted to improve the performance of the network over time.

2.6 NETWORK-LEARNING SUMMARY

In the previous sections, we have described several different methods for determining the connection-weight values needed to produce a neural network that will solve a particular problem. In so doing, we have (hopefully) conveyed the idea that each network paradigm has its own quirks and foibles, determined by the structure of the particular network, the learning process employed by the network, and the method by which units compute their activation values. The point of this discussion was to show that there are many different kinds of neural networks, and that each has a very particular kind of problem that it is designed to solve. The misuse of a neural-network paradigm is very often the reason why applications fail. Now that we are armed with an understanding of the internals of the various neural-network paradigms, we can begin to better determine which networks are most appropriate for a particular problem.

SUGGESTED READINGS

There are a number of excellent textbooks that describe the detailed operation of the various networks we have discussed in this chapter. For those interested in the underlying algorithms, as well as understanding how to go about writing programs to implement the simulations of these networks on conventional computers, an excellent text is *Neural Networks: Algorithms, Applications, and Programming Techniques* by James A. Freeman and David M. Skapura [4]. Another excellent book describing the operation of these and various other network paradigms, as well as many applications of the technology is *Introduction to Artificial Neural Systems* by Jacek Zurada [14]. For those interested in exploring the variety of data representation schemes used to address specific applications, the series of books edited by Branko Soucek and The IRIS Group [15–17] presents an outstanding compilation of papers describing the implementation of neural-network applications on a variety of computer platforms. Of course, the proceedings of any of the major conferences on neural networks, such as the IEEE Conference on Neural Networks or the INNS World Congress on Neural Networks, always contain an excellent cross section of the theory and application of the technology.

BIBLIOGRAPHY

1. Gail A. Carpenter and Stephen Grossberg. Invariant pattern recognition and recall by an attentive self-organizing ART architecture in a nonstationary world. In Maureen Caudill and Charles Butler, editors, *Proceedings of the IEEE International Conference on Neural Networks.* San Diego, CA, pp. II(727–735), June 1987.

2. Gail A. Carpenter, Stephen Grossberg, and Courosh Mehanian. Invariant recognition of cluttered scenes by a self-organizing ART architecture: CORT-X boundary segmentation. *Neural Networks,* 2(3):169–181, 1989.

3. James A. Freeman. *Simulating Neural Networks with Mathematica.* Addison-Wesley Publishing Company, Reading, MA, 1994.

4. James A. Freeman and David M. Skapura. *Neural Networks: Algorithms, Applications, and Programming Techniques.* Addison-Wesley Publishing Company, Reading, MA, 1991.

5. Stephen Grossberg. A neural model of attention, reinforcement, and discrimination learning. *International Review of Neurobiology,* 18:263–327, 1975.

6. Masifuma Hagiwara. Multi-directional associative memories. In *Proceedings of the International Joint Conference on Neural Networks,* pp. II(3–9), Washington, DC, January 1990.

7. Robert Hecht-Nielsen. Counterpropagation networks. In Maureen Caudill and Charles Butler, editors, *Proceedings of the IEEE International Conference on Neural Networks.* San Diego, CA, June 1987.

8. Bart Kosko. Bidirectional associative memories. *IEEE Transactions on Systems, Man and Cybernetics,* 18(1):49–60, January–February 1988.

9. Terrence J. Sejnowski and C. R. Rosenberg. Parallel networks that learn to pronounce english text. *Complex Systems,* (1):145–168, 1987.

10. Branko Soucek, editor. *Fast Learning and Invariant Object Recognition.* John Wiley, New York, 1992.

11. Branko Soucek, editor. *Fuzzy, Holographic and Parallel Intelligence.* John Wiley, New York, 1992.

12. Branko Soucek, editor. *Neural and Massively Parallel Computers.* John Wiley, New York, 1988.

13. David W. Tank and John J. Hopfield. Collective computation in neuronlike circuits. *Scientific American,* 257(6):104–114, December 1987.

14. Jacek Zurada. *Introduction to Artificial Neural Systems.* West Publishing Company, St. Paul, MN, 1992.

Application Design

The journey of a thousand miles begins with one step.

— Lao-Tsze

In the first two chapters of this book, we discussed how neural networks operate microscopically and macroscopically. We have seen how all neural-network models share certain operational characteristics, such as the distribution of knowledge throughout the network structure, and the massively parallel operation of the system. The most important characteristic shared by all of these networks, however, is that they all perform some useful information-processing function that can be exploited to solve other problems.

However, simply knowing how these neural-network models behave is quite often only half of the problem in creating practical applications. The other aspect of building successful neural-network applications is the process of acquiring and modeling the application data, selecting the most appropriate network model for the application, and training the network to perform the application. In this chapter, we shall focus on the process of application-data modeling, showing the interrelationship between the chosen data representation scheme and the operation of the neural-network processing model.

We shall begin our study of neural-network application design by first describing some of the issues that an application developer will likely encounter when building a neural-network application. We shall then tie together the concepts of data representation and network paradigm selection, showing why the behavior of the network model must be considered when developing an application. We conclude this chapter by describing, in detail, a specific example of a viable neural-network application, illustrating the process of collecting and refining the training data for the network.

3.1 DEVELOPING A DATA REPRESENTATION

From our discussion of neural-network operational characteristics in the first two chapters of this book, we know that all of the popular neural-network paradigms process information in the form of input pattern vectors. We also know that all of the neural models produce an output pattern that must be interpreted by a higher-level process, although the actual form of the output will vary depending on the specific network model. For example, the BPN produces an output pattern that is completely independent of the input pattern; that is, the output produced by the network is generated by a different set of processing elements than those that accept the input pattern. In contrast, the Hopfield memory produces an output pattern that is actually an altered form of the original input pattern.

In all cases, the pattern vectors propagated through the network model always comprise one of two types of signal[1] components: **analog,** or *continuously variable,* signals; and **discrete,** or *quantized,* signals. In Figure 3.1, we illustrate the different types of informational signals used in neural-network models. Notice that both types of signals share one common trait: Both are finite-amplitude signals, varying in amplitude between their minimum and maximum values, although the range of the variance may differ dramatically from signal to signal.

As we already know, most of our neural-network models are designed to detect, and respond to, the presence of *features* in an input pattern vector that is presented as a static pattern to the network. Here, then, is the crux of the dilemma that we face as application developers: How can we capture a myriad of time-varying signals and represent them so that a neural-network model can process them as spatial pattern vectors?

Because our job as applications designers is to create a network that performs the correct input-to-output transformation across a wide variety of different input patterns, we must consider how our choice of pattern representation will interact with the network model when information is propagating through the network. In essence, we must design the data representation scheme for the application to maximize the ability of the selected network model to detect, and respond to, any features that may exist in the input pattern that will enable the network to produce the correct output pattern. Here, we must concern ourselves with the issues of deciding how to capture the application data, and properly format it prior to presentation to the network.

Then, too, we must consider the representation of the output pattern that we will ask the network to produce, and balance that against the intrinsic ability of the network model to produce the desired output. All too often, novice applica-

---

1. In the ensuing discussion, we shall describe the operation of the neural models as though the network exists as a physical entity. Because most network models are (at least, initially) implemented as software simulations, the idea of "signals propagating through connections" is clearly an abstract concept.

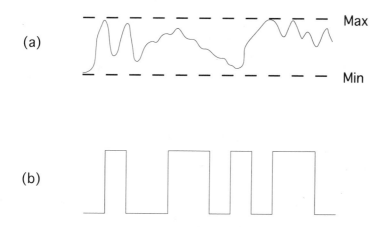

Figure 3.1 This diagram depicts the two different types of information-bearing signals that can be used by a neural model. Notice that the signals do not need to be periodic, nor does the time base need to be consistent between different signals. (a) Analog signals vary in amplitude smoothly, allowing the signal to take on any value between its minimum and maximum amplitude. (b) A discrete signal behaves as a step function. A signal of this type can take on only one of two values: its minimum and maximum amplitudes. Values between the minimum and maximum are never valid.

tion developers select a "natural" representation for the output, only to find after hours[2] of training time that the network cannot produce the desired output.

In the remainder of this section, we shall consider these issues in depth, and provide a set of guidelines that can be used to maximize the success rate of an application using neural-network models. We begin this discussion by addressing the issue of scaling input signals prior to presentation to a neural-network model.

3.1.1 Internal Representation Issues

All of the neural models described in Chapter 2 of this book, and all of the paradigms used to construct the applications described in subsequent chapters, are defined to process patterns that are composed of signals that are limited in amplitude. Typically, these signals are held in the range of zero and one.[3] We impose these limits on the pattern signals to allow the network to use its interconnection weights to encode the representation of the application pattern vectors.

If we did not limit the amplitude of signals in the network, pattern components with very large amplitude swings would dominate the behavior of the network. This is true because, as we described in Chapter 1, the instantaneous

2. Or perhaps weeks.

3. Some network models require that signal values vary in range between -1 and 1. We will henceforth use the term *bipolar* to distinguish these networks from their *binary* counterparts.

behavior of each processing element in the network is governed by the total stimulation received by the unit, which we have defined as the algebraic sum of all of the weighted input signals to the unit. Recall from Chapter 1,

$$\text{net}_j = \sum_{i=1}^{n} o_i w_{ji} \tag{3.1}$$

where net_j is the activation of the jth unit in the network, which is determined by gating the output of the ith unit (o_i) through the modulating interconnection between the units (w_{ji}), for all input signals.

Inspection of Eq. (3.1) tells us that, to allow the network connection-weight values to control the activation of each unit, we must ensure that the output signal from each unit (or external input) be limited in amplitude to a fairly narrow range, typically between zero and one. Otherwise, signals with very large amplitudes will saturate the activation function of the unit during training, and diminish the effective range of the interconnection weights in the network. This issue is particularly relevant when we consider that most of the activation functions used in neural-network models are designed to switch between the active and inactive states at approximately zero activation. Moreover, signals propagating through a network structure are transient, generated in response to the instantaneous input to the network. Therefore, if we were to allow signals of significantly different amplitudes to propagate through a given network, the network would have no way of determining which units were activated in response to large, instantaneous signals, and which were activated because a connection weight (or set of weights) was set to amplify a specific, but low-amplitude, signal.

In contrast, by limiting the amplitude of the signals propagating through the network to the range between zero and one, we give the network a much greater effective range for connection-weight values. As shown in Figure 3.2, large, positive connection weights will enhance a unit's response to a signal, while large, negative connection weights will suppress a unit's response. Also, we can effectively *disconnect* an input to a unit by setting the connection-weight value for that input to zero. In this manner, the network can encode information by selectively varying the values of the weights in each of the interconnections.

3.1.2   External Interpretation Issues

Another important concept to consider when developing an application using neural networks is how the output from each layer in the network is to be interpreted. From an application perspective, we shall be primarily concerned with the interpretation of the input and output patterns, because the behavior of the network will, for the most part, govern the internal representation of information in the network.

In this regard, it is important to recognize that, individually, the processing elements within a network have little or no understanding of the application the network is being asked to learn. The only thing the processing elements know

Figure 3.2 This diagram illustrates how very large input signals can dominate the behavior of a neural network. Using line thickness to depict the effective range of values for each connection weight, this diagram shows that the interconnections from the unit with the large amplitude signal have a narrow effective range, between -1 and $+1$, because values outside this range will only amplify the magnitude of the input signal. However, by limiting the magnitude of the input signal, the connection weight has a much larger effective range, and thus can be used to amplify, attenuate, or squelch the input signal. It is this characteristic of selectively enhancing or diminishing certain input components that enables a neural network to perform complex pattern matching. It is also the reason why we must limit the magnitude of the signals within the network.

how to do is to compute an input stimulation and produce a corresponding output signal. Similarly, the patterns that are propagated through a neural network consist of a set of component signals that, individually, reveal very little about the entire pattern.

Even when viewed collectively, the patterns often do not take on a meaning until we define how the information is to be interpreted *externally*. As an illustration, consider the binary patterns

$$\mathbf{x} = 00010001011111000100011001011001001$$
$$\mathbf{y} = 10000100001000010000100001000011110$$

Without an interpretation, all we can say about $\mathbf{x}$ and $\mathbf{y}$ is that these two patterns are significantly different from each other. But how different are they? There are many methods we could use to analyze the degree of difference between them. For example, we could choose to interpret $\mathbf{x}$ and $\mathbf{y}$ as binary numbers. We

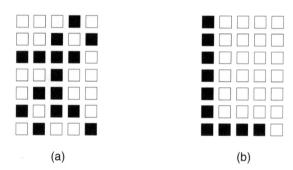

(a)   (b)

Figure 3.3   This diagram illustrates how the character *L* can be represented as a bit-mapped vector. We interpret the pattern vectors by first chopping each 35-element vector into a 7 row × 5 column matrix. Then, by replacing each 1 in the resulting matrix with an opaque dot, and each 0 with a transparent dot, we obtain a pattern that resembles the symbol "L" as might be written (a) cursively, and (b) in block form.

could then say that the difference between **x** and **y** is the mathematical difference, given by $x - y$. Another interpretation might cause us to consider **x** and **y** as pattern *vectors*, with significance in both magnitude and direction in hyperspace. Using such a scheme, each bit position in the pattern vector would be interpreted as an indication of the status of the individual components in the pattern. To analyze the difference[4] between patterns, we might employ a vector inner-product calculation to determine the projection of **x** onto **y**.

   In both of these examples, every bit position in each pattern has significance. We cannot change the state of a single bit anywhere in either pattern without (perhaps significantly) altering the interpretation of the pattern. Fixed pattern representations, such as those just described, are common in computer applications because modern digital computers are designed to efficiently perform explicit comparisons. However, many applications that are now considered "difficult" on conventional computers involve the analysis of patterns that do not have an explicit representation. Quite often in problems of this kind, significantly different patterns must be associated together in order to produce the same results. Such is the case with the patterns contained in **x** and **y**.

   Surprisingly, as different as **x** and **y** appear on initial inspection, there is at least one easily observed interpretation that produces two different representations of the same thing: The image of the letter "L." Figure 3.3 illustrates how we produce this interpretation.

   Given this new interpretation scheme, it is easy to see how **x** and **y** are related. Prior to having that interpretation, however, comprehending the information in the patterns was difficult. By extension, we cannot expect our neural-

---

4. Or, perhaps more importantly, the *similarity*.

network models to have any inherent understanding of an application; *we* must provide that interpretation outside the network.

3.2 PATTERN REPRESENTATION METHODS

There are a variety of techniques that can be used to represent an external parameter for a neural-network model. The selection of an *appropriate* technique, however, is often complicated by a number of application-specific factors, including

- *The nature of the data source.* Specifically, is the parameter being modeled a continuously variable signal, or is it a discrete value?

- *The range of the parameter.* Because we want to compress the effective range of all external signals to values between zero and one, we must consider the entire range of values for the parameter *across the entire training set.*

- *Any interrelationship between parameters.* Often, an application will use a number of parameters from different, but related, data sources. In such cases, it often (but not always) makes sense to treat these parameters in a similar fashion.

- *Any interrelationship between patterns.* The most common mistake made by novices is to assume that there is no duplication of information in any of the training patterns they have collected, when, in fact, *they* have introduced duplications by their selection of data-formatting schemes.

Unfortunately, there are no hard and fast rules that can be used to determine how each parameter in an application data set should be represented. Often, the determination of the best technique comes from an innate understanding of the application. For the novice neural-network practitioner, however, the choice of an appropriate representation scheme for the application data also requires some insight into how the network will treat the data internally. For that reason, we shall now explore several common techniques for neural-network application-data formatting, emphasizing the interaction between the data-representation scheme and the network operation.

Obviously, the following review is not meant to be an exhaustive summary of all possible techniques for data formatting. Quite often, the application designer must be creative when developing a suitable representation scheme for a specific application. The following summary is, however, a good synopsis of the most common, and practical, techniques used to format data for neural-network applications.

3.2.1 Binary Patterns

As we now know, neural-network processing elements produce output signals that vary in magnitude, usually in the range from zero to one. We have also assumed throughout our discussions that input and output patterns are comprised of a set of numerical values in the range of the output signals produced by the units in the network. It is therefore not very difficult to understand why binary patterns are the easiest patterns to represent for a network; they provide a very direct method of representing an input pattern. We simply list the features of the input that we deem important to distinguish the pattern, associate each feature with a bit position in a pattern vector, and use the binary digits {0, 1} to indicate the presence or absence of the features in each pattern instance. Usually, because of the way information is propagated through a neural network, we choose 1 as the representation of an active pattern element, and 0 to indicate the absence of a feature.

With regard to output patterns, most applications that utilize a binary-data format can be thought of as performing a *classification* function; that is, the outputs produced by such a network are interpreted as an indication that the input pattern belongs to a particular class of patterns seen during training that share common attributes. Sometimes, the classifications are exclusive. In such cases, only one output unit is active for any given input pattern, and the active output is interpreted as an indication of the category to which the input pattern belongs. In other cases, the classifications are more general, and multiple output units can be active simultaneously.

In all cases, however, whenever a binary representation is chosen for a particular application, any processing element that must produce binary output signals will employ some form of nonlinear function as its activation function, such as the sigmoid. The reason for choosing a nonlinear function can be found by relating the binary nature of the data representation to the activation response of the function. In order to classify patterns into one of two states, the network units must utilize an activation function with a bistable response.

Exercise 3.1: Consider a neural-network application to map a set of attributes to a room designation. For example, in a house, a living room normally contains a sofa, a coffee table, and a floor lamp, while a kitchen contains an oven, a refrigerator, and a table. Devise a data representation for a network that will accept an attribute pattern vector and produce a corresponding room designation for five different rooms. Generate a set of training patterns, consisting of a number of attribute-designation vector pairs, to show how your data representation solves the problem. ∎

3.2.2   Tertiary and *n*-ary Patterns

The binary representation scheme maps nicely into all neural-network paradigms. In fact, it can be used in any situation where patterns are composed of elements that are either present or absent, such as in video displays, where luminescent dots are used to produce monochromatic images, or in diagnostic applications, where the presence or absence of symptoms can be used to deduce problems. Unfortunately, not all applications can be modeled using a simple binary representation.

In many situations, pattern elements are not always simply present or absent—
sometimes, they are also in an intermediate, or a *don't care*, state.

A good example of this kind of situation can be found in the representation of
the state patterns for a game such as tic-tac-toe. In tic-tac-toe, each board position
can have *three* states: It can be occupied by the "X" token, occupied by the "O"
token, or vacant. If we attempt to model the game situation by using a binary
representation of the current board state, we quickly find that it is not possible
to map three conditions into two indicators. To resolve problems of this type, we
shall now consider an extended form of binary representation.

Many successful neural-network applications overcome the *n*-ary representation problem by using multiple binary inputs (or outputs) to represent non-
binary states. The most straightforward approach is to consider each feature in
the pattern as an individual subpattern. Then, for each subpattern, choose a data
representation that allocates as many positions in the pattern vector as there are
possible states for the feature. Finally, concatenate the multiple subpatterns into
one long pattern vector. Figure 3.4 illustrates this concept for the tic-tac-toe example.

Exercise 3.2: Modify your data representation scheme from Exercise 3.1 to include attributes that are common to more than one room. For example, a *fireplace*
could be an attribute of a living room and a game room. Show how your modified
representation scheme deals with shared attributes when the attribute is unknown
for a certain room. ■

A significant benefit of this representation scheme is that it lends itself to
many neural-network applications where the network must discriminate between
similar patterns. This data-representation scheme supports that behavior in a network by insisting that different subpattern vectors are orthogonal to each other.
Because most network units compute their input stimulation using an inner-
product calculation, orthogonal vectors are easily detected by the network.

There are drawbacks to this approach, as well. The most significant is the
issue of network size. As we have seen previously, the addition of a single unit in
a layered network structure increases the number of connections that have to be
modeled by the number of input units plus the number of output units connected
to the new unit. Because most neural networks are simulated in software (at least
initially), each connection in the network consumes memory, and requires CPU
time to process. Therefore, by using a very large number of input units to model
n categories, we have geometrically increased the amount of memory needed
to model the network and the amount of time needed to propagate information
through the network structure.

3.2.3   Analog Patterns

Another method for representing *n*-ary data in a neural network is to use a single
unit to represent each feature, but, rather than simply indicating the presence
or absence of the feature with binary numbers, we **scale** the value to indicate

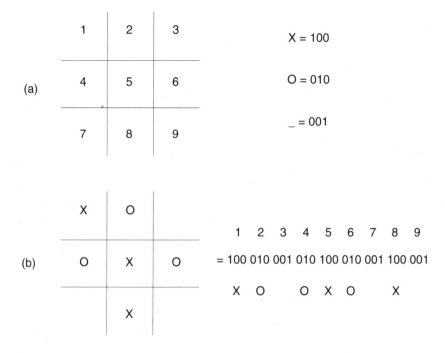

Figure 3.4 A scheme for representing the tertiary tic-tac-toe game situation is shown. In this example, each board position is allocated three pattern elements, one to indicate that the position is occupied by the "X" token, one to indicate that the position is occupied by the "O" token, and one to indicate the position is vacant. The entire data game situation is then the concatenation of the nine subpattern representations, where the first three pattern elements indicate the state of the first board position, the second three indicate the state of the second position, and so on.

the degree to which a feature exists in a particular pattern. As before, when a feature is present in a pattern, we denote that fact by representing the feature with a 1 at the corresponding position in the pattern vector. Likewise, when the feature is absent, we indicate that condition by setting the corresponding pattern component to 0. To indicate that a feature is in a third (or n^{th} state, we use a value proportional to the state of the unit, scaled between 0 and 1. If, for example, a feature can take on three states, we might represent the third state with a value of 0.5. It is important to recognize, however, that the values chosen to represent the different states ought to reflect the magnitude of the change in the feature.

In the tic-tac-toe game representation problem, for example, our first attempt at assigning values to the different position states might naturally cause us to use a 0 to indicate an unoccupied position, a 0.5 to indicate the "O" token occupies the position, and a 1 to indicate the "X" token owns the position. However, using this representation scheme is an error, in that asking a network unit to learn to produce an intermediate output (the target value 0.5) is significantly more difficult than expecting a binary unit to learn to saturate one way or the other under certain conditions. A much better representation for this example would be to let a 0 indicate that the "O" token owns the position, a 1 indicate that the "X" token owns the position, and the 0.5 to indicate the unoccupied state.

The same situation exists when using large-scale, continuously variable, or **analog**, signals in pattern vectors. Suppose, for example, that one component of an input pattern vector that we might need is a measurement taken from some data-acquisition device that provides an analog signal in the range of 0.0 to 1000.0. Suppose, further, that the signal that we want to model for the network normally varies in the range from 900 to 950. We can incorporate that signal into our pattern vector by simply scaling the signal to fit within the range corresponding to output signals produced by the neural-network units. In this case, we simply take the analog value provided by the instrument, subtract out the bias value (900), and scale it down by dividing by the valid range of the signal (50).

However, care must be taken when choosing to represent an output pattern component in this manner. The activation function chosen for the output layer of network units must allow the unit to produce a continuous output in the desired range. Alternatively, the network unit could produce a scaled-down output, which we would then convert to its true value by postprocessing the output. In either case, be certain that you have selected an activation function for the unit that is linear, or very nearly linear, in the range of the expected outputs.[5]

Also, we must be wary of the fact that a continuously variable network output unit that is expected to produce a very precise signal is being restricted to a very precise input stimulation value. Any network used to perform this function must be able to set its connection weights very precisely. In practice, it is extremely difficult to create a network that performs a complex transformation across a variety of patterns and still generates very precise output values, unless the network incorporates some type of pattern memory[6] as part of its structure. Thus, we must be careful to avoid using the wrong network paradigm when we expect the network to produce very precise output signals.

Exercise 3.3: Develop a general equation to scale a single component (x_i) to a value between two variable limits, which we will denote as L for the lower limit and U as the upper limit. You may assume that you have access to a function called max($\mathbf{x}$) that extracts the largest value from a set of values, $\mathbf{x}$, and another called min($\mathbf{x}$), which returns the smallest value. Note that negative numbers are legal. ■

---

5. Many times, I have seen students carelessly attempt to use sigmoidal units to produce analog outputs, and then wonder why the network could never produce an accurate solution.

6. Such as the competitive unit, as described in Chapter 2.

3.2.4   Temporal Patterns

One of the most confusing aspects of creating a data-formatting scheme for an application is the question of how to model parameters in the time domain for presentation to a spatial pattern network. Fortunately, not all applications require temporal patterns. However, some do, and most of the networks that are now in common use are not designed to process time-dependent data patterns. Instead, most network models respond to instantaneous pattern vectors that persist at least until the network has completely propagated the pattern through its internal structure. That being the case, we must devise a method for representing patterns that have a temporal relationship as spatial patterns for our networks.

The most natural, and commonly used method for accomplishing this task is to simply concatenate multiple, discrete time patterns into a single pattern vector. In this manner, the network will learn to distinguish the relationships between the different temporal patterns exactly as it learns to identify relationships in spatial patterns. For example, if we were to build a network that could recognize the differences between two monochromatic photographs of the same scene, taken a few seconds apart, our approach to formatting the image data would consist of the following steps:

1.   Digitize the photographs to produce two matrices of pixels, each describing one photograph.

2.   Scale each pixel to a value between zero and one. Notice that because the pixels all come from the same image source, we can use the same scale factor for all pixels.

3.   Create an image vector for each photograph by concatenating the rows in each matrix. This produces two image vectors.

4.   Create a pattern vector for the network by concatenating the two image vectors.

In Figure 3.5, we illustrate the process of concatenating temporal patterns.

The primary benefit of this approach to representing temporal data is that it maps cleanly into most real-world applications. For example, while comparing digitized photographic images is not usually considered a task for automation, comparing millions of sequential video frames is considered extremely difficult, even for people. Even for a neural network, such a task would prove impossible. Fortunately, most applications only require two or three frames of data to be compared during any given analysis. In this case, the network simply performs the same analysis repeatedly, shifting sequential video frames through a multiframe window.

Obviously, the drawback to this approach is the same as the problem associated with n-ary data patterns—the additional memory and CPU time needed to create and process a network that can accept twice (or three times) as much input data as is required for a single image is daunting. Another problem associated with this scheme is that, sometimes, it is not possible to capture the temporal

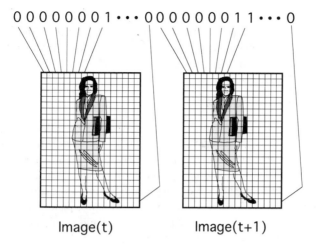

Figure 3.5   This diagram illustrates how temporal data can be encoded as a spatial pattern for examination by a neural network. Even though we show the pixel values as binary here, they could just as easily be analog values representing gray-scale intensity, or even color hue. The details of the pattern-generation process are described in the text.

aspect of the pattern data by simply concatenating discrete time pattern vectors. Fortunately, these situations are rarely encountered by the novice application developer.

3.3 EXEMPLAR ANALYSIS

The next step in building a successful neural network after collecting the application data that will be used to train the neural network and formatting that data for presentation to the network is to perform an analysis of the data. As part of the analysis process, we must ensure that

- The data collected provides an accurate representation of the application problem space;

- There are no inconsistencies in the data that the network will not be able to resolve; and

- Any problems uncovered as part of the analysis can be corrected without compromising the effectiveness of the network.

In the remainder of this section, we shall describe a methodology for performing such an analysis. For simplicity, we have assumed that the application uses a BPN model, although the concepts discussed could be easily adapted to other network models. We shall begin with an approach to ensuring that the training data provide a complete representation of the problem space. We shall then investigate some techniques for verifying that there are no anomalies in the data that would prevent the network from learning the desired transformation, and discuss methods for correcting such anomalies. We then conclude the discussion of our analysis strategy with some general suggestions for correcting the deficiencies that we might discover in our training set.

3.3.1 Ensuring Coverage

In any neural-network application, it is imperative to ensure that the data patterns used to train the network provide a complete representation of the problem space. If we do not, the network may learn how to perform the requested transformation on our training set, as well as *every* input pattern presented to it. When this situation occurs, we find that the network has learned only how to produce the desired outputs—not how to identify the features of the input pattern that characterize the desired outputs, which is the real reason for building the application in the first place. To ensure that the network can perform the desired transformation in production mode, we must provide it with example patterns during training that not only represent the desired output but also are contra-indicative of the desired output.

Ideally, the mix of patterns in an application where the network is being used to *classify* input patterns into an appropriate output pattern should be about one-to-one; that is, approximately half of the training patterns should represent the desired input-to-output pattern classification, while the other half of the exemplars should represent what we shall refer to as **null patterns,** which are simply patterns that do not indicate the desired output. However, caution is required when creating an application in this manner. After training such a network, the application developer must ensure that the network not only can perform the desired classification on valid input patterns but also can correctly identify all null patterns.

There are also exceptions to the 1:1 coverage rule. Specifically, we can forego the 1:1 pattern-mix requirement on any application where we can *guarantee* that the network will never be used to classify an input (after training) that can not be classified. In cases such as this, we assume that the process that runs to collect and format the data prior to propagation through the network also ensures that the data collected represent a viable pattern for classification.

For example, consider an application similar to the one described earlier in this chapter, where a neural network was to be used to classify an input image pattern consisting of monochromatic video pixels into a corresponding character representation. In this case, we could train a network to perform two simultaneous classifications: one indicating the character represented by the input image pattern, and another indicating the type of character represented by the image. In Figure 3.6, we illustrate a typical structure for a network designed to perform this character classification function.

By inspection of the output layer in this network structure, we can conclude that this network will *always* try to classify the input as one of the predefined character set, even if the input pattern is garbage. Because we have provided no

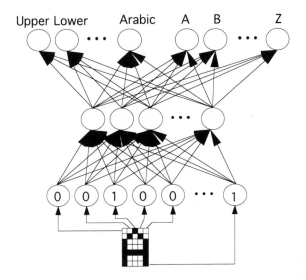

Figure 3.6 This diagram illustrates how a three-layer BPN could be constructed to classify a pixel image of a character into its corresponding type and identification. As shown on the output layer, we train the network to perform two simultaneous classifications, with a subset of the output units indicating the type of the character image, and the remainder identifying the character itself.

direct mechanism for the network to indicate that an input pattern is *not* one of the desired outputs, we must either ensure that the network is never asked to classify an invalid input, or we must use an indirect method to recognize an invalid pattern.

Unfortunately, there are drawbacks to both methods. If we attempt to filter out all possible illegal input patterns prior to propagating the pattern through the neural network, we will have effectively nullified the function of the network. Put another way, if we can identify all of the legal input patterns before we use the network to classify them, have we not already classified the input? If so, what purpose does the neural network serve? Moreover, by filtering the input patterns, we will have eliminated the benefit of using a network to classify noisy inputs.

However, we might be tempted to add another output unit to the network, which we would train to activate whenever the input pattern does not contain a valid character representation. Then, we must concern ourselves with collecting a representative sampling of null patterns that we could use as part of the training set. The problem we face with this approach is the definition of a null pattern for this application. What are the characteristics of an input pattern that does *not* contain a valid character image, and how shall we collect a representative sampling of those patterns?

The most practical approach to resolving dilemmas such as these is to combine the neural network with a data-collection routine that performs a coarse filtering of the patterns passed on to the network. This is not to say that we have to verify that the image pattern contains one of the characters used to train the network, because that would be defeating the purpose of the network. Rather, we need only ensure that the image pattern that we will ask the network to classify contains some nonblank pixels, that the image of the character is properly framed, and that the image contains only one character. These tests are easily performed using conventional programming tools, and patterns that pass can then be classified by a neural network without compromising the effectiveness of the network. Finally, we can employ an indirect analysis of the output of the network to determine if the input were successfully classified.

3.3.2   Exemplar Consistency Checking

One of the most common errors made by novice application developers is the "presumption of innocence" mistake made when collecting training data. Unlike the criminal justice system in the United States, where an individual is presumed innocent until proven guilty, we cannot assume that, just because we have collected a set of empirical data that faithfully represents the desired function of the neural network, there will not be errors in the training set that will prevent the network from learning the application. The sources for errors in data collection are many: Temporal inconsistencies, data formatting errors, and conflicting exemplars are just a few of the common errors that can be inadvertently introduced into a pristine training set.

From a training perspective, the most difficult problem to recognize is the issue of conflicting exemplars. A conflict occurs when two or more identical (or very similar) input patterns are associated with different outputs. To see why this is a problem, consider the behavior of the BPN, which is designed to transform a given input into a specific output pattern. For this example, let us suppose that we have collected a set of exemplars containing two instances of input pattern A, which we shall refer to as A_1 and A_2. We shall further suppose that pattern A_1 is associated with output pattern B, and pattern A_2 is associated with output pattern C. Finally, we shall assert that pattern B is different, by at least a single component, from pattern C.

During training, the BPN learns to reproduce the input-to-output transformation by sequentially propagating a given input through to the output, then modifying its connection weights to produce a better approximation of the desired output. So, when pattern A_1 is applied to the network, the network adjusts itself to produce a better version of pattern B at the output. Later, pattern A_2 is applied to the network. This time, however, the desired output pattern is C, which is different from B. When the network adjusts itself to produce a better approximation of C, it is effectively *unlearning* its representation of B. Similarly, when pattern A_1 is again presented to the network during the next epoch, the network unlearns its encoding of output C in favor of B, which is the output associated with input A_1. However, A_1 and A_2 are identical, creating a situation in which the network is faced with an unresolvable conflict: It cannot produce both *B and C* from a single output layer when presented with *A*, because *B* and *C* are different. Thus, a conflict represents a situation that prevents the network from ever learning the application.

Fortunately, conflicts can usually be corrected by adjusting the data representation scheme for the exemplars. Unfortunately, an adjustment usually cannot be made until the conflict is identified. Because a training set may contain hundreds, or even thousands, of exemplars that have been collected and formatted for use by the neural network, identifying the specific exemplars that are causing the conflict can be a very tedious task. Because of the large number of patterns involved, and the combinatorial nature of the problem, it is impractical for a developer to manually inspect each pattern to ensure that it does not represent a conflict with another pattern in the training set. There are, however, training techniques that a savvy application developer can employ to assist in the identification of exemplar conflicts.

One simple technique is to perform a binary search of the exemplar set to identify conflicting patterns. When training a BPN, the global error begins to drop quickly after a few (relatively speaking) training epochs, and eventually "flattens" out as the number of errors generated by the network decreases. This fact is easily observable by plotting the global error during training versus training epoch, which we illustrate for a typical BPN application in Figure 3.7. However, the number of epochs that constitute a "few" depends on a number of application-specific factors, including the topology of the network, the number of exemplars in the training set, the specific learning rate (η) and momentum (α) values used, and the number of components in the input and output patterns. For purposes of this discussion, we shall assume that 30 epochs is sufficient to lower the global error of the network to a value around 0.2, which is usually low enough to indicate that the network will learn all the exemplars in the training set. However, readers should note that the actual number of epochs needed to lower the global error for any given application may be as high as 10,000, or as low as two or three, depending on the application and the network.

We can exploit this characteristic drop in global error during training when attempting to identify exemplar conflicts by breaking the entire training set into successively smaller subsets and using each subset to train the network for a "few" epochs. For example, if we suspect an exemplar conflict exists in a given training set, we can first train the network for 30 epochs on the complete training set and note the global error. We then split the training set in half, and train another network using just the first subset. If the error after 30 epochs is *significantly* lower than the error after the previous test, we can assume that the conflict exists between some pattern in the first subset and another pattern in the second subset. If not, we simply halve the training set again, and repeat the process until we find a subset that produces an acceptably low global error after the required 30 epochs.

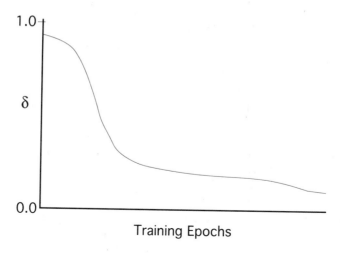

Figure 3.7 This graph shows the typical reduction of the global error as training progress in a BPN application, assuming that there are no conflicts in the data. Notice that the change in the error is initially very small, followed by a period of rapid improvement. During this rapid drop, the network has found a configuration that encodes most of the training exemplars, and is merely reinforcing that configuration. However, there are always a few patterns (or pattern components) that do not fit into the initial encoding scheme, and must be individually corrected by the network. This is the phase following the knee of the curve, when the global error is reduced very slowly.

We can then identify the specific pattern(s) causing the conflict by gradually adding patterns from the second subset back to the first, and retraining the network for 30 epochs. When the error jumps back up, we will have included the conflicting pattern in the training set. We then repeat the process, using successively smaller groupings, until the specific conflict has been identified.

Once all of the conflicts have been identified and corrected, training can proceed in the normal manner. The primary disadvantage of this approach is the amount of time involved in identifying the conflict. Because most neural-network applications are initially prototyped in software, it can take hours, days, or even weeks to perform all of the training needed to identify, and correct, all of the conflicts.

3.3.3   Resolving Inconsistencies

In the previous section, we alluded to the process of correcting exemplars without providing a description of how to perform that correction. We shall now describe some approaches for resolving inconsistencies in the training data. We cannot, however, recommend a specific technique from the set of techniques that we shall present here, because each approach has its own benefits and drawbacks. We shall therefore summarize each approach, describing the advantages and disadvantages of each, and trust that the reader can make his or her own determination about the appropriateness of each with respect to the application.

3.3.3.1 Eliminating Patterns

The most intuitive method for eliminating conflicts in training data is to simply exclude the patterns causing the conflicts. The benefit of this approach is that it is simple and easy to implement. The disadvantage is, of course, that by discarding a training pattern, we have reduced the effectiveness of the neural-network solution.

More often than not, a pattern conflict can be corrected by other means, and eliminating valid training exemplars is not required. There are, however, a few, rare, occasions when it is more appropriate to discard a training exemplar rather than trying to force it to fit into an application. For example, when it can be determined that a specific, conflicting exemplar represents an invalid, or inaccurate, data point in the training set, it is better to throw out the conflict than to try to massage it to fit the application requirements. Such a conflict might occur when the training data were collected with a noisy, or uncalibrated, sensor.

Another case where eliminating an exemplar would be considered a viable option is when it can be determined that the exemplar in question represents a situation that, while possible, is not likely to occur in practice. For example, while it is possible for a snowstorm to occur in Houston in August,[7] it is certainly not likely. We could therefore discount such an exemplar if we were building a weather-prediction application for southeastern Texas, *and* the encoding of such an exemplar were causing a conflict in our data-representation scheme.

3.3.3.2 Combining Patterns

Often, conflicting patterns in a training set occur because the application data were collected over some period of time, during which the input situation was duplicated, but the resulting output situation differed. Thus, our empirically obtained training set will contain conflicting exemplars that will prevent the network from ever learning the application.

One method for countering this situation is to combine similar patterns; that is, associate an output pattern that is the *union* of all of the output patterns associated with the exemplars that have duplicate input patterns. For example, consider the three binary exemplars

$$x_1 = 010110, \quad y_1 = 10000$$
$$x_2 = 010110, \quad y_2 = 00100$$
$$x_3 = 010110, \quad y_3 = 00001$$

---

7. For those readers unfamiliar with weather patterns in Houston, temperatures in August rarely drop below $20°$ C, and often exceed $35°$ C.

Obviously, if we were to try to build a network to learn just these exemplars, the network would never be able to produce a solution, no matter how long we trained it. If, however, we combine the three conflicting patterns into one, we eliminate the conflict and create a training set that the network *can* learn. In this example, the three conflicting exemplars reduce to

$$x' = 010110, \quad y' = 10101.$$

While this technique is guaranteed to eliminate conflicts in the training set, we must advise caution on the part of the developer. Depending on the application, it may not make sense to combine the output patterns. If, for example, the outputs from the network were expected to be mutually exclusive, combining output patterns in this manner would defeat the entire purpose of the network. In cases such as this, the developer must either revise the data representation scheme for the input pattern in order to differentiate "identical" inputs, or alter the interpretation of the output pattern to allow combination.

3.3.3.3 Altering the Representation Scheme

Another effective technique for eliminating conflicts in a training set is to simply change the way in which the exemplars are encoded for the network. As we mentioned in the previous section, a one-to-many conflict is usually the result of data collected over some period of time, without providing a means of indicating the sample time as part of the pattern encoding. Therefore, one of the most straightforward techniques for resolving such a conflict is to simply encode a unique indicator as part of the pattern itself.

If the three patterns described in the previous section were actual data samples taken from a set of sensors from a piece of equipment that we were monitoring at different time periods, we could simply add a few additional components to the pattern to distinguish them for the network. For example,

$$x_1 = 001010110, \quad y_1 = 10000$$
$$x_2 = 010010110, \quad y_2 = 00100$$
$$x_3 = 100010110, \quad y_3 = 00001$$

where we have simply appended the x_i pattern to a three-bit code indicating the discrete time of the sample.

This approach has several benefits, not all of which are obvious. For example, while it may seem as though we have now rendered the significance of the former pattern irrelevent (because we might assume that the output can be directly determined from the time stamp), most applications that we are likely to create will contain many other patterns that the network will have to learn. By adding these three bits to each input pattern, we have guaranteed that we have eliminated a conflict without inadvertantly introducing another conflict, as it is impossible to create a "new" conflict by appending information to a pattern, unless the original patterns were conflicting anyway.

Moreover, this technique can be used to resolve nontemporal pattern conflicts. If, for example, conflicting patterns occured because the data were collected from different locations, the conflict could be easily resolved by appending location bits, instead of time codes.

3.4   TRAINING AND PERFORMANCE EVALUATION

The final step in creating a neural-network application is training and testing the network. Most of the time, training is an operation that occurs before the network is tested, although some network models (the ART networks, or Hopfield memory, for example) do not have two separate phases of operation. In this section, we shall summarize some of the commonly accepted guidelines for training a network that has separate learning and production phases. We shall also describe several techniques that allow an application developer to evaluate the performance of a trained network after training has been completed.

While these techniques are obviously slanted toward the network models that are trained prior to use, many of the guidelines presented in the remainder of this section can be adjusted for those paradigms that do not fit the mold.

3.4.1   Training Guidelines

In all of the network models that we have described, there is a measurement defined that will allow us to evaluate how well the network has encoded the patterns in the training set. For the BPN, that measure is the global error, while, for the ART networks, the measure is indicated by the number of resets that occur in the orienting subsystem. In every case, however, we must address the issue of determining what constitutes an "acceptable" error for the network.

For the ART networks, an acceptable error is a situation in which no resets occur after we have presented the network with all of the patterns that we expect it to learn. Such a condition almost always requires that we expose the network to all of the exemplars at least twice: once to allow the network to encode the patterns, and a second time to evaluate whether all of the patterns were learned (recall the issue of supersets and subsets, described in Chapter 2).

Determining an acceptable error for the BPN, however, is a much more complicated process, because the global-error parameter computed during training is a function of not only the state of the network but also the *specific training set* the network is being asked to learn. Therefore, a minimal error for one application may be rather high (0.1), while, for another, the network may easily achieve a very small global error (0.01).

Practically speaking, a BPN should always be able to obtain a global error of 0.2, *if* there are no conflicts in the training set. The guideline for the BPN, then, is to train the network until the global error falls below 0.2. When that occurs, note the training epoch, and save the state of the network for archival purposes. Then continue training until the error falls below 0.1. If the number of additional training epochs required to achieve that error is fewer than 30% of the number of epochs required to obtain the original error (0.2), repeat the process and shoot for an error of 0.05.

Continue this process, successively halving the target error value, until the number of additional epochs exceeds the 30% guideline, *then stop*. Any training performed beyond that point will not significantly improve the performance of the network; indeed, it is possible to **overtrain** a BPN. In such cases, the network becomes predisposed to favor the desired output patterns, and tends to organize itself to produce those output patterns, even when the input pattern is outside the training domain.

3.4.2   Partial-Set Training

After training is complete, we must evaluate the *effectiveness* of the training by testing the operation of the network. In so doing, we are not only evaluating how well the network has learned the application but also how complete our training set was for the application. As we shall now describe, it is entirely possible to create a network that can successfully learn a specific training set, but still not perform adequately in an application because the training set was incomplete.

Typically, network effectiveness is measured by presenting the trained network with patterns that were not part of the training set, and evaluating how well the network interprets those new inputs. Depending on the network (and the application), we would expect the trained network to be able to produce output patterns that correspond favorably with outputs that we would expect the network to produce, assuming that our data-representation scheme is consistent with the scheme that we employed during training.

For example, if we were to train a BPN to recognize the image patterns of a set of handwritten English characters, we would evaluate the effectiveness of the trained network by presenting it with a set of new (and slightly different) input patterns, then comparing the actual output of the network with the output that we expected. If the training were sufficient, and the new input is not outside of the range of characteristics that the network learned to recognize, it should be able to correctly identify the new character pattern. If, however, the new input pattern is sufficiently different from the training set, we should not expect the network to perform any reasonable classification. In other words, while it is entirely reasonable to expect the network to **interpolate** patterns, we should never expect it to be able to **extrapolate** patterns.

To be able to evaluate the effectiveness of the trained network, we must be able to present the network with a set of **control patterns** that were not used during training, but which are similar to the training patterns. There are a number of techniques that we might employ to obtain the required control patterns for our evaluation. The easiest, and most common technique is to simply withhold a number of patterns randomly extracted from the original training set, then use those withheld patterns to determine the effectiveness of the training.

This technique is quite viable, and is almost always sufficient to measure the effectiveness of the training for a neural network. However, you should be aware that there are some potential failings with this approach that can cause misleading results. The most common problem encountered is the sequencing of the training set during network training. Essentially, it is possible for the network to learn that some patterns always precede others, and therefore become predisposed.

This situation is often only found when the application developer deliberately changes the sequence of the pattern presentation during training. In fact, a colleague of mine reported that during one application-development effort, a BPN that learned a training set in one trial failed to learn the same training set when the sequence of pattern presentation during training was changed, even though the initial configuration of the network was the same.[8] Thus, the problem with simply withholding a portion of the training set as a control set to measure network effectiveness is that complete coverage of the application domain is not guaranteed.

3.4.3 Hold-One-Out Training

Another technique used to measure the effectiveness of network training is called, appropriately enough, the *hold-one-out* technique. In this approach which is described in detail in *Computers That Learn,* [2], one exemplar is extracted from the training set, the network is trained using the partial training set, and the withheld pattern is used to determine the effectiveness of the training. However, unlike the partial-set training approach, this process is repeated for *every* exemplar in the training set. Thus, for a training set containing n exemplars, the network must be trained n times.

The benefit of this approach is that, once we have obtained a network that can successfully recognize the withheld exemplar on all trials, we have ensured that the training set is complete, and that the network will be able to recognize the similarities in any new input pattern. The problem with the approach, unfortunately, is time. As we have already discussed, training a network to correctly recognize an entire training set *once* is a time-consuming process. Repeating the entire training process n times, where n is the number of exemplars in the training set, will often make this approach untenable.

3.4.4 Pathology Analysis

The final approach we shall describe for evaluating the effectiveness of network training is perhaps the most difficult of the three techniques described in this section for the novice practitioner to implement. However, actually performing the analysis is often a very enlightening experience. In essence, what this technique

---

8. Kenneth Marko, speaking at IJCNN '90.

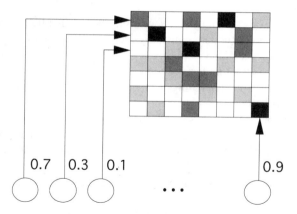

Figure 3.8 A Hinton diagram illustrating the activity of a layer of units in a neural network is shown. In this diagram, each indicator is assigned to a specific unit in the network, and behaves like an analog "thermometer," visually indicating the amplitude of the output of the unit. When viewed collectively, the Hinton diagram can tell us, at a glance, which units are strongly active, which units are off, and which are indeterminate.

ascribes is to dissect the network after training, examining the configuration of the connection weights and identifying the features of the input pattern that the network configured itself to recognize.

The easiest method for accomplishing this analysis is to use a graphical tool called the **Hinton diagram** [1], named for its originator, Geoffrey Hinton. As shown in Figure 3.8, the Hinton diagram allows the developer to view the activity of each unit in the network, and to visualize the relative importance of each component of an input pattern to each unit in the network.

Using the Hinton diagram to visualize activity in the network, the application developer can identify the units in the network that respond to different pattern components. This analysis can be performed using the exemplars from the training set, or can be used only when specific pattern components are tested. For example, consider an input pattern containing components representing several independent parameters. During training, the network learns to recognize the inputs and to produce the corresponding outputs. After training, however, we can selectively activate just the individual unit(s) on the input that represent one, or any combination of the external input parameters. Then, using the Hinton diagram to visualize the activity in the network, we can identify those units that respond most strongly to the individual inputs.

Similarly, we can use the Hinton diagram to visualize the input connection weights to each unit in the network. In this manner, we can identify the features, or combinations of features, in the input pattern that excited each unit. Likewise, we can easily identify connections that inhibit the activation of each unit. By performing such an inspection after training a network, we can determine the characteristics of the input that the network deemed important to successfully recognizing the exemplars. In practice, we often find that a trained network has found the underlying relationships in the data. We can then use that knowledge to further refine the training set, usually by eliminating input components that the network did not use during training.

3.5   A PRACTICAL EXAMPLE

Now we shall try an exercise to reinforce the concepts we have studied in this chapter. Let us suppose that we are given the task of developing an automated system to predict the weather in a certain region of the country. Because this task inherently requires a good bit of speculation and guesstimation, we have decided to use a neural network to provide the prediction. We know that we have access to a plethora of empirical data describing current conditions and surrounding weather patterns, so all that remains to complete the forecasting system is the task of building and training the neural network.[9]

3.5.1   Defining the Data Sources

We begin the development of our neural-network weather-forecasting system by first defining the data sources we have available for the network to use as a basis for its forecasts. These are

- The current temperature, measured in degrees Celsius.
- The current atmospheric pressure, in inches of mercury.
- The current relative humidity, as a percentage.
- The current wind speed, in kilometers per hour (KPH).
- The current wind direction, in compass direction (N, NE, E, ..., W, NW).
- The current cloud cover, in a decimal scale from zero to nine, where zero indicates clear skies and nine indicates total overcast.
- A subjective indication of the current weather condition (e.g., rain, thunderstorms, snow, sleet, hail, sun, fog, windy, and mild).

Moreover, we shall assume that we have access to the same information from several surrounding weather stations. For this exercise, we shall assume that there are eight other weather stations with which we share information, each located 100 kilometers from our position. Furthermore, we shall assume that each remote station is situated so that it lies in one of the primary compass directions from our position, as depicted in Figure 3.9.

---

9. Actually, we would also have to define and implement all of the preprocessing and postprocessing functions needed to collect the current data, coerce it for the network, and interpret the output produced by the network. For clarity, we have omitted those tasks in this discussion.

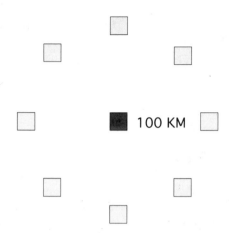

Figure 3.9 A map showing the position of the nine weather stations described in the text is shown.

3.5.2 Selecting a Network

Once we have defined the data that we will use to train the network, the next step in developing the network application is to decide on an appropriate network paradigm. We do this by first identifying the characteristics of the application that will influence the paradigm selection, then selecting a network paradigm that can account for the application requirements.

For our example application, we know that the network must produce an output that is different from its input. Specifically, we shall require this network to produce a forecast of the weather for the next day, given the current situation and recent weather conditions. We also know that the network will be required to find general relationships in the input patterns presented to it, to produce the corresponding output, as opposed to recalling the patterns that it has learned. We can therefore conclude that we will need one of the **mapping** networks for this application.

From our discussions in Chapter 2, we know that the BPN, or possibly the forward-mapping CPN, could be used to satisfy the mapping requirement for this application. However, we can probably eliminate the CPN from consideration due to the requirement to produce a *generalized* mapping between the input and the output patterns. The CPN will not satisfy this requirement due to the way that it processes input patterns. As an illustration of why this is so, recall from our discussions in Chapter 2 that the instar layer in the CPN attempts to match inputs by measuring the distance between pattern vectors in Euclidian space. While this pattern-matching characteristic is useful in some applications, it is more appropriate as a pattern *memory* than as a *feature detector,* which is the essence of this application. Thus, we should select the BPN as the best network model for this application, although we may decide to try another paradigm later, if, after training, the BPN proves ineffective.

Exercise 3.4: Would an ART network also be appropriate for this application? Explain your answer in terms of the internal operation of the network. ■

3.5.3 Defining the Input Pattern

Now that we have selected a network model, we can define a data formatting scheme that will allow us to represent the input parameters that the BPN will learn. We know that the BPN requires input patterns to be represented as vectors composed of elements that range in magnitude between zero and one. Therefore, we must find a way to translate each of the data elements that will comprise the input pattern into a value (or set of values) such that no pattern component exceeds the range between zero and one.

We begin by examining the form of the raw data that will be used as the input to the network. Inspection of the data sources tells us that there are only two different types of inputs that we will have to consider: Scaled, continuously variable values (in some arbitrary, but practical, range), and n-ary representations of category values. The data parameters that can be scaled include

- Temperature, which will vary between $-10°$ C and $40°$ C.
- Atmospheric pressure, which will vary between 26 and 34 inches of mercury.
- Relative humidity, which will vary between 0 and 100 percent.
- Wind speed, which will vary between 0 and 250 KPH.
- Cloud cover, which will vary from 0 to 9.

If we scale each of these inputs between zero and one, using the range identified for each parameter, we will be able to represent each of these parameters as a single component of an input pattern for our BPN. Practically speaking, however, we also observe that wind speeds will normally vary between 0 and 40 KPH. By scaling wind speed in the range of 0 to 250 KPH, we have accounted for all possible variations in the parameter, but we have also diminished the influence of the parameter on the weather prediction for all but the most extreme weather conditions. Therefore, we shall now refine our representation for wind speed to better reflect the normal variations in the parameter.

Rather than scaling wind speed as a single value in the range of 0 to 250 KPH, we shall henceforth consider wind speed on two different scales: normal wind speed, which will range from 0 to 40 KPH inclusive, and windstorm speeds, which will encode wind speeds above 40 KPH. Both of these parameters will be scaled in their respective ranges, and thus, the wind-speed indicator for the network will consist of two scaled parameters in the input pattern vector.

Finally, we define a representation for the two remaining parameters that will be monitored.

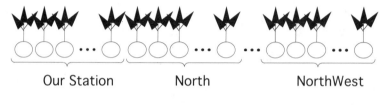

Station	T	P	H	C	W₁	W₂	N	S	E	W	NE	SE	SW	NW	R	TS	S	Sl	H	Su	F	W	M

Station | T P H C $W_1 W_2$ N S E W NE SE SW NW R TS S Sl H Su F W M
N | T P H C $W_1 W_2$ N S E W NE SE SW NW R TS S Sl H Su F W M
NE | T P H C $W_1 W_2$ N S E W NE SE SW NW R TS S Sl H Su F W M
E | T P H C $W_1 W_2$ N S E W NE SE SW NW R TS S Sl H Su F W M
SE | T P H C $W_1 W_2$ N S E W NE SE SW NW R TS S Sl H Su F W M
S | T P H C $W_1 W_2$ N S E W NE SE SW NW R TS S Sl H Su F W M
SW | T P H C $W_1 W_2$ N S E W NE SE SW NW R TS S Sl H Su F W M
W | T P H C $W_1 W_2$ N S E W NE SE SW NW R TS S Sl H Su F W M
NW | T P H C $W_1 W_2$ N S E W NE SE SW NW R TS S Sl H Su F W M

Figure 3.10   This diagram illustrates the encoding of the current weather situation as a pattern vector for presentation to the BPN described in the text.

- Wind direction can be represented by eight different categories. Thus, wind direction can be encoded by an eight-component vector, where only one (or possibly two adjacent) elements are active for any given pattern.

- The current weather condition can be represented by a nine-component vector, with at least one but possibly several elements active simultaneously.

Using this encoding scheme, we can represent the seven data parameters that describe the current conditions as a vector with 23 components: one for each of the four scaled parameters, two for wind speed, eight for wind direction, and nine for subjective assessment. Because we have eight other stations from which we can obtain data, we can encode the parameters from each of those stations in a similar fashion, and represent the entire weather picture as a 207-component vector, as shown in Figure 3.10.

3.5.4   Defining the Output

Now that we have an idea of what the input patterns will look like for the example application, we shall next consider the format for the output pattern that we will expect the network to produce. The first step in this process is to decide *exactly* what we want the network to tell us when it is presented with a new input.

We have already decided that the network should provide us with a forecast of what the weather will be 24 hours from now. What we have not yet decided on is a definition of the indicators that the network must produce that we can interpret as a weather forecast. To define these indicators, we can call on our experience with the local meteorologist on the evening news, and decide that an acceptable forecast contains (at least) the following information:

• A temperature prediction.

• A prediction of the chance of precipitation occuring.

• An indication of the expected cloud cover.

• A storm indicator, to signal a potential for extreme weather conditions.

Notice that, while we could have chosen to ask the network to produce a more comprehensive forecast by including specific indicators for rain, snow, and sleet, we have chosen instead to limit the network to a generic *precipitation* forecast. We have done so for the following two reasons:

1. The weather characteristics that point to a chance of precipitation are more general, and therefore easier for the network to learn to recognize, than are the specific indicators for rain, snow, and sleet.

2. Normally, the temperature indicator will allow us to infer the type of precipitation that will occur. For example, if the temperature is forecast to be $-4°$ C, we should expect any precipitation that occurs to fall as snow.

Having defined the expected outputs from the network, all that remains to complete the encoding of the output pattern is to define a representation for each expected output. There are several ways in which this can be accomplished, and no one technique is necessarily better than any other. As a learning aid, we leave the specification of the output encoding for this application to the reader as an exercise.

Exercise 3.5: Define a suitable data-representation scheme for the output of the weather-forecasting network application. As part of your answer, be sure to define the activation function that will be used by each output unit in the network. ∎

Exercise 3.6: Having completed Exercise 3.5, describe how the output layer on this BPN will be trained. Keep in mind the BPN training algorithm we discussed in Chapter 2. Note any issues that you feel will have to be addressed during the training process. ∎

3.5.5 Collecting the Training Exemplars

Having defined the format of the input and output patterns that we will expect the BPN to learn for this application, we must next determine how we will collect the data that we will use to train the network. To accomplish this goal, we must consider how the network will be expected to operate after training has been completed.

In production mode, we will present the network with a pattern vector formed by the encoding of the current weather conditions as collected from the nine weather stations. This pattern vector will then be propagated through the network structure, and the output produced by the network will be interpreted as the forecast for tomorrow's weather conditions. In other words, the training set for this application must consist of a set of exemplars that associate the known weather conditions at a specific point in time with the conditions that preceded the current situation by 24 hours. In order to successfully train our network, we must therefore have collected a set of historical exemplars where we know the correct output for every input.

There are two methods we can employ to collect the necessary data: The first assumes that we have no historical information available, and must therefore begin tracking the weather for some period of time; the second assumes that we have an extensive collection of data records, and merely need to extract the required information. For discussion purposes, we shall assume that we already have available all of the required information.

There remain two questions that we have to resolve to build our training set. First, How far back in time do we have to go to have a complete training set? Second, What granularity do we need to have to develop an accurate forecast? The answers to these questions will determine size of the training set we must create, and, to a large extent, the amount of time needed to train the network.[10] To answer the first question, we must decide how much time is required to obtain an accurate picture of the weather.

If we are going to forecast the weather in Honolulu, Hawaii, we probably only need a few month's worth of data, because the variation in the weather in Honolulu is very slight. If we are going to forecast the weather in Pittsburgh, Pennsylvania, however, we probably need at least a year's worth of data because the weather changes dramatically with each of the four seasons. In either case, we need to go back far enough in time to ensure that we can accurately capture the entire domain of the problem.

The answer to the second question is not quite as easy to obtain. The natural choice is probably to limit the granularity to a daily sample, because we are only expecting the network to provide us with a forecast for the next day's weather. However, if we limit the granularity to a daily sample, we will likely omit a great deal of pertinent information, simply because the weather can change quite dramatically in a very short period of time, certainly much faster than once a day. However, if we reduce the sample time to once an hour, we introduce the possibility of developing an error-riddled training set, because we are associating an *instantaneous* snapshot of the current weather conditions with an instantaneous snapshot of the weather conditions 24 hours hence. Using this scheme, it is very likely that we would encode many conflicting exemplars—one exemplar indicating rain today at noon means sunny conditions tomorrow at noon, while another exemplar indicates that rain at noon today means rain tomorrow at noon—which would have to be resolved before we could successfully train the network.

---

10. Assuming, of course, that the initial network is developed using a software simulator.

We shall therefore compromise on this question, and refine our definition of the output pattern. We will collect input data on an hourly basis, but the corresponding output pattern will be the *average* of the instantaneous patterns over a 12-hour period. By using this refined scheme, we have significantly reduced the possibility of conflicts in the training set while simultaneously increasing the amount of information that the network will have available to make its forecast.

3.5.6 Training the Network

After gathering and formatting the 8,760 exemplars that comprise our training set, we can construct the network and start the training process. We begin by defining the number of hidden layers we will need for this network (normally one), and the number of units that we will implement on each layer (the prevailing wisdom among researchers suggests that we should start with approximately one-fifth of the number of input elements on the hidden layer, then gradually increase or decrease that number based on how well the network trains). Because the number of units on the input and output layers is fixed by the specification of the input and output patterns for this network, we need only define the number of hidden-layer units we shall require. For this application, we shall begin with 42 sigmoidal units on a single hidden layer.

As we indicated earlier in this chapter (in Section 3.4.3), the most comprehensive method for ensuring that the network has learned the desired mapping is to train it with the *hold-one-out* technique. Unfortunately, this method is not very practical for our application. If we were to employ this training method, we would have to perform 8,760 different training sessions, holding one exemplar out during each training session, then test the network using the withheld exemplar.

Given that our network contains approximately 9,000 connections, and assuming that we are training the network using a software simulator, we can expect such an exhaustive test to consume months of development time.

Exercise 3.7: Compute the amount of time needed to perform the *hold-one-out* training method for the weather-forecasting application. Assume that the BPN simulator is running on a serial machine rated at 1 MFLOPS (million floating-point operations per second); that each connection requires two floating-point calculations for the feed-forward computation, six floating-point calculations for the backpropagation computation, and 10 floating-point calculations for the sigmoid; and that 100 epochs are needed to determine if the network is going to converge.

A much more practical technique for training this network is to randomly select a portion of the training set, and withhold those randomly selected exemplars as a *control* group. Then, train the network with the remaining exemplars until the global error has lowered sufficiently, and test the operation of the network with the control exemplars. If the training set provides the necessary coverage, the network should produce outputs that closely match (but are not necessarily identical to) the outputs associated with each of the control patterns.

3.5.7   Completing the Application

Normally, the first network created by a developer to address a new application can be expected to have a number of problems associated with it. It may not converge during training, or, after converging, may not do well predicting the output when presented with a new input.

There are a number of things that an application developer could, and probably should, do to improve the effectiveness of the network. Herewith, we provide a brief summary of some of the more commonly accepted techniques for improving the effectiveness of the network.

- Monitor the progress of the training by plotting the global error of the network versus the training epoch. Global error should *always* decrease, even if only slightly, from epoch to epoch. When the error begins to oscillate, note the training epoch, and proceed with the following tests, training the network in each case to the point where the oscillation originally began.

- If the network does not converge during training, try reducing the size of the training set. If the network converges with the smaller training set, a conflict may exist in the data that prevents the network from learning the entire application.

- If the network does not learn the reduced training set, continue the process of pruning the training set until a network *does* converge. Then start adding training exemplars back gradually, retraining a new network after each addition. When you obtain a training set that again does not converge, examine the training set for conflicts.

- If no conflicts are found and the network still does not converge, examine the state of the network connections to see if any of the hidden-layer units have become saturated. If saturated units are found (they are indicated by input connections that are predominately very positive, or very negative, in their weighting values), add a few more (approximately 20% of the number of units already on the layer) and repeat the training process.

- If no saturated units are found, but the network does not converge, try lowering the learning rate parameter (η) and training longer. A lower learning rate will slow the amount by which connections are adjusted, thereby allowing the network to more easily find a minimal error location on the weight surface.

- If the network converges but does not produce accurate outputs, evaluate the coverage of the training set. It could be that the network has learned a subset of the problem domain very well, but the control set consists of patterns that are outside of the application domain described by the training set.

- If the network converges but does not produce accurate outputs, and you have determined that the training set provides adequate coverage, consider refining the pattern representation to include additional indicators (in this example, consider adding a *season* indicator to the input) to help the network discriminate between similar inputs that produce very different outputs.

Readers should note that these suggestions are primarily for applications that use the BPN. Other network paradigms require other techniques, although those methods are not *strategically* much different from the ones outlined here. Rather, the other techniques are tailored to the operation of the different network models, just as these are specific to the operation of the BPN.

Exercise 3.8: Build the weather-forecasting network described in this section. Collect your own data using daily weather reports obtained from local newspapers (which are usually archived by libraries). Train the network, and evaluate its effectiveness after training. ∎

3.6 APPLICATION-DESIGN SUMMARY

In this chapter, we have examined the details of designing a neural-network application, and shown how the selection of a data-representation scheme can influence the success of the application. We have also taken our first steps toward developing applications of our own design, by working through a detailed example of a viable neural-network application.

With these foundations well established, we are now ready to begin a detailed investigation of the other successful applications of the technology. In subsequent chapters, we will draw heavily from the concepts presented in this chapter as we describe how each application was constructed, and show how other researchers have overcome many obstacles to produce successful applications.

SUGGESTED READINGS

At this writing, there are not very many good textbooks available that address the idea of application design and data preparation; hence, this book was written in an attempt to fill that void. However, there are a number of conferences held annually that sponsor an applications track, where researchers describe successful applications of the technology. The interested reader will find a variety of data modeling techniques described in the technical papers in the proceedings of those conferences. The best source for applications papers can be found in the proceedings of the annual Neural Information Processing Systems: Natural and Synthetic conference and workshop, the IEEE Conference on Fuzzy Logic and Neural Networks, and the World Congress on Neural Networks, sponsored by the International Neural Network Society.

BIBLIOGRAPHY

1. G. E. Hinton and T. J. Sejnowski. *Parallel Distributed Processing.* MIT Press, Cambridge, MA, p. 301, 1986.

2. S. M. Weiss and C. A. Kulikowski. *Computers That Learn,* Morgan-Kaufmann Publishers, Inc., San Mateo, CA, 1991.

Associative Memories

An idea is a feat of association.

—Robert Frost

An associative memory is, quite simply, any device that associates a set of predefined output patterns with specific input patterns. A computer-memory chip is an excellent example of a simple associative memory: It produces a single output datum from a set of predefined data patterns when presented with a specific address as input (along with the appropriate control signals). An important characteristic of the memory is that there is no requirement for a specific *mapping* from the input to the output; that is, the output produced can take on any legal value for any given input, so long as each output pattern was stored at a specific location in the memory at some earlier time.

However, to say that a computer-memory chip is equivalent to an associative memory is somewhat misleading. The behavior of a computer memory resembles the behavior of an associative memory only as long as the input patterns to the device are members of the set of addresses that were initialized with a desired output pattern. Moreover, we must also have some guarantee that the address patterns sent to the memory are accurate. If the input address to the memory deviates from the desired pattern by a single bit, the output pattern produced by the memory will either be the wrong one or be correct only through happenstance.

In this chapter, we shall explore the applications of associative-memory networks. In the process, we shall show how the structure of the network endows the applications with a robustness that is not found when other techniques are employed. We shall begin this discussion with a brief review of associative-memory definitions, to illustrate the different types of behavior obtainable with an associative memory. We then discuss the implementation of several applications of the technology, showing how the associative-memory network provided a solution for each application that could not have been easily obtained using conventional methods.

4.1 ASSOCIATIVE-MEMORY DEFINITIONS

Compare the behavior of the computer memory described earlier with that of natural memory. When we see the face of another person that we know, it makes no difference to us whether that person's appearance has changed slightly. We continue to recognize that person even if he or she has changed hairstyle, has grown a beard, or is wearing sunglasses. We will almost certainly note the differences, but unless the changes have been many and significant, we will recognize the face nonetheless. From this example, we can see that the behavior of biological memory is significantly more robust than the behavior of the computer memory.

In many applications, the robustness of the biological memory is a desirable quality. There are many situations where we would find it desirable for a computer system to do something intelligent (but predictable) when presented with a situation that differs slightly from anything we may have anticipated prior to deploying the system. Intelligence in the face of noisy or incomplete input information is especially desirable. Thus, we pose the following question: How can we endow a computer with the ability to mimic the robustness found in biological memories?

The most intuitive answer to this question is to construct memory devices that operate in a manner similar to the biological-memory systems. In Chapter 2, we described the operation of several different neural-network structures. In retrospect, we can see that the behavior of many of these networks is remarkably similar to the behavior we expect from an associative-memory device. Yet, with so many different networks to choose from, how can we be sure that the network we select for an application is the most appropriate? To assess the applicability of these networks to the kinds of automation problems we intend to address, we must first define a set of categories that describe certain predictable behaviors. We can then distinguish the network paradigms based on these categories. One such classification for associative memories is as follows:

- A **heteroassociative memory** is a device that produces an output pattern that was stored as one of a set of output patterns. The specific pattern generated is the one associated with the input that is most similar to the current input.

- An **interpolative associative memory** generates an output pattern that differs from the predefined output associated with the input closest to the current input by an amount that corresponds to the difference between the current input and the closest training input.

- An **autoassociative memory** converts a corrupted input pattern into the pattern that most closely resembles the current input. Notice that, in this definition, the output from the network is equivalent to the input.

After the connection weights have been configured for an application, the BPN, CPN, BAM, and MAM can all operate as heteroassociative and autoassociative memories, although each can also be used in distinctly different ways. Similarly, the CPN with more than one winning competitive unit illustrates the behavior of an interpolative associative memory. In the remainder of this chap-

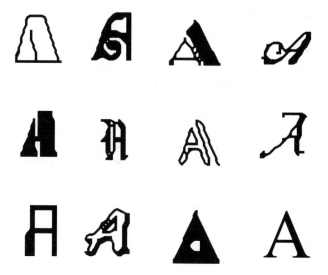

Figure 4.1 All of these images represent the same character. Notice the variety of shapes, and consider that there are 25 other letters (not to mention the ten digit characters, the 26 lower-case letters, and punctuation marks) that can take on the same variety in their representations.

ter, we shall investigate how these networks can be used to address associative-memory applications.

4.2 CHARACTER RECOGNITION

As we described in the beginning of this chapter, the process of associating a meaningful interpretation with a visual image is quite often a complex task, especially when the form of the images to be processed can vary significantly. For example, consider the images of the characters illustrated in Figure 4.1. While *we* easily recognize that all of these images represent the same character, the process of programming a computer to perform the same task is daunting. Moreover, if we were to add to this set of characters another form, one that was similar to, but not exactly the same as one we had seen previously, we would likely recognize the character, but our computer program may not.

As we have already alluded, a neural-network can quite easily be constructed that will perform the character-recognition function. However, as we saw in Chapter 2, there are many different neural-network paradigms, with many different types of behavior. Several of those paradigms can be used to successfully solve this problem, and at least one cannot. Of those that can be used, two networks are very appropriate for this problem, and the others will merely suffice.

The issue that we must address, then, is how do we select the proper network for the given application?

To construct a network that will perform the character-recognition task, we must first define the data-representation scheme we will use to model the problem. This is an important point, and unfortunately, one that is commonly neglected by a novice neural-network application developer. As we shall describe in this section, the choice of the data-representation scheme for an application will quite often imply the use of certain neural-network paradigms.

Let us begin, then, by defining a suitable data representation for our neural-network character recognizer. Referring again to Figure 4.1, you should first notice that each image is approximately the same size as all the other images, both horizontally and vertically. We shall therefore assume that the network that we will construct to recognize these images will not have to deal with differently sized characters,[1] and restrict our network design to the recognition of differently shaped images.

4.2.1   Input Pattern Definition

To build a neural network that can associate character images with character meaning, we must first determine the means of image acquisition for the application. The most common method of acquiring image information (in the sense that a computer processes information) is through the use of *raster video* techniques. As shown in Figure 4.2, a video image can be thought of as a two-dimensional matrix of pixels. A monochromatic pixel, in its simplest form, is a binary indicator of the illumination status of the pixel: a logic "1" is usually interpreted as a white (or illuminated) pixel, while a logic "0" is typically used to indicate a black (or nonilluminated) pixel. For images more complex than simple text characters, a gray-shade (or color) pixel representation is often used, but that requires additional information about each pixel. For this application, binary information will be sufficient to construct images of all the characters the system will ever process.

Using the video pixel matrix as the basis for our character-image representation, we must next select the resolution that we will need to adequately model the character image for the neural network. Because our application is to build a network that will correctly recognize a variety of different character shapes as a limited number of characters, we will require a character matrix that provides only a moderate resolution—say, eight pixels horizontally and ten pixels vertically. However, if our application required that the network be able to discriminate between characters that have only subtle differences, a higher resolution image would be necessary, because each additional pixel in the image would give the associative memory a corresponding increase in information that it can use to differentiate characters.

---

1. If we cannot guarantee that the images will be approximately the same size, we could *prescale* the character images before asking the neural network to classify them.

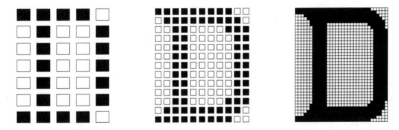

Figure 4.2   A variety of video-matrix representations for the character D are shown. Notice the difference in the resolution of the character as the number of pixels in the image matrix varies—more pixels provide a higher-quality, easier-to-distinguish image while fewer pixels result in a character image that is jagged looking.

By concatenating the ten row vectors of eight pixels that comprise the character matrix into a single, 80-element vector, we will have formed a pattern that is suitable for input to an associative-memory neural network. Moreover, by considering the input image as a *vector*, with both magnitude and direction in *n*-dimensional hyperspace, we have provided the network with the inherent ability to *compare* images of new characters with images of characters it has already learned to recognize.

4.2.2   Output Pattern Definition

The next step in constructing the data representation for the application is to define the form of output that we will interpret as the meaning of the input image. There are several schemes we can use to define the form of the output pattern. The most straightforward approach is to use a *classification* scheme in which one, and only one, output element is active for any given input pattern. The position of the active output element will determine the corresponding character. A neural-network implementation of this scheme is depicted in Figure 4.3. Using this strategy has the advantage of simplicity: It is relatively easy to construct a layer of processing elements in a neural network that will produce a one-and-only-one output across the layer. It is also very easy for the external application to interpret the output from the network: It need only determine which output unit is active, and then use the character associated with the active unit.

Unfortunately, the classification scheme we are using at the output also has some implicit disadvantages. For instance, it requires that we must be able to completely specify beforehand the number of different characters that the memory must recognize. If, at some later time, we should need to add another character to the set of recognized characters, the output must be extended to accommodate the new character.

While this simple extension may not seem devastating from a system perspective, remember that we are using interconnected processing elements to represent each pattern element. Thus, the addition of a single output unit to an associative memory network adds a relatively large number of interconnections

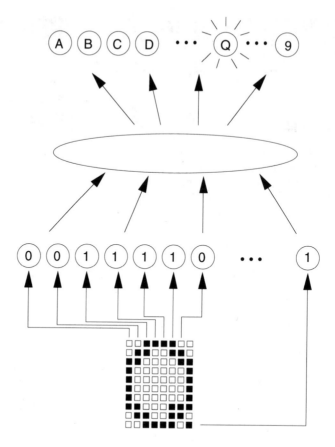

Figure 4.3 A neural-network structure arranged to identify characters using a video pixel input pattern and an output classification scheme is shown. In this diagram, the input image pattern becomes the output from the input layer of units. After propagating this input pattern through the internal network structure (shown in this diagram in a simplified form), each unit on the output layer of units produces an output signal based on the stimulation it has received from the rest of the network. If the network has been trained appropriately, only one unit on the output layer will produce an active output—in this case, the unit associated with the character Q.

(along with the corresponding time to process the new connections), and forces us to completely retrain the network. Retraining will be necessary[2] because it is unlikely that the newly created input connections to the new unit will have any *a priori* understanding of the application.

---

2. The need to retrain the network will vary with the network paradigm being used. See Chapter 2 for more information on this topic.

(a)

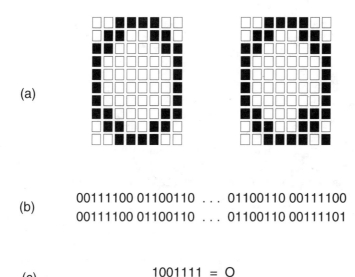

(b)
00111100 01100110 . . . 01100110 00111100
00111100 01100110 . . . 01100110 00111101

(c)
1001111 = O
1010001 = Q

Figure 4.4   This diagram illustrates how small differences in the input to an associative-memory network can result in substantially different outputs from the network. (a) The raster images of the characters *O* and *Q*. (b) The input vectors of the two images in binary form. (c) The ASCII codes for the two characters, also in binary form. Note the number of bit differences between these two output patterns.

Another data-representation scheme we might use to interpret the output from the network is to use some predefined code, such as an ASCII representation, to indicate the meaning of the image pattern. This scheme has the advantage of fewer processing elements on the layer (seven, to represent 128 different characters versus 62 to represent the 26 upper-case, 26 lower-case, and ten digit characters), a significant consideration with regard to simulation time and network storage requirements. Unfortunately, it also has the disadvantage of being more difficult to train. Subtle differences in the images of two similar characters will often result in significantly different output responses from the network. An example of this situation is shown in Figure 4.4.

4.2.3   Network Specification

Recall from our previous discussion the objective of this application: to *correctly* recognize the images of characters that will often have very great differences in shape, even between identical letters, due to differences in style. The fact that we want the associative memory to produce an *exact* output, even though the input pattern used may be slightly different from any of the images the network has learned to recognize, suggests that we should use a classification scheme (e.g., allowing each output unit to uniquely represent exactly one of the desired output classes) for generating outputs, because this approach provides us with a greater separation between output patterns, and thus improves the ability of the network to successfully *categorize* new input patterns.

Next, let us consider the comparison process that a neural network will perform when processing new input images. Recall from Chapter 1 that each processing element in a neural network produces an output signal that is derived from the aggregate stimulation the unit receives from all of it inputs. Because there are many different types of comparisons that can be performed by such a processing element (e.g., Euclidian distance metric, Hamming distance, and feature extraction), we must decide which is best suited to the application at hand. We have already decided the form of the input pattern to the network for this application—image data in the form of a binary vector containing 80 pattern elements. If we consider each input pattern as a vector in Euclidian space, we could use a competitive layer of elements to process the input, with the winning unit being designated as the unit that has been encoded with the training image that best matches the current input image. Such a comparison is illustrated in Figure 4.5.

However, a simple Euclidian comparison such as the one performed by a competitive layer has two significant problems with respect to this application:

- The number of patterns that can be distinguished will be limited to the number of units on the competitive layer.

- Spatial comparisons cannot easily distinguish subtle differences between similar, but different, patterns.

Referring again to Figure 4.5, notice that a competitive layer can only perform comparisons between the current input pattern and those patterns associated with each unit on the competitive layer.[3] Thus, a competitive layer is restricted to comparisons between the current input and a fixed number of prestored patterns. If, at some later time, we wish to extend the application to include recognition of some characters that were not part of the original training, we would have to reconstruct the entire application with a network containing a similar number of additional competitive units, one for each new character to be recognized.

Now consider the characters shown in Figure 4.6. Two of these are the lowercase letters g and q, and two are different images of the decimal character 9. If we were to use a competitive network, three different units would be needed to distinguish the g, the q, and the 9. But, with only three units to recognize these four characters, and with each unit using a Euclidian distance comparison, how can we guarantee that the appropriate unit wins the competition? Specifically, which unit would win the competition if the input pattern were the distorted image of the 9? If the image vector of the g is closer to the image vector of the distorted 9 than is the image vector of the 9, how can we prevent the network from

---

3. As defined by the weight values in the input connections to each unit.

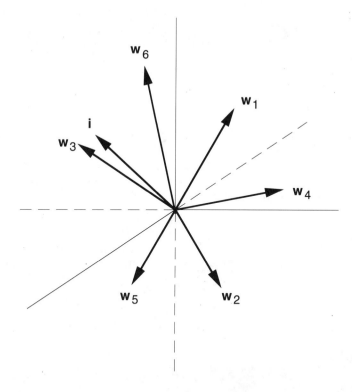

Figure 4.5 The comparison of pattern vectors in Euclidian space is shown. In this diagram, each of the vectors labeled w_i represent image vectors of characters the competitive layer has learned to recognize. The current input image vector, labeled i, is *closest* in Euclidian distance to vector w_3. Unit 3 will therefore win the competition, and generate the output that was associated with this unit during the training process.

misclassifying the distorted 9 as a *g*? The answer to these questions, if we are using a competitive layer to compare vectors in Euclidian space, is that we must again add more units to the layer, to ensure that each subtle nuance in character images is captured within the network.

Practically speaking, however, building a neural network that will contain a distinct unit to detect each unique variation of each possible character image is no solution at all. A network cannot contain an infinite number of units, nor can it be realistically expected to *exactly* recognize each of an infinite number of possible input patterns. A much better approach for this application would be to use a network that can recognize the *features* of the input that tend to correctly classify the image patterns. The BPN, also described in Chapter 2, does an excellent job of categorizing outputs based on generalizing input patterns into their feature components.

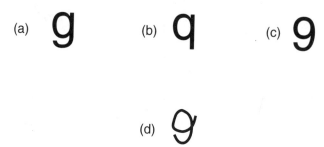

Figure 4.6 Four similar character images are shown. (a) A lower-case *g*. (b) A lower-case *q*. (c) The digit 9. (d) A distorted 9. The details of the comparison among these image patterns is described in the text.

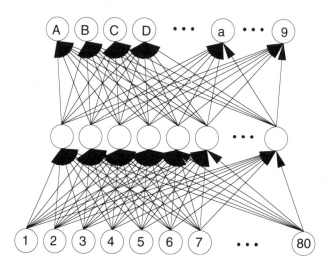

Figure 4.7 The BPN structure needed to solve the character recognition application. The operation of the network is described in the text. *Source:* Neural Networks: Algorithms, Applications, and Programming Techniques [2]. *Copyright ©1991, Addison-Wesley. Used with permission.*

We shall therefore specify the network for our character-recognition application as a three-layer BPN, similar to the network illustrated in Figure 4.7. In this approach, the first layer will act as a fan-out layer that will simply hold the input image pattern for the rest of the network, the second layer will act as a *feature-identification* layer, with each unit responding to the presence (or absence) of features that tend to classify the input, with an output layer consisting of *n* units, where *n* is the number of characters to be recognized. Using this encoding scheme, we shall expect the output of the network to produce only a single active unit for each input pattern presented, and we shall interpret the *position* of the active output unit as the indicator of the character itself.

Because the output units in this application are essentially binary, we shall employ the sigmoidal activation function on both the hidden and output layers for this network. The hidden-layer units will require the nonlinearity in the activation function to help the network distinguish between nonlinearly separable patterns. The output layer units will use the sigmoid function to relax the restrictions on the range of input signals each unit must receive to produce a specific output, while creating a situation where it will be relatively easy for the units to produce either strongly active or inactive output signals.

Using the input and output data-representation schemes described previously, we know that there must be 80 input units and 62 output units (one for each upper- and lower-case letter character, and one for each of the ten digit characters). All that remains to complete the network specification is to determine the number of hidden-layer units for the application; select a learning-rate parameter (η) and, if required, a momentum term (α); and to train the network.

Unfortunately, there is no hard-and-fast rule that can be used to precisely determine any of these parameters for every application. As a general rule, however, a learning rate of 0.5 and momentum value of 0.2 should be about right for a first trial. We select these values for the following reasons:

- As the learning rate approaches unity, learning in the BPN becomes deterministic. This means that connection-weight changes are made to eliminate the instantaneous pattern error every time the network adapts. Unfortunately, the network must be able to learn more than one pattern, which it cannot do under these circumstances, because changes to completely eliminate the error in one pattern almost always result in the introduction of errors in other patterns.

- Conversely, as the learning rate approaches zero, learning in the BPN slows equivalently. While slower learning increases the ability of the network to encode patterns, it also increases the likelihood of entrapping the BPN in a local minimum on the error surface during learning, creating a situation where the network never converges to an acceptable solution.

- Choose a fairly small, but nonzero, value for the momentum parameter to reduce the ability of a single outlyer in the training set from adversely affecting the direction of the weight update during training. If momentum is too high, any outlyer patterns can overwhelm the connection-weight update on the next pattern, thus preventing the network from encoding that pattern.

The guideline for specifying the number of hidden-layer units in the BPN is as follows: Start with a fraction of the number of input units, train the network, and adjust the number of units based on how well the network trained. Generally, for a BPN that contains more inputs than outputs (as do most BPN applications), a good place to start is with one-quarter to one-third as many hidden units as input units. Then, after training has been completed, the number can be adjusted up or down, based on whether the network learned the application (if not, adjust up), or if many hidden-layer units never activate for any of the input patterns (adjust down).

Exercise 4.1: Specify a neural-network solution for a character-recognition application, this time using the ASCII representation of each character as the desired output. Indicate the type of network used, the number of units on each layer, and the activation function for each layer of units, and describe any potential issues that must be addressed in order to make the application successful. ■

4.3 STATE-SPACE SEARCH

We have all played games that require us to perform pattern-matching and state-space searches. For example, when we played tic-tac-toe as children, we quickly learned which strategies offered us the best prospects for winning, and which strategies tended to result in ties or losses. We probably learned to recognize the game situations that produced those results without consciously realizing that we were, from a computational viewpoint, performing a rapid search of a relatively large state-space. To put this notion in perspective, consider that in the simple game of tic-tac-toe, there are precisely 362,880 (9!) different ways that the game board can be completely filled. To be fair, however, the number of possible situations that can be encountered in a typical game is significantly smaller, because we usually do not continue after one player has won.

If we were to model this game so that a computer could play against a human opponent, we would likely begin by defining a state-space for the game that the computer could search and evaluate. We would probably use a graph to model the state-space for the computer, representing each legal game situation by a node, and using the arcs between nodes to represent the move made to transition between the legal situations. Finally, we would program the computer to construct and search partial game state-graphs, with each search beginning at the node representing the current game situation, and proceeding forward using an algorithm like the *minimax* to determine the best move for the computer, given the current situation.

Let us separate ourselves from the classical perspective of modeling situations for computer processing for a moment, and consider the process whereby *we* learned to play the game. Usually, our first experience with tic-tac-toe comes as a child, and involves a series of trial-and-error attempts to learn the strategies of the game. After being told the rules and objectives, we begin by making moves randomly, eventually winning or, more likely, losing as a result of luck and our opponents skill. After many trials, we learn to associate desirable next-state situations with current-state patterns. Eventually, after much practice, we achieve a level of competence that virtually guarantees that any future game we play will be either won or drawn, simply because we have progressed to a point where we quickly recognize any situation that we will likely encounter, and have associated the proper response with that situation.

This process of associating patterns is the essence of a heteroassociative memory. Therefore, it seems reasonable to assume that we could teach an associative memory network to play tic-tac-toe against a human opponent. The only question that remains is: *How?*

4.3.1   Input-Output Specification

From an application perspective, it is clear that the neural network we want to build will use the current game situation as input, and will output a recommendation of the proper move based on the current situation. Using this scenario, let us first consider how to unambiguously model the current game situation for an associative-memory network.

We know, from our experience, that any position on the tic-tac-toe game board can legally exist in three distinct states: unoccupied (or *blank*), occupied by the *X* token, and occupied by the *O* token, which we will henceforth denote as *b*, *X*, and *O*. We also know that input pattern elements to a neural network are usually binary values, although they can be continuously variable in the range between their limits. We therefore have a situation where we are attempting to describe three distinct states using network-processing elements that are designed to operate on primarily binary values. We can address this issue in one of the following two ways:

- We could map one input pattern element to each legal board space, and let each pattern element have three legal values, say {0.5, 1.0, 0.0}, to represent {*b*, *X*, *O*}, respectively.

- We could map multiple input pattern elements to each legal board space, and then use combinations of binary patterns to represent the three legal game states.

We shall select the second of these two options for the reasons described in Chapter 3.[4] We will further specify the use of three inputs for each of the nine board positions, one to represent each of the possible position states (*b*, *X*, *O*) using a one-and-only-one representation technique. Thus, we will require a total of 27 inputs to the network, only nine of which will be active for any valid input state.

To produce the desired output from the network, we will need only nine units, one for each of the nine board positions. We shall expect the network to activate units on the output layer when presented with the current game situation at the input layer. The units activated by the network will be interpreted as the position on the game board where the next token should be placed. As before, the internal configuration of the network (i.e., the number of hidden-layer units, if any) will depend on the network paradigm selected to implement this memory. Figure 4.8 illustrates the general form of the network needed to play tic-tac-toe.

---

4. See Section 3.2.2, Tertiary and *n*-ary Patterns, for the details on this issue.

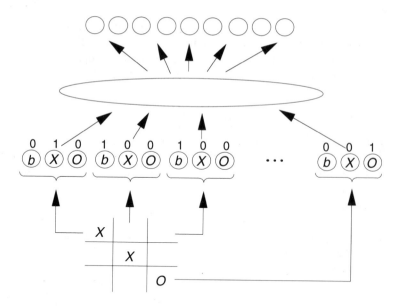

Figure 4.8 The structure of a neural network designed to learn to play tic-tac-toe is illustrated. Notice that the network is used only to assess the current situation and recommend the next move. External software (or possibly even hardware) will be necessary to sense the state of the game, to convert that information into the form needed by the network, and finally to implement the recommended move.

4.3.2 Exemplar Acquisition

In this application, there are several issues associated with acquiring the exemplar data that we did not encounter in the character-recognition application. These issues are

- A lack of immediate feedback with regard to the *quality* of a particular move. Usually, the results of a move made early in the game do not become apparent until the game is almost over.

- Temporal constraints on the exemplars acquired across multiple games, possibly creating a situation where the network might never learn the application due to conflicts in the training exemplars.

- Rotational duplication of training patterns, resulting in many exemplars that are functionally redundant, but necessary, depending on the network paradigm selected for the application.

To illustrate why these issues are a concern, we must take into account the process by which a neural network *learns* to reproduce a target output from certain input patterns. Depending on the network, training is usually implemented from *instantaneous* exemplars; that is, a network learns to reproduce a set of

exemplars by slowly adjusting its internal connection weights based on the presentation of a single input and a desired output. Training continues by repetitively
showing the network the same set of exemplars, until the network can accurately
reproduce all of the target outputs when presented with the corresponding input
patterns, one at a time. This learning process means that the network being trained
has no specific memory of patterns previously seen, nor does it have any fore-
knowledge of patterns that have not yet been seen.

With those constraints in mind, consider the process of collecting the training
data that we will need to construct our exemplars for this application. Because
the neural network is intended to be an opponent for a human player, we might
expect the game to be played interactively; that is, players would be expected
to alternate turns. However, we have no way of telling the network whether the
first move it makes, be it defensive or offensive, is good or bad until the game
is almost over. This time lag between action and feedback, coupled with the lack
of explicit pattern memory in the network, will make it impossible to train the
network interactively. Therefore, we shall back off from our interactive training
requirement, and create a situation that will allow the network to observe and
learn from other players before ever making a move.

We can create such a situation by playing several games either against ourselves or against another human player, and recording each move made as a
situation-move ordered pair. Then, after recording the evolution of many different
games, we can transcribe the sequence of moves into exemplars for the network.
The network can then be trained normally. Once it has learned the exemplars, we
can then test the memory by allowing it to effect its own moves interactively. If
training has been sufficient, the network should be able to play the game as well
as the user. If not, additional exemplars should be added to the original training
set, and the network retrained.

The scenario just described addresses the issue of dealing with a lack of immediate feedback. The other two issues are also significant concerns, especially
when using certain networks. For example, consider what might happen if we
simply used the training data acquired as previously described to teach a BPN the
tic-tac-toe application. The BPN is a spatial mapping network, meaning that it
will always try to find a way of producing a given output when presented with a
given input. It has no mechanism built into it to allow it to learn *many* different
outputs that are associated with *one* input, which, unfortunately, is quite likely the
case in this application.

For example, if we have collected our exemplars by playing many different
games and recording each and every situation-move pair as a separate exemplar,
we will have multiple exemplars that have exactly the same input pattern—say,
the empty game board—with different associated outputs. This situation, which
is illustrated in Figure 4.9, presents a problem for the BPN because it has no
explicit memory of any exemplars, other than the one that it is attempting to learn.
Thus, every time a conflicting exemplar is presented to the BPN, the network
will attempt to learn the new target output by *unlearning* any conflicting output

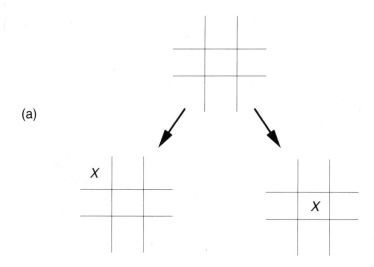

(a)

(b)   100 100 100 100 100 100 100 100 100   100 000 000
       100 100 100 100 100 100 100 100 100   000 010 000

Figure 4.9 This diagram illustrates how conflicting training information might be acquired for the tic-tac-toe example. (a) The initial game-board situation commonly results in one of two next-state situations. (b) The two exemplars resulting from situation (a). Notice that both have the same input pattern, but the output patterns are significantly different. We refer to exemplars that exhibit this quality as *conflicting*.

pattern it may have already seen, creating a situation where the network will never converge to a global solution.

We could solve this problem by choosing to use one of the BPN-variant networks—for example, the Jordan network—as the basis for this application. The Jordan network allows us to deal with the one-to-many mapping problem by virtue of the feedback provided from the output layer to the input layer. In a sense, the state units provide a discrimination pattern that the Jordan network can use to separate the duplicate patterns.

Exercise 4.2: We have just described why conflicting exemplars present a training problem for the BPN. Identify another network paradigm, different from the BPN and its variants, that will not have a problem with conflicting exemplars. Explain why the selected network can deal with a one-to-many pattern mapping. ∎

With regard to the rotational issue, we can offer no easy solution, other than to say that it is a common problem in neural-network applications, and must be dealt with on an application basis. For this particular application, the best solution might be to ensure that the training exemplars include several instances of every possible variation, with the frequency of the various instances mirroring the occurrence of the situations.

Exercise 4.3: Based on the previous discussion and your knowledge of the different neural-network paradigms, define the architecture of a neural network that could learn the tic-tac-toe application. Specify the network-learning paradigm, the number of layers needed, and the number of units and activation function for each layer in the network. ■

4.3.3   Network Specification

Now that we have defined the input and output data representations for the network, we can complete the application by selecting the appropriate network-learning paradigm, and by constructing the network from the specifications. To select an appropriate network paradigm, we shall first review what we already know about the tic-tac-toe application, because the requirements of the application will influence the selection of the proper network paradigm.

- The form of the input and output patterns in each exemplar will be binary vectors. If the selected network prefers the use of continuous or bipolar[5] patterns, we must convert the exemplar format accordingly.

- When the network receives an input pattern after training has been completed, the output produced by the network should be the pattern that most closely resembles the current situation, as indicated by the input pattern vector. The best technique for accomplishing this comparison is via the Hamming-distance measure.

- It would be preferable to have the memory learn the application interactively, if possible. If not, we must be able to collect a representative sampling of exemplars to train the network offline.

- The network selected must be able to deal with a one-to-many (1:M) mapping of inputs to outputs, in order to learn different strategies for similar situations. If the selected network cannot handle 1:M pattern associations, then we must preprocess the exemplars to eliminate conflicting exemplars.

- Rotational duplication of situations cannot be dealt with easily within the network without some preprocessing of the input patterns. The most straightforward approach for resolving this issue is to simply ensure that the training set includes many examples of rotated situations.

There is no one network paradigm that will satisfy all of these constraints. Instead, we shall compromise, and select a modified ART1 network as the best choice for this application. The network, as shown in Figure 4.10, is functionally

---

5. In this text, we reserve the term *binary* to refer to elements from the set $\{0, 1\}$. Similarly, the term *bipolar* is reserved for patterns containing elements from the set $\{-1, 1\}$.

Linear Outputs

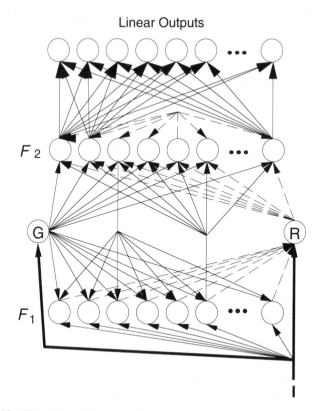

Figure 4.10 The ART1 network, modified with the addition of an outstar layer from F_2 to the linear-output layer, is shown. Recall that the F_2 layer is a competitive layer in the art model, meaning that after the network achieves resonance (when it has either matched or stored the input pattern), the associated output pattern can be stored in the connection weights between the winning F_2-layer unit and the linear-output layer. © *David M. Skapura, 1990. Reprinted from* A Connectionist Approach to Heuristically Pruning Large Search Trees. *Used with permission.*

identical to the ART1 network described in Chapter 2, with the exception of the outstar layer that we have combined with the F_2 layer, and the linear-output units that will serve to identify the next move position. Why do we need this modification to the ART network? Quite simply, ART1 acts as a constantly learning pattern memory, but it has no built-in provision for storing patterns to be associated with the memory patterns. The addition of the outstars, which are merely a logical extension of the existing F_2-layer units, provide the network with the ability to store the associated pattern memories. The linear-output layer acts as a pattern multiplexer, providing a common output location for all of the patterns that can be produced by the F_2-layer units. More importantly, though, the outstar learning law allows the outstar to learn the *average* of all of the pattern vectors associated with the unit, thereby solving the 1:M pattern issue.

4.4 IMAGE INTERPOLATION

Earlier in this section we saw how video imagery could be used as an input to an associative memory designed to recognize text characters in the image. We shall now investigate a variation of that application, this time showing how an interpolative associative memory can be used to produce meaningful responses when an input pattern varies from the training exemplars. For this application, first described by James Freeman [1, 2], the input to the memory is the two-dimensional (2D) image of a model of the space shuttle that can be rotated about a single axis. The output from the memory is then expected to be the angle of orientation of the shuttle model with respect to a fixed reference position.

The purpose of this application, as described in the original paper, was to show how a neural network could be used to perform the rudimentary functions associated with image understanding. The original experiment was conducted as a precursor to the more complicated problem of stereoscopic computer vision, where the third dimension (depth) becomes a concern.

4.4.1 Input Pattern Specification

As we saw in the character-recognition application, computer image processing usually begins with some form of video camera being used to acquire the image information. The video data, in the form of raster pixels, is then digitized[6] and collected together as a *frame* of imagery. Each frame of data represents a snapshot of the scene, essentially a moment frozen in time, that can be used to perform a static analysis of the image.

In the character-recognition application, the image processing was fairly straightforward—the application expected the image data to contain a recognizable character, and the character image was expected to be well behaved (i.e., positioned and oriented in a particular manner within the character matrix). Because we were only concerned with the identification of monochromatic text images, the pixels in the character image could be represented as binary values.

For the spacecraft orientation system, monochromatic video was also used to provide the input image for the system. In this case, however, each pixel was digitized into one of 256 gray shades, rather than simply on or off. While not necessary to the success of the application, the gray shading was used to assess the ability of a neural network to handle complex image data. Because gray shades allow for shadows on the image, and provide softer transitions at areas

---

6. A quantizing process, where each pixel is assigned an integer value indicating its luminescence, and, if appropriate, its color.

of high contrast, it was felt that gray shading provided a more comprehensive test of the associative memory than if the input image were simply binary.

The original image obtained from the video input system was a 256×256 pixel matrix, with the image of the shuttle model positioned at the center of the frame. Using conventional pixel compression techniques, the video image was then reduced to a 32×32 pixel image in order to reduce the computational complexity to a size that was manageable in a neural-network *simulation*.[7] The 1,024 pixels from the compressed image were then each scaled to a value between zero and one, by translating each pixel according to the equation

$$i_i = \frac{p_i}{\max\{p_j\}} \quad j = 1, \ldots, 1024 \tag{4.1}$$

where i_i represents the value of the ith pixel in the input pattern (**i**), and p_i represents the value of the ith pixel in the image pattern (**p**). The resulting values were thresholded into binary pattern elements, and concatenated into a pattern vector comprised of 1,024 binary elements, each representing a gray-shade pixel from the compressed image of the shuttle model. Figure 4.11 illustrates the form of the input pattern, and shows how it corresponds to the original, digitized image of the shuttle.

4.4.2   Output Pattern Specification

For this application, the associative memory was expected to provide an interpolated estimate of the orientation of the space-shuttle model from the image of the model. Because the model had only one axis of rotation, the neural network had merely to provide an indication of the rotational orientation of the model given the input image. To see how that was accomplished, let us now consider the method used by the application developers for representing the rotational orientation in a manner that can be reproduced by a neural network.

First, given that the model had only one degree of freedom, we can conclude that the orientation, while continuously variable, can always be expressed by an angular difference between the current position and some predefined reference position. For this application, the nose-up orientation was selected as the reference position.

Next, we must determine how we should model outputs from the network so that we might interpret the network response as an indication of the angular difference between the current input image and the reference position. One method for satisfying this requirement is to specify the output value from the network as an indication of the sine (or cosine) of the angle between the two positions. Us-

---

7. In this application, as in most of the applications described in this text, the neural network was implemented as a software program running on a conventional computer system. Simulators tend to be extremely slow when running large networks; hence, smaller networks are preferred.

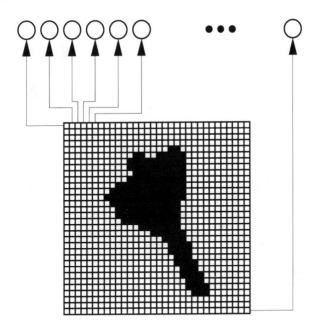

Figure 4.11   This diagram illustrates how the input pattern vector was formed from the digitized image of the space shuttle. The image of the shuttle has already been preprocessed to compress the image to 1,024 pixels. *Source: Adapted from* Neural networks for machine vision: the Spacecraft Orientation Demonstration [1]. *Copyright ©1988. Used with permission of the author.*

ing this interpretation, we can guarantee that the output from the network will be limited to values in the range of $-1 \ldots 1$ (because the sine and cosine functions have those minimum and maximum values). This representation scheme also maps well into the kind of output that can be easily produced by a neural processing element; in this case, as a continuous bipolar output.

Finally, because in this application we expect the output to be interpolated between specific training points, we can improve the ability of the network to resolve points if we ask it to provide *both* the sine and cosine values for the input orientation. By so doing, when the network interpolates an output, we will have an external measure of how accurate the interpolation was by having two different indications of the interpolated value. If the interpolation produces an exact (or very near exact) response, the difference of the angles that produce the resulting sine and cosine values will be very small. However, the interpolation is somewhat less accurate, we should expect differences in the angles indicated by the sine and cosine outputs. When this occurs, we can choose to externally refine the approximation provided by the network by averaging the two angles indicated. Such a situation is illustrated in Figure 4.12.

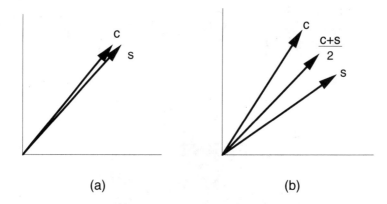

(a)   (b)

Figure 4.12 This figure depicts the use of two interpolated output signals as a measure of the confidence in the interpolation process. (a) When the angles indicated by both outputs agree, confidence in the interpolation process is very high, and no external averaging is required. (b) When the output angles differ, confidence in the interpolation is diminished, but externally averaging the output angles can produce better results.

4.4.3   Network Specification

Having completed the specification of the input and output patterns for the associative memory, we are now able to complete the application by selecting an appropriate neural-network paradigm. To choose the most appropriate neural model, let us first review the two primary requirements of the memory for this application:

- The memory must be able to accept digitized video images as input. The outputs to be produced by the network will be the numeric value of the sine and cosine of the angle between the reference position and the current position of the shuttle model, as contained in the input image pattern.

- The network must be able to recall exact matches to input patterns, or to interpolate between training examples when the current input differs from one of the training inputs.

Based on these requirements, the developer of this application selected the forward half of the CPN as the most appropriate network paradigm. The forward half of the CPN is a logical choice for this application, due to the fact that the CPN can produce outputs that are analogous to linearly interpolated, continuous mathematical functions. Specifically, by constructing a CPN containing 1,024 inputs, 12 hidden units, and 2 outputs, and training the network to recognize 12 different images of the shuttle model, each rotated by 30 degrees from its neighboring image, the network became a heteroassociative memory for the 12 images.

After training was completed, the behavior of the network was altered to allow two hidden units to win the competition for any new input pattern. This modification allowed the CPN to perform a linear interpolation between the angles associated with the images that most closely correspond (in Euclidian space) to the current input image. Thus, if the input image indicated that the shuttle was at an orientation of 41 degrees, the competitive units that learned to recognize the image at 30 degrees and 60 degrees would win the competition, with the first having a slightly higher activation than the second. When these two units then sent their respective angle information to the output layer, the linear units at the output of the CPN integrated the responses from the two winning units, and provided a linear interpolation between them.

There were, however, two problems with this particular implementation: First, the CPN offered no method for internally detecting when an input pattern exactly matched one of the training patterns, and, thus, an interpolation between two units was performed even when the input was one of the training inputs. Second, the method of interpolation was a problem; linear interpolation between angles is at best a crude method of approximating an angle. We can illustrate this concept with an example.

Using the scenario described above, let the current input image represent the shuttle at 45 degrees, halfway between two training points. After propagating that image pattern to the hidden layer, the units associated with the input image at 30 degrees and 60 degrees will win the competition, with identical activation values. The values propagated to the linear output units are then given by the equations

$$s = 0.5 \sin(30°) + 0.5 \sin(60°)$$
$$= 0.25 + 0.433$$
$$= 0.683$$

and

$$c = 0.5 \cos(30°) + 0.5 \cos(60°)$$
$$= 0.683$$

because each of the two winning units contributes an equal share of its output pattern to the total output. Now, by taking the inverse sine and cosine of the values produced by s and c, we find that the angle indicated by unit s is 43.08 degrees and that the angle indicated by unit c is 46.92 degrees. Only by averaging the results provided by the network can we compensate for the error introduced by the linear interpolation process.

Exercise 4.4: Determine the output from the interpolative CPN if the input pattern were 120 degrees. Assume that, as before, two units win the competition when the input pattern is propagated forward. ■

Exercise 4.5: Describe the modifications you might make to the CPN to detect when an input pattern exactly matches one of the training inputs. Be sure that your solution does not rely on any external information beyond the input pattern being provided to the network. ■

4.5   DIAGNOSTIC AIDS

The last example of an associative-memory application that we will study is based on an unpublished application developed by one of my students. The objective of the project was to determine if an associative-memory neural network could be used to assist in the diagnosis of equipment failures in large, complex computer systems. Specifically, an autoassociative memory was trained to recognize patterns that consisted of a variety of symptoms that, in specific combinations, indicated certain failure modes in the equipment. After training the network, the memory was used to match a partial list of symptoms against the complete patterns stored in the memory. The output pattern produced by the network was compared to the partial pattern to determine if the operator may have overlooked certain symptoms during the diagnostic process that, if present, could help pinpoint the source of the problem.

This application was found to be very useful in practice, because, as with most fairly complicated systems, many failure modes tend to produce identical symptoms: For example, a blank cathode-ray tube (CRT) screen in a desktop computer system can be indicative of a power-supply problem, a bad graphics card, incorrectly connected cables, or a defective power switch. Only by looking at the complete list of symptoms can we identify the source of the failure (e.g., if the CRT is blank, the light over the switch is on, the cables are all connected correctly, and the computer produces an abnormally long *beep* during the bootstrap process, we can identify the source of the problem as the graphics card).

Compounding the problem, the diagnosis of equipment failures is often complicated by the fact that certain failures sometimes induce other failures that, in turn, produce a whole new set of symptoms. The symptoms of the induced problem can ultimately mask the symptoms of the original problem, complicating the diagnosis. Often, the only method that exists for identifying and correcting these kinds of problems is to have specialized technicians perform an analysis of the failure. The problem with this solution, however, is the loss of generality with the technicians—if a technician becomes so specialized that he or she can only diagnose problems in certain kinds of equipment, the diagnostic skills of the technician cannot be reapplied to another system without significant retraining.

A possible solution to this dilemma lies in the ability of an autoassociative neural network to match partial input patterns, producing as output the training patterns that most closely resemble the partial input. In this manner, the autoassociative memory can be used to capture the specialized symptom knowledge available from a system designer, which can then be integrated into a field-diagnostic system. By automating the diagnostic process, equipment failures can be rapidly, and accurately, diagnosed by technicians who require fewer equipment-specific diagnostic skills, thus lowering the cost of maintenance to the end user of the systems.

4.5.1 Symptom Representation

To illustrate the method used to represent symptom patterns for an autoassociative memory, we will select a fairly common application as an example. Specifically, we will focus on the diagnosis of the failures that may occur in a desktop computer system. We must begin by identifying all possible problem symptoms[8] that are recognizable without specialized test equipment. Examples of such symptoms might include the following:

- There is no fan noise (indicating the fan is not turning).
- The CRT screen is blank.
- The cursor is present on the CRT screen.
- The computer sounds two quick *beeps* during boot.
- The computer sounds one long *beep*, followed by two quick *beeps* during boot.
- An error message appears on the CRT during boot.
- The computer does not respond to keyboard inputs.
- The disk light does not turn on during boot.
- The stepper motor in the diskette makes no noise when the disk light is on.

Inspection of this symptom list reveals that there are interdependencies in the symptoms, meaning that the presence of one symptom may imply the absence of another. For example, if the CRT screen is blank, we can infer that no error message appeared on the CRT screen during the boot process; if one had appeared, it would have persisted until the computer was rebooted. Such interdependencies are common in diagnostic applications, and will not present a problem for an autoassociative network. However, the fact that there are interdependencies in the symptoms means that the application developer must ensure that there are no conflicts in the diagnostic exemplars prior to training the network. Otherwise, the network will learn incorrect diagnosis patterns, and, in production, will reproduce the same faulty patterns.

Having completed the list of symptoms that we will use to diagnose the failures in our desktop computer system, we must now determine an appropriate representation scheme for processing by a neural network. As in all previous applications, it is preferable to cast each component of the training pattern into a binary form to make it compatible with the form of the output signals produced by neural processing elements. However, there are at least three states that we must be able to represent for most of the symptoms (e.g., *present*, *absent*, and *unknown*). This means that our pattern representation scheme must allow us to accommodate tertiary patterns.

---

8. For brevity, we will not identify *all* possible problem symptoms. Rather, we shall identify a subset of typical symptoms, and expect that the reader can extrapolate from those examples.

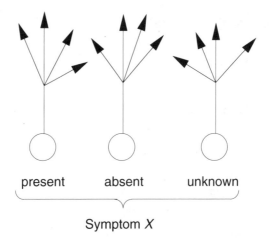

Figure 4.13   This diagram illustrates the use of three binary units to represent one of three possible states for each symptom in the pattern. Notice that, by using this scheme, only one of the three units can be active at any given time.

We have already seen one example of how to represent three states using binary pattern components in our discussion of the tic-tac-toe application. We will utilize the same scheme here, assigning one unit for each of the three possible states we can assign to a symptom. Then, for each symptom we have identified, we will set the output of the unit corresponding to the state of the symptom to the active mode, leaving the other two units associated with that symptom inactive. An example of this scheme is shown in Figure 4.13.

The input pattern to the autoassociative network can therefore be defined as the concatenation of all of the symptoms identified for the application, with the three units associated with each symptom set to the proper states. Units associated with symptoms that are unknown or irrelevant are set to the *unknown* state prior to propagating the complete pattern through the network. With respect to the output, we know that the network is going to be expected to produce the pattern from the training set that best matches some partial input pattern. Thus, we know that the output layer from the network must have exactly the same number of elements as the input layer, and must be interpreted in exactly the same manner as the input pattern, even if the input and output layers are not physically the same layer in the network structure.

4.5.2   Network Specification

There are three network paradigms that lend themselves to performing the kind of pattern matching required by this autoassociative application: the Boltzmann-completion network [2, 3], the BPN, and the BAM.[9] The Boltzmann network is probably the best suited of the three for this application, but, because of significant processing constraints, was eliminated from consideration.

Of the two remaining networks, both can be specified in the same manner, with respect to the input-output layers. The number of units on both layers will be exactly the same, and that number can be determined by multiplying the total number of symptoms that define the application by three, because each symptom requires three units. Furthermore, as the input and output patterns are composed of binary elements, we can use the sigmoidal activation function for the units in the BPN, and the BAM activation function if the BAM is selected.[10]

Which of these two networks will provide a better solution? A cursory analysis of the processing required by the application tends to indicate the BAM, due to its use of Hamming distance to compare patterns. For this application, the Hamming-distance measure seems to be indicated because we are interested in matching patterns that may differ from training exemplars by only a few symptoms. However, because we are using a tertiary pattern representation, the BAM (and its MAM counterparts) may settle into invalid output states (e.g., one where more than one unit is active for a single symptom) if the partial input pattern used to start the pattern-matching process is relatively sparse.

For that reason, we selected a three-layer BPN for this application, and achieved excellent results. The BPN learned to recognize the combination of symptoms that distinguished the different pattern vectors, and was able to recognize and reconstruct complete symptom patterns from partial patterns containing only 50% of the total information needed to uniquely identify the pattern. Moreover, when presented with partial inputs that tended to indicate multiple exemplars, the BPN produced reduced outputs from the ambiguous units that, if known, would uniquely distinguish the patterns. Thus, the BPN provided us with a means of identifying which of the unknown symptoms had yet to be positively determined, something that the BAM could not have done.

4.6 ASSOCIATIVE-MEMORY SUMMARY

In this chapter, we have investigated the application of associative memories to several real-world problems. We have defined the three basic types of associative memories (hetero-, interpolative, and autoassociative) and shown how each of the three has been successfully applied. We have seen how some of the neural processing models described in Chapter 2 can be used to construct associative memories, and investigated the issues associated with acquiring and formatting the application data for use by the neural-network. While the applications described in this chapter are somewhat simplistic, they nevertheless illustrate the

---

9. The BPN and BAM architectures are discussed at length in Chapter 2.

10. If the BAM is selected, bipolar outputs must be substituted for the binary format.

basic concepts associated with building neural-network applications, and provide the first examples of the process of engineering practical applications. In later chapters, we will build on these foundations, as we develop more sophisticated applications of neural-network technology.

SUGGESTED READINGS

Although there are precise mathematical definitions for each of the three associative-memory models described in the first part of this chapter, space precludes us from providing the details of those definitions in this text. The reader interested in exploring these definitions further is referred instead to [2] for details.

With respect to associative-memory applications, the literature abounds with applications that utilize neural networks as their base technology. The best source of technical papers describing applications of associative-memory networks is in the proceedings of the International Joint Conference on Neural Networks (IJCNN), a conference sponsored by the Institute of Electrical and Electronic Engineers (IEEE) and the International Neural Network Society (INNS). The IJCNN conferences were held annually from 1987 through 1992 (with one mid-year conference held in 1990), and proceedings are available from the IEEE. Another good source of applications papers is the *Advances in Neural Information Processing Systems* (NIPS) conference proceedings, published annually by Morgan Kaufmann Publishing Company.

The tic-tac-toe application described in this chapter was taken from a more complete assessment of the ability of neural networks to perform parallel state-space searches, the results of which were published in 1990 as my master's thesis at the University of Houston–Clear Lake [5]. Likewise, the spacecraft-orientation application described in this chapter was based on a research project conducted by an associate of mine, Dr. James Freeman, while under contract to the NASA/Johnson Space Center Artificial Intelligence Section [1].

Readers interested in a more formal mathematical treatment of associative memories are referred to *Foundations of Neural Networks* [4] by Tarun Khanna. Finally, for a formal investigation into the theoretical limits of several different associative-memory network models, readers are referred to Chapter 6 of *Introduction to Artificial Neural Systems* [6] by Jacek Zurada.

BIBLIOGRAPHY

1. James A. Freeman. Neural networks for machine vision: the spacecraft orientation demonstration, $e^x ponent$, *The Ford Aerospace Technical Journal*, Fall 1988, pp. 16–20.

2. James A. Freeman and David M. Skapura. *Neural Networks: Algorithms, Applications, and Programming Techniques*. Addison-Wesley Publishing Company, Reading, MA, 1991.

3. G. E. Hinton and T. J. Sejnowski. *Parallel Distributed Processing, Vol. 1*. MIT Press, Cambridge, MA, pp. 282–317, 1986.

4. Tarun Khanna. *Foundations of Neural Networks*. Addison-Wesley Publishing Company, Reading, MA, 1990.

5. David M. Skapura. *A Connectionist Approach to Heuristically Pruning Large Search Trees*. Master's thesis, University of Houston–Clear Lake, 1990.

6. Jacek Zurada. *Introduction to Artificial Neural Systems*. West Publishing Company, St. Paul, MN, pp. 313–388, 1992.

CHAPTER

Business and Financial Applications

All our knowledge has its origins in our perceptions.

— Leonardo da Vinci

In the business world, success is measured by the financial bottom line—an organization that makes money flourishes, while an organization that loses money (or merely breaks even) flounders. Often, the most profitable organizations are the ones that do the best job anticipating the marketplace. Because crystal balls have not yet been perfected, businesspeople often attempt to anticipate the market by interpreting innumerable external parameters, such as prevailing economic indicators, public opinion, and even the current political climate. Many larger businesses currently employ full-time statisticians to construct models of a specific market, then evaluate individual business opportunities based on the model. Recently, however, many smaller businesses have found success using neural networks, instead of statistical models, to anticipate changes in the marketplace.

In this chapter, we shall investigate a diverse set of neural-network applications that businesses and financial institutions[1] have employed to help make better predictions about investment opportunities. In several of the applications we shall study, the neural network is used to analyze trends in large quantities of empirical data. In others, the network performs an **information-fusing** function—that is, from many pieces of (apparently) unrelated data, the network learns to produce abstractions that imply more about the problem domain than is discernible from the component pieces. In all cases, the neural network adds value to the application by learning to recognize the general characteristics of a specific financial model, and then provides a mechanism for using the learned generalities to predict the success of an investment at some future time.

---

1. Not to mention individual investors.

We shall begin our investigation of the business and financial applications of neural networks by first examining some of the general issues associated with modeling a financial application for use by a neural network. We then present a survey of several successful applications of the technology, showing how each application was constructed, and illustrating the role of the neural network in the final system implementation.

5.1   FINANCIAL MODELING

Time is always the underlying component in any financial-analysis model. Depending on the application, we may be interested in understanding the history of how a market has responded to some external stimuli, or we may simply be evaluating the personal credit history of a loan applicant. Unfortunately, most neural-network paradigms are fairly limited with respect to temporal pattern recognition and classification. If we are to successfully apply the current generation of neural networks to financial applications, we must first develop a strategy for converting a temporal sequence of indicators into a spatial pattern that the network can process. We can accomplish this goal through the use of several popular financial-analysis techniques, which we shall now describe in detail for readers who are not experts in market analysis. Readers already comfortable with financial-modeling techniques may skip the remainder of this section without fear of missing anything important with regard to the neural-network applications that we shall describe.

5.1.1   Discrete Time Sampling

In general, the technique that provides the most general approach for converting temporal sequences into spatial patterns is the process of *discrete time sampling*. As the name suggests, discrete time sampling is the process of quantizing a continuously variable signal by sampling it at regular time intervals. A sequence of n samples can be concatenated to form a single pattern that encapsulates a quantized *signature* of the signal.

To illustrate this concept, consider an application to analyze the performance of the stock market over a period of time. As indicated by the bar chart depicted in Figure 5.1, the stock market is a prime example of a financial model that varies (sometimes drastically) with the passage of time. On any given business day, a single value can be computed from a set of key stocks that provides an instantaneous indication of the state of the market; one such value is the Dow Jones Industrial Average. However, the Dow Jones average, by itself, offers almost no insight into what the market might do *tomorrow*. A more meaningful interpretation of what the market is doing[2] is obtained by observing a trend of the average.

---

2. As well as what it might be doing in the near future.

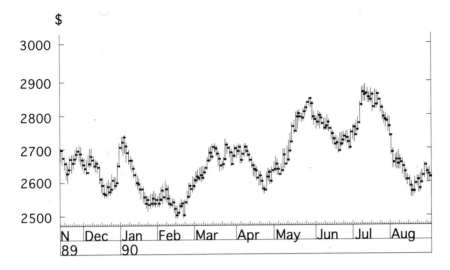

Figure 5.1   This graph shows the daily high and low of the Dow Jones Industrial Average from November 1989 through August 1990. In this chart, the vertical axis represents the numerical value of the average, while the horizontal axis depicts the passage of time. Each bar represents the range of the average during the day, while the tick mark on the range indicates the closing average. Thus, we have quantized the dynamic behavior of the market by taking a daily sample of the high, low, and closing points of the average. When looking at this chart, do you see a series of discrete points, or do you see a line moving from left to right, indicating the long-term behavior of the market?

However, a simple time series only conveys a sense of how a particular market (in this case, the stock market) is changing over a fairly long period of time. To gain an insight into the direction the market (or a particular stock) may be going, a good financial analyst will also consider a number of other mathematical indicators. There are many such indicators in common use. For our purposes, we will consider only three of the most popular: a market-intensity indicator called the ADX [11], which is used to provide a sense of whether the market is trending; a moving-average convergence/divergence (MACD) [1] analysis, which will indicate optimal buy and sell signals in a trending market; and a slow stochastic analysis [6], which is typically used to complement the MACD, because it works well in a nontrending market.

5.1.2   Average Directional Movement

To determine whether a market is trending, we can calculate an n-period ADX for each discrete time sample. The ADX, as it was originally described by J. Welles Wilder, is computed in a five-step process that begins with an assessment of the basic directional movement of the market. Specifically, the high and low values of the market at the current time are compared with the high and low values at

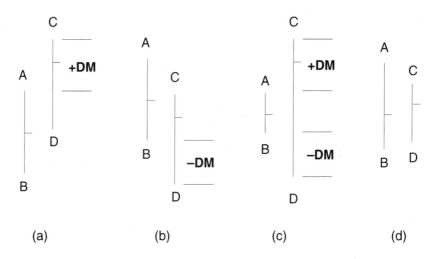

Figure 5.2   The computation of the market directional indicators is shown. (a) The value of +DM is given by determining the absolute difference between the high point of the average at the previous time interval and the high point of the average at the current time. (b) The value of −DM is given by the absolute difference between the low points at the two time samples. (c) When the trading at the current time is **outside** the trading range at the previous time, the larger of +DM and −DM is used as DM. (d) When trading at the current time is **inside** the trading range at the previous time, DM is zero. *Source: From The Average Directional Index (ADX), by Thom Hartle, Technical Analysis of* STOCKS & COMMODITIES, *Vol. 9, No. 3, (Mar. 1991), p. 101. Copyright ©1991, Technical Analysis, Inc. Used with permission.*

the previous time. The difference values obtained indicate the *plus directional movement* (+DM) and the *minus directional movement* (−DM), respectively. Next, we must determine a single value that we will use to indicate the overall *directional movement* (DM) for the current time period. Wilder defines this value as a function of the range of the averages from the two time periods: If the trading range at the current time is outside the range of trading at the previous time, then the larger of +DM and −DM is used as DM. However, if the trading range at the current time is inside the range of trading at the previous time, then the value of DM is zero. Figure 5.2 illustrates the computation of these values.

Next, Wilder computes a *directional indicator* (DI) value, which is defined as the percentage of the price range that is directional for the given time period. DI is obtained by dividing DM by the true-range (TR) value for the current time period, where TR is the largest of

- The difference between the high and low value at the current time.
- The difference between the high at the current time and the closing value at the previous time.

- The difference between the low at the current time and the closing value at the previous time.

The value of DI can be either positive or negative, while all of the previously calculated values are positive (or zero). To retain the positive notation scheme, Wilder defines two separate indicators, $+$DI and $-$DI, where $+$DI simply indicates a time period with a positive DI and $-$DI is the absolute value of the DI for a time period with a negative DI.

The average directional movement (ADX) indicator for a market is a smoothed moving average of the DI values across an interval of n time periods. Thus, for an n period ADX, we initially compute the average DIs across the n time periods. This calculation is given by

$$+\mathrm{DI}_n = \frac{\sum_{i=0}^{n-1} +\mathrm{DM}(t-i)}{\sum_{i=0}^{n-1} \mathrm{TR}(t-i)} \qquad (5.1)$$

$$-\mathrm{DI}_n = \frac{\sum_{i=0}^{n-1} -\mathrm{DM}(t-i)}{\sum_{i=0}^{n-1} \mathrm{TR}(t-i)} \qquad (5.2)$$

where the subscript n is used to indicate the span of the average, and the terms have been given a parenthetical index $(t-i)$ to indicate how many time periods *prior* to the current time period the value occurred (eg., $-\mathrm{DM}(t-4)$ is used to indicate the minus directional movement value four time periods prior to the current time, and $+\mathrm{DM}(t-0)$ indicates the plus directional movement at the current time period).

Once the average DIs have been initially computed, they may be updated for each new time period (t) by recomputing the three DM indicators ($+$DM, $-$DM, and TR) according to the equation

$$X_n(t) = X_n(t-1)\frac{n-1}{n} + X(t) \qquad (5.3)$$

where X represents each movement indicator, and subsequently recomputing $+\mathrm{DI}_n$ and $-\mathrm{DI}_n$ according to Eqs. (5.1) and (5.2).

We next convert the average DIs to a *directional movement index* (DMI) to indicate the magnitude of the trend on a scale of 0 to 100. The computation is performed according to the equation

$$\mathrm{DMI} = \frac{\| +\mathrm{DM}_n - -\mathrm{DM}_n \|}{+\mathrm{DM}_n + -\mathrm{DM}_n} \qquad (5.4)$$

Finally, the ADX is computed as an n-period moving average of the DMI. After the first n ADX values have been computed for a particular market, the ADX can then be updated for each subsequent time period (t) according to the equation

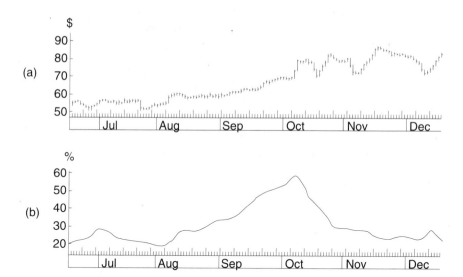

Figure 5.3   These diagrams illustrate the relationship between market prices and the adx. (a) This graph illustrates the discrete time behavior of a particular stock listed on the New York Stock Exchange over a six-month period. Notice how the value of the stock fluctuates on a daily basis, yet exhibits a long-term increase. (b) The ADX computed for the same stock, over the same six-month period. Notice that the ADX peaks at the same point in time as the stock growth trend diminishes. *Source: From* The Average Directional Index (ADX), *by Thom Hartle, Technical Analysis of* Stocks & Commodities, *Vol. 9, No. 3, (Mar. 1991), p. 101. Copyright ©1991, Technical Analysis, Inc. Used with permission.*

$$\mathrm{ADX}_n(t) = \mathrm{ADX}_n(t-1)\frac{n-1}{n} + \mathrm{ADX}(t) \tag{5.5}$$

The primary benefit of the ADX is its ability to determine when the monitored signal, or market, is in a trending state. For example, consider the graphs illustrated in Figure 5.3. If we restrict our analysis to just the temporal sequence of data, it is difficult to determine when the market really begins a long-term trend. The ADX, however, rises rapidly at the onset of a trend, and levels off when the market again begins normal fluctuations.

5.1.3   Stochastics

A *stochastic oscillator*, as it is referred to in the financial industry, is actually a misnomer for a signal that is designed to anticipate sudden reversals in market values. The oscillator[3] was originally developed by George C. Lane, as a method

---

3. The term *oscillator* is not exactly appropriate, either, in that it is taken from the appearance of the computed signal, not from the fact that the signal is intended to oscillate. Nevertheless, we shall abide by the language of the financial industry, to lessen the confusion when reading financial papers.

to anticipate when the stock market was about to reverse itself. Mr. Lane actually developed more than 50 separate indicators, but for our discussion we will concern ourselves with only two: We shall refer to these signals as %D and %K, because they were the fourth and eleventh signals developed by Lane.

The indicators achieve their desired function by taking advantage of a well-known stock-market phenomenon—a market **top**, or high point for a particular stock, is usually indicated by daily closing prices that tend to cluster around the high value for the stock. Conversely, a market **bottom** is indicated when daily closing prices cluster around the low value of the stock. Because stock prices tend to reverse their trends during a top (or bottom) period, we can anticipate reversals by detecting when a stock is at (or near) its limit. In a mathematical sense, we can develop such an indicator by comparing the current closing price of a stock with its highest high and lowest low values over a period of time. By assessing the tendencies of the indicator with respect to the trend of the true market value, we can interpret the derived signal as a market indicator that can portend sudden changes in the value of a stock.

Lane's indicators are simply a mathematical comparison, over some fixed period of time (usually between five and 14 days) of the closing value of a stock to its highest highs and lowest lows. Both signals are designed as percentage indicators; hence both are limited to numerical values in the range of 0 to 100. The two signals are also remarkably similar in their design: The %D indicator is actually a three-day smoothed version of the %K indicator. Specifically, the signals are calculated from the raw market data according to the equations

$$\%K = 100 \frac{C(t) - \text{LOW}_{14}(t)}{\text{HIGH}_{14}(t) - \text{LOW}_{14}(t)} \tag{5.6}$$

$$\%D = 100 \frac{\sum_{i=0}^{2} C(t-i) - \text{LOW}_{14}(t-i)}{\sum_{i=0}^{2} \text{HIGH}_{14}(t-i) - \text{LOW}_{14}(t-i)} \tag{5.7}$$

where $C(t)$ indicates the closing market value for time period t, $\text{HIGH}_{14}(t)$ indicates the highest, high value for the market over each of the 13 time intervals preceding, and the one including, interval t, and the term $\text{LOW}_{14}(t)$ indicates the lowest, low value from the same interval.

As shown in Figure 5.4, the %D and %K indicators developed by Lane can be interpreted in two different, but meaningful, ways. First, because the indicators are actually calculations of the percentage difference between a stock's closing value and its low and high points over some time interval, a saturation of the indicator can be thought of as an *overage* condition on the stock. Specifically, a stock is considered *overbought* when the stochastic indicator goes above 80%. Similarly, a stock is considered *oversold* when the indicator goes below 20%. Second, by examining the tendencies of the indicator with respect to the true market value of the stock over a period of time, the stochastic oscillator can be used to indicate *buy* or *sell* signals.

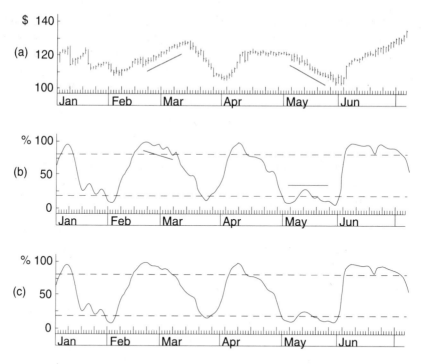

Figure 5.4   The relationship between the stochastic oscillator and a typical *blue-chip* stock is shown. In each of these figures, the top graph depicts the daily closing price of the stock, while the bottom graphs illustrate the plots of the stochastic signals. (a) In this diagram, the stochastic indicates a *sell* period when the value of the indicators go over 80% and the direction of the indicators tend to diverge from the direction of the market prices. (b) Similarly, a *buy* signal is indicated when the indicators go below 20% and the stock value declines with respect to its stochastics. (c) The same market data is smoothed with a slow stochastic oscillator. *Source: From* Stochastics, *by Thom Hartle, Technical Analysis of* STOCKS & COMMODITIES, *Vol. 9, No. 3, (Mar. 1991), p. 103. Copyright ©1991, Technical Analysis, Inc. Used with permission.*

Another variation of the stochastic oscillator uses a three-day moving average of the %D indicator instead of the %K indicator. This model is called the *slow stochastics oscillator*, and is considered by many market analysts to be an improvement over the stochastic oscillator, because the resulting analysis tends to be less susceptible to transitory fluctuations in the input data.

5.1.4   Moving-Average Convergence/Divergence

The MACD indicator, developed by Gerald Appel [1], has gained popularity as a stock-market indicator to measure the *trend* of a stock over a period of time. The indicator is developed by comparing the difference between two exponentially smoothed price data (called the MACD line), and an exponentially smoothed series of the difference (referred to as the signal line).

Exponential smoothing is a relatively intuitive method for computing an average of a dynamic indicator (such as a stock price) that accounts for the behavior of the signal over an arbitrary period of time. In financial applications, it also has the advantage of being able to rapidly respond to fluctuations in the price data. The computation of an exponentially smoothed moving average (EMA) for any time period t over an arbitrarily long duration is given by the equation

$$\text{EMA}(t) = \alpha(x(t) - \text{EMA}(t - 1)) + \text{EMA}(t - 1) \qquad \textbf{(5.8)}$$

where α is the smoothing constant, the term $x(t)$ represents the instantaneous value of the indicator at time t, and $\text{EMA}(t - 1)$ indicates the value of the EMA at the previous time interval.

In this formulation, α is actually a weighting value designed to allow the EMA to approximate a simple moving average across an arbitrary time period. Thus, α can be approximated as

$$\alpha = \frac{2}{(n + 1)} \qquad \textbf{(5.9)}$$

where n is the number of discrete time periods over which the moving average will be calculated. For example, for a nine-day EMA analysis, α would be approximated as $\frac{2}{9+1}$, or 0.20.

Interpreting the MACD to anticipate market trends is also relatively simple. As shown in Figure 5.5, a *buy* signal is indicated when the MACD line crosses above the signal line, while a *sell* signal is generated when the MACD crosses below the signal line. Moreover, because the MACD is a trend-following technique, it also has the advantage of providing an early indication of market reversal. As with the stochastic oscillator, market reversal is indicated by comparing the MACD with the instantaneous indicator—in this case, the closing stock price— over a period of time. When the MACD and instantaneous indicators begin to diverge, a reversal is indicated.

5.2   MARKET PREDICTION

In the previous section, we examined several mathematical tools that a financial analyst might use to predict the future of the stock market by examining several key indicators. However, if predicting the stock market were simply a matter of correlating three or four indicators, most people could develop a high-yield portfolio without the assistance of a financial analyst. In truth, a good financial analyst will often evaluate *hundreds* of indicators, some derived mathematically from empirical market data, others simply subjective evaluations of the current market situation. Compounding the problem is the depth of the historical data that the analyst has available—the Dow Jones Industrial Averages, for example,

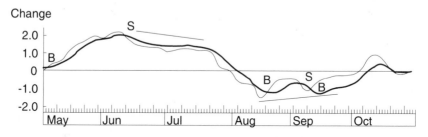

Figure 5.5   The use of the MACD to indicate market trends is shown. In these diagrams, we employ appel's MACD calculations using a 12- and 26-day EMA to compute the MACD line, and a nine-day EMA to compute the signal line. As before, the top graph represents the closing price of the stock we are monitoring over a specific time period, while the bottom graph illustrates the macd computed from that data. *Buy* signals are indicated when the MACD line crosses above the signal line, while *sell* signals are produced where the MACD line crosses below the signal line. Notice how the *buy* signals tend to precede periods of increasing value in the stock price, while *sell* signals tend to precede periods of declining stock price. *Source: From* Moving Average Convergence/Divergence (MACD), *by Thom Hartle, Technical Analysis of* Stocks & Commodities, *Vol. 9, No. 3, (Mar. 1991), p. 104. Copyright ©1991, Technical Analysis, Inc. Used with permission.*

have been published (in their current form) daily since October 1928. If we are to develop high-yield portfolios, we, as financial analysts, must first decide how much of the available data is relevant to the current market.

To be successful in the capital-management business, it is essential to beat the market; that is, to forecast what the market is going to do in the near future, and trade accordingly. However, some market researchers have advocated the notion that the market is chaotic [7], and therefore unpredictable. If that assertion is true, it would be impossible to create a "crystal ball" that would accurately forecast the future in the market. We will not dispute the validity of the *random-walk* theory here. But, given the cyclical nature of the market, and the undisputed near-term accuracy of the mathematical indicators available to assess current market conditions, several researchers have developed computer applications using neural networks to help them make better financial decisions.

One such application was described in a series of articles published in a stocks and commodities trade journal [4]. In the first of these articles, investment managers Dean S. Barr and Walter J. Loick at LBS Capital Management, together with Professor Mark B. Fishman of Eckard College, reported constructing a neural network to predict the U.S. equity market (the Standard & Poors (S&P) 500 Index) five days into the future. Moreover, they reported remarkable success using a relatively simple neural network trained with only six financial indicators derived from the recent performance of the S&P 500. In their subsequent papers, however, Barr and Loick reported that the complexity of the network increased rapidly as additional indicators were incorporated into the training set, as several other components were added to refine the analysis process.

Because this financial "crystal ball" provides LBS with an obvious competitive advantage, the details reported become increasingly less specific as the application becomes more refined. Nevertheless, the details of the first network application are sufficient to illustrate how such a neural network could be constructed and trained. We shall therefore focus on the neural-network component of that system in the ensuing discussion.

5.2.1   Network Architecture

In their original paper, Barr and Loick reported investigations using a variety of network arrangements, although all of the networks were based on the backpropagation learning algorithm. The input layer in each network contained n inputs, where n was cited as the number of market indicators used for the specific network. We can therefore surmise that Barr and Loick use a 1:1 mapping between the market indicators they have selected and the number of input units used to represent those indicators. This also implies that they are normalizing the indicator values prior to training, because the BPN requires that input values have values in the range from zero to one, while the unnormalized values of the indicators may vary drastically.

The number of layers in each network is not explicitly indicated. It seems reasonable, however, to assume that most of their work was done using a typical three-layer network architecture. However, Barr and Loick indicate that they had their best results using a four-layer BPN, the fourth layer being an additional hidden layer containing approximately 12% of the number of input units.

As shown in Figure 5.6, the output of the network was a single, linear unit, the output of which is interpreted as a scaled prediction of the amount of change in the S&P 500 average five days in the future. In this example, Barr and Loick restrict their input to four derived market indicators and two raw data points for each training exemplar.

Exercise 5.1: In their articles, Barr and Loick do not provide any specific guidance with regard to selecting indicators (beyond the four described here) that might improve the performance of the network, although they do indicate that their best network contained a total of 26 indicators. From your understanding of the BPN, describe the selection criteria you would apply to determine if a financial indicator could improve the performance of the network. ∎

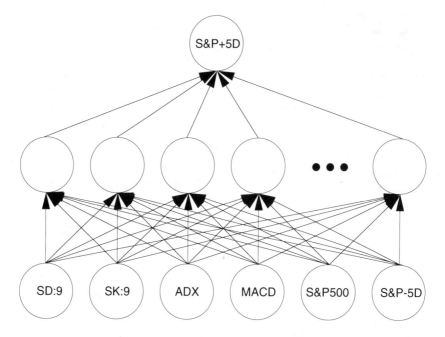

Figure 5.6 The three-layer BPN architecture used at LBS Capital Management to predict the S&P 500 average five days in the future is depicted. In this example network, the indicators used are the slow %D and slow %K stochastic indicators, using $n = 9$, an 18-day ADX, and histogram (difference) MACD values. Also used as input to the network are the current value of the S&P 500, as well as the net change in the S&P 500 value from five days prior. The output of the network is a continuously variable signal that is interpreted as a scaled estimate of the change expected in the market five days hence. *Source: Adapted from* Using neural networks in market analysis [4]. *Used with permission. Copyright ©1991, Technical Analysis, Inc.*

5.2.2 Market-Prediction Exemplars

To train their neural network, Barr and Loick describe the development of the training exemplars that will be presented to the network during the learning phase. Obviously, the primary source of information will be the recent history of the S&P 500. With respect to the network architecture they selected, the initial training patterns will consist of a set of associated pattern vectors comprised of six input components and a single output. From an application perspective, each training pattern is essentially a snapshot of the market at a specific, discrete time step, while the corresponding output is the difference between the current market value and the value of the market five time steps ahead of the input data. Thus, the training exemplars for the network can be developed from historical market data, while the performance of the trained network can be evaluated by comparing actual market performance with the projections made by the network using current market data.

In the ensuing discussion, we shall reconstruct the network Barr and Loick described in their original article by using data points consisting of the closing value of the S&P 500 at 20 different discrete time intervals (in this case, days). We shall refer to these values as a function of time, $S(t)$, with a value that is simply the closing value of the S&P 500 at discrete time t. In this notation, we shall refer to the most recent time period as t_0, with t_n representing any arbitrary discrete time period. Further, we will let n be positive to indicate a future time period, and negative to indicate a previous time period.

To construct the training exemplars for this network, we shall require a history of the S&P 500. The depth of information required will depend on the number of training exemplars we shall need to train the network. Barr and Loick suggest that, contrary to the "popular wisdom" it was possible to "confuse" the network by overwhelming it with too many training patterns.

Without knowing the specific details of the training set used to build this application, it is impossible for us to know if Barr and Loick were truely overwhelming the network with too much information, or if they were simply training on conflicting patterns, as we described in Chapter 2. Based on a conversation that I had with one of their researchers, I suspect that the problem was more likely the latter than the former, although it is entirely possible to overwhelm a BPN with too much data.

Nevertheless, we shall follow the example presented by LBS and limit our initial training data to 20 exemplars. However, because four of the six inputs that will be used to construct each input pattern require additional historical data to compute,[4] the total amount of market data we will need will be determined by the amount of information needed to construct the financial indicators for the 20 intervals of interest.

The indicators used by Barr and Loick to construct their training exemplars were

- A slow %D stochastic using a nine-day observation window, denoted as SD:9.
- A slow %K stochastic, also using a nine-day window (SK:9).
- An 18-day ADX.
- The *histogram* values for an 18- and 26-day MACD, where the histogram values are determined as the difference between the MACD and signal lines for the given data.

In addition to the derived indicators, Barr and Loick include the true value of the market at each time step, as well as the change in the market value from five days prior to the current time step. To determine the corresponding output value for each input pattern, we will need to know the difference between the value of the market at the current time step and its value five days in the future.

---

4. See the earlier discussions in Section 5.1, Financial Modeling.

Exemplar	Input						Output
Number	SD:9	SK:9	ADX	MACD	$S(t)$	$S(t_{-5})$	$S(t_5)$
1	26.651	45.756	14	0.152	272.02	8.53	−0.87
2	47.921	77.664	14	−0.209	272.21	7.53	−2.23
3	72.664	92.885	14	−0.423	272.06	6.87	−5.57
4	87.218	91.106	14	−0.597	272.98	10.48	−11.08
5	90.180	86.547	14	−0.617	271.93	5.91	−9.18
6	86.758	82.621	14	−0.553	271.15	−0.87	−8.60
7	80.678	72.867	14	−0.417	269.98	−2.23	−11.29
8	70.953	57.370	14	−0.100	266.49	−5.57	−5.93
9	54.672	33.780	14	0.379	261.90	−11.08	−1.13
10	36.640	18.771	16	0.608	262.75	−9.18	−1.72
11	21.992	13.426	17	0.730	262.55	−8.60	−2.31
12	14.302	10.708	18	0.995	258.69	−11.29	−1.71
13	11.864	11.458	19	0.992	260.56	−5.93	−3.47
14	11.867	13.435	20	0.918	260.77	−1.13	0.36
15	15.345	21.141	21	0.796	261.03	−1.72	−1.85
16	18.983	22.373	22	0.714	260.24	−2.31	−0.56
17	20.156	16.953	23	0.806	256.98	−1.71	5.35
18	16.994	11.654	24	0.799	257.09	−3.47	5.42
19	17.284	23.245	24	0.493	261.13	0.36	0.39
20	25.299	40.997	24	0.373	259.18	−1.85	−0.83

Table 5.1 The market data used by Barr and Loick to construct the 20 exemplars used to train the market-prediction neural network are shown.

Based on these requirements, we will need at least 51 days of the most recent S&P 500 averages to construct the 20 exemplars needed to train this network. In Table 5.1, we recreate the training data described by Barr and Loick in their original article. As mentioned earlier, these data should be normalized according to the formula

$$x_{ij}^* = \frac{x_{ij} - \min\{x_{ik}\}}{\max\{x_{ik}\} - \min\{x_{ik}\}} \forall k \in \{T\} \qquad (5.10)$$

where $\{T\}$ is the set of all training patterns and x_{ij}^* refers to the normalized value of the ith value in the jth pattern, prior to training the network.

Once trained, new input patterns are created by simply continuing the data-collection process. These new patterns are then presented to the neural network for estimating the value of the S&P 500 five days in the future. Figure 5.7 illustrates the performance achieved by the network we have just described for a period of 17 days beyond the training date. The close correlation between the

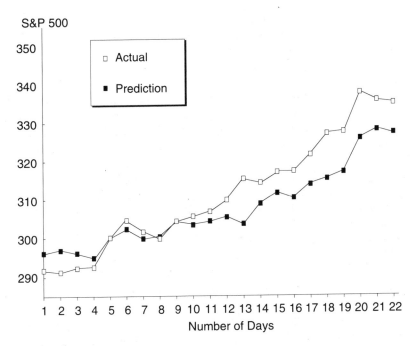

Figure 5.7   The response of the market-prediction BPN after training is shown. As this graph illustrates, the network has its lowest error in the earlier estimates, and tends to diverge from actual market values as time goes on. *Source: Adapted from* Using neural networks in market analysis [4]. *Used with permission. Copyright ©1991, Technical Analysis, Inc.*

market value predicted by the neural network and the true value suggests that such networks may indeed become very powerful tools in financial applications. In support of this belief, the Suggested Readings section at the end of this chapter contains references to several texts and many papers that describe other market predicting applications of neural networks, indicating that the financial world has become very interested in the potential of this technology.

Exercise 5.2: The graph in Figure 5.7 shows that the neural network tends to become less accurate as the prediction date becomes more distant from the time when the training data were collected. Suggest a strategy that could be employed to reduce this error in the network's response. Explain the advantages and disadvantages of your approach. ■

5.3 BOND RATING

Debt financing is a method by which corporations and government organizations can raise capital for immediate needs by offering *bonds* to investors. These bonds are guarantees by the offerer of repayment to the investor, over a period of time, of the face value of the bond plus interest. To make the bonds attractive to investors, bonds are often issued at a higher interest rate than can be attained through normal investment opportunities. However, if an offerer ends up over-extended financially and cannot repay the debt, investors are faced with legal proceedings to recover their investment, or they can lose their investment entirely.

To help potential investors accurately assess risk associated with bonds and securities, a *bond-rating* metric has been established by various independent financial organizations; among them, Standard and Poors (S&P) and Moody's Investor Service. These ratings describe the bond's potential for default, taking into account a number of factors about the issuer, including the issuer's ability and willingness to repay, and any other protective provisions for an issue.

From the perspective of the offerer, the bond rating has a significant effect on the yield of the issue—a lower bond rating means many fewer investors, which in turn means a much lower capital influx. Therefore, it is in the offerer's best interest to maintain as high a bond rating as possible.

However, because bond ratings are made by organizations that do not advertise the system (if any) that they use to determine a specific bond rating, it is difficult for a private investor or financial institution to independently assess the **default risk**[5] of a bond investment. Further complicating matters is the belief that different rating organizations use different criteria to measure the offerer's willingness to repay, making it extremely difficult to construct a precise mathematical model that could be used to determine bond ratings with any degree of consistency.

In the remainder of this section, we shall review two neural-network applications [3, 9] to predict bond ratings using a number of financial variables about an offerer that can be easily determined by an independent investor. We shall also show how the original authors compared the performance of their neural-network solutions to traditional statistical analysis methods.

5.3.1 Bond-Rating Networks

Both of the bond-rating neural-network applications we shall examine are very similar in their design. As shown in Figure 5.8, the primary differences between them are the number of layers in the networks and the actual financial variables used to determine the input training exemplars. The first application, originally described by Soumitra Dutta and Shashi Shekhar in 1988 [3], used two- and three-layer BPNs with six and ten input variables to perform its bond-rating function. The second application, described in a paper published by Alvin J. Surkan and J. Clay Singleton in 1990 [9], used three- and four-layer BPNs, with the four-layer networks varying in the number of processing elements per hidden layer, and seven financial variables as input. In both of these applications, the output from the network was interpreted as an indicator of the classification of the bond

---

5. The default risk of a bond is the likelihood that a promised coupon and par value will not be paid.

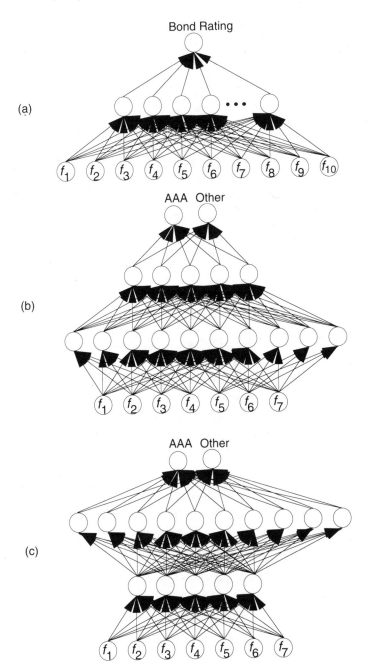

Figure 5.8   The architectures of the networks used to perform bond rating are shown. (a) The Dutta network, which is designed to classify bonds into one of the four major bond-rating categories (AAA, AA, A, BBB). (b) The Surkan network with four layers, which is designed to classify bond offerers as either AAA or A. (c) The reversed Surkan network, which was developed only for experimental purposes.

rating that should be applied to an offerer having the financial data described by the input pattern.

5.3.1.1 Three-Layer Network Application

The Dutta network, which predates the Surkan application by several years, was developed to determine whether neural networks could be used to correctly categorize bond issuers into one of the four major bond classifications, as defined by S&P. The degree to which the neural network classification agreed with the S&P classification was used to determine the accuracy of the network.

For their application, Dutta and Shekhar first established which financial variables were most appropriate for classifying bond ratings. Based on the results of other researchers, they decided to use nine, easily obtainable financial measures and one subjective estimate of the health of the bond issuer. The variables they selected were

1. Liability divided by (cash + assets).
2. Debt proportion.
3. Sales divided by net worth.
4. Profits divided by sales.
5. Financial strength.
6. Earnings divided by fixed costs.
7. Previous five-year revenue growth rate.
8. Projected next five-year revenue growth rate.
9. Working capital divided by sales.
10. Subjective prospect of the issuer.

Next, data from a total of 47 randomly selected industrial bond issuers were gathered from a recent issue of the Valueline Index, and the corresponding bond ratings for those issuers was obtained from the S&P Bond Guide. From those 47 data sets, 30 were again randomly selected as the training exemplars, while the remaining 17 were set aside to be used as validation sets.

Each of the 47 data sets was then converted into a form usable by the neural network. In the case of the input variables, each of the numerical inputs was normalized to eliminate any bias in the pattern. Similarly, the single output value was assigned according to the formula

$$y = \frac{C}{4}$$

where C is simply a numerical value assigned to the rating category (e.g., AAA = 4, AA = 3, A = 2, BBB = 1).

The BPN was then constructed in software, using the sigmoidal activation function for each of the hidden-layer units, and a linear activation function for the output unit. The resulting network was trained using the 30 training exemplars, and subsequently tested on the 17 validation exemplars. The output of the network was finally compared to the S&P rating assigned to those 17 issuers. For reasons not completely described in their paper, Dutta and Shekhar limited their analysis of the success rate to the ability of the network to correctly classify only one of the bond-rating categories (AA). Their results indicate that the neural network correctly classified AA offerers 82.6% of the time, with 8.3% classified as false-negatives and 9.1% classified as false-positives.

Finally, to illustrate the robustness of their solution, Dutta and Shekhar retrained the network, this time using only the first six variables as the components of the input pattern. Their results showed absolutely no difference between the smaller network and the larger implementation with respect to successfully classifying bond issuers.

5.3.1.2 Four-Layer Network Application

The Surkan network is functionally identical to the network used by Dutta with respect to its design and implementation. The only significant differences between these two applications are the number of layers used by Surkan (four, as compared to the three used by Dutta), the selection of the data used to construct the training exemplars for the application, and the interpretation of the output produced by the network.

As in the earlier application, Surkan and Singleton first selected a set of financial variables that would act as input patterns for the network. The variables selected for their experiments were determined by independent research [8] based on the bond ratings of the 18 Bell Telephone companies divested by American Telephone and Telegraph in 1982. The selected variables are defined as

1. *Leverage:* Debt divided by total capital.
2. *Coverage:* Pre-tax interest expense divided by income.
3. *ROE:* Return on equity or income.
4. *CV of ROE:* Coefficient of Variation of ROE over five years.
5. *TA:* Logarithm of total assets.
6. *Flow:* Construction costs divided by cash inflow.
7. *Toll:* Toll revenue ratio calculated as intradivided by inter-LATA.

Unfortunately, the authors do not provide the actual data that they used to train and test the performance of their networks, so it is difficult for us to attempt to assess the difficulty of the classification problem. However, they do provide a table listing the statistical mean and sample size of their original data, which we recreate in Table 5.2. Using these data, it is possible for the ambitious student to construct a set of synthetic exemplars that have the same general characteristics as the original training data. We encourage you to do so, and use that data to train your own network.

Variable	Bond-Rating Symbol						
	AAA	**AA1**	**AA2**	**AA3**	**A1**	**A2**	**A3**
Leverage	0.39	0.41	0.39	0.36	0.36	0.39	0.39
Coverage	4.50	4.48	4.99	5.69	5.02	4.30	4.46
ROE	0.25	0.14	0.14	0.15	0.12	0.14	0.15
CV of ROE	0.10	0.10	0.08	0.10	0.14	0.09	0.07
TA	14.70	15.75	13.00	14.25	15.15	16.36	16.43
Flow	1.05	0.92	1.05	1.05	0.85	0.74	0.83
Toll	1.34	1.08	0.82	1.24	1.04	1.01	0.90
Frequency	30.00	23.00	20.00	27.00	10.00	11.00	5.00

Table 5.2 The statistical mean of each of the financial variables used to classify bonds into one of seven different quality ratings. The last row in the table provides the size of the sample for each classification.

5.3.2 Network Results vs. Statistics

In both of the bond-rating applications, the authors compared the performance of the neural network to conventional, statistical methods to validate the network performance. Dutta and Shekhar reported that their three-layer BPN correctly classified bonds described in the training set 92.4% of the time, compared with a 66.7% accuracy obtained using a multiple-regression analysis. When presented with bond data from the 17 untrained exemplars, the neural network responded correctly on 82.4% of the inputs, while the multiple-regression analysis yielded only a 64.7% accuracy.

Surkan and Singleton reported a success rate of 90% using a four-layer BPN arranged with seven inputs, 10 units on the first hidden layer, five units on the second hidden layer, and two output units. When they reversed the arrangement of the two hidden layers, the network accuracy dropped to 83%. In contrast, a linear discriminant function that was estimated by using the seven financial features as explanatory variables produced only a 39% success rate.

Based on these observations, the researchers in both of these applications concluded that neural networks provide a powerful method for independently determining bond ratings. Given the ready availability of representative training data, these applications also provide us with an easily reproducible model illustrating the ability of the technology to address real-world financial applications.

5.4 PREDICTING COMMODITY FUTURES

As the name implies, commodities are raw materials, such as grains, meats, or metals, that are used to create finished products for sale in the retail marketplace. Buying and selling commodities is yet another way of investing money to (hopefully) realize financial gain. As in any other form of commerce, the objective is to buy while the price is low, and sell when the price is high, thereby realizing a profit. However, as we have seen in our previous examples, recognizing when a commodity price has reached its low (or high) point is a fairly complex task, and is often prone to error. We shall now review an application developed to assist commodity traders that use a neural network trained with raw market data to recognize the *buy* and *sell* points for certain commodities before they occur. As we shall see, successfully anticipating the market highs and lows can yield significant financial returns over a relatively short period of time.

5.4.1   Market Variables

In an application originally described by Joseph E. Collard [2], a standard BPN was trained on market data comprised of six key indicators[6] over a period of one year. The indicators used were the opening price (OPEN), the closing price (CLOSE), the lowest price for the commodity during a single business day (LOW), the highest price during the day (HIGH), the open interest (INTEREST) for the commodity, and the trade volume (VOLUME), or the number of futures actually exchanged during the day. Each of these indicators was obtained for a single, unnamed commodity for each business day during the year 1988. Because the commodities markets operate on a normal business week, 253 exemplars were obtained to train the network.

In his first experiments with a neural network, Collard reports that he augmented the training data by including 18 subjective variables, which he describes as assessments of the weather (which plays an important role in determining the future price of commodities that are influenced by prevailing weather conditions), and other "seasonal indicators." Additionally, because all of the training data used were historical, one other variable was included in each training pattern—a long/short indicator obtained by evaluating, in retrospect, whether the commodity was overbought or oversold. After training and testing his network, Collard decided to account for trend conditions in the training data by including his six market indicators from each of the two business days immediately prior to the day represented by the training pattern in the input pattern. Thus, in his final application, each input pattern to the neural network consisted of 37 variables—the six market indicators, 18 subjective indictors, and one long/short indicator for the current business day, and six market indicators from each of the previous two business days.

---

6. The use of the term *indicators* differs slightly from our previous usage of the word. Here, we use the term to refer to specific price values, as opposed to derived measurements of performance. We have altered our usage of the term only to remain consistent with the nomenclature used by the original author of the paper.

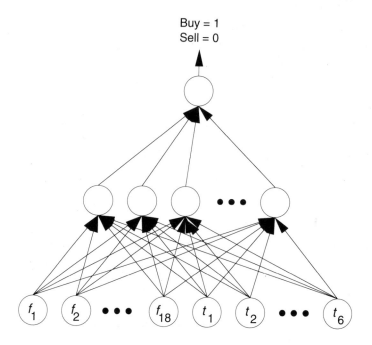

Figure 5.9 This figure illustrates the architecture of the BPN used to predict commodity futures. As described in the text, the input patterns are each scaled, analog indicators of market state, and the output generated by the network is interpreted as a *buy* or *sell* signal for the selected commodity. Once trained, the network was tested by presenting it with data from selected periods in 1989, a year after the data were used to train the network. The output produced by the network was then compared to the actual market performance during the same interval, to assess the accuracy of the system.

5.4.2   Market Data Representation

Unfortunately, in the original paper describing the commodity-prediction network application, Collard does not provide any real detail regarding either the data-representation scheme used to construct his 37 inputs, or the source of the subjective data. We can surmise from his description of the application, however, that each indicator was represented by a single node in the network input, and that the indicators were linearly scaled to values between zero and one prior to presentation to the network. Even if this is not the case, this data representation scheme will be sufficient for this application, because each of the inputs is essentially an analog measurement of a single parameter.

As shown in Figure 5.9, the output generated by the network was a single, binary signal that was interpreted as a *buy* or *sell* indicator for the commodity. Collard indicates that several variations on this network structure were evaluated, primarily with respect to the number of units on the hidden layer. As expected, the network that achieved the lowest overall training error (1%) also produced the largest expected profit when tested with new market data.

Exercise 5.3: In this discussion, we have assumed that the subjective variables (e.g., prevailing weather conditions) can be represented as an analog measurement. Using this technique, we might have several units dedicated to weather, one of which might be called "precipitation." We might then model the precipitation indicator such that drought conditions are represented by a value of zero and flooding conditions with a value of one. Describe the limitations of this approach. Suggest an alternative method for representing the subjective variables, and describe how your technique improves on the analog representation.   ■

5.4.3   Network Performance

Using historical data, it is a relatively straightforward process to evaluate how well the trained network generalizes the training data, and successfully predicts the future—we simply present the network with input taken from the market in a time period after the training data were obtained, and compare the market performance predicted by the network with the actual market activity. Collard reported evaluating his trained network against actual market conditions using input taken from the first 205 business days of 1989. As shown in Figure 5.10, the BPN successfully anticipated changes in the selected commodity market. In fact, according to Collard, the network did so well that, had it been used to make buy and sell decisions during that same period, an investor would have realized a $10,000 profit on an initial investment of $1,000 over nine months, or a 1,000% return on the investment in less than one year.

Again, it is unfortunate (for educational, as well as financial reasons) that the actual data used to train the network is not available for us to evaluate directly, due to the competitive nature of the application. However, it is not impractical to test the performance of such a network by creating a data base of financial indicators, and to construct and test a market-prediction network similar to the one we have just described. We encourage you to perform such tests on an application of your own design.

A note of caution, however, before you begin investing money in commodities futures (or in any other market, for that matter) based on the recommendation of a neural network. This network, like all of the other networks in the applications we have examined in this chapter, is only as good as the data used to train it. Neural networks, and in particular, the BPN, are very good at *interpolation* and finding relationships in complex data sets (*generalization*); however, no neural network yet defined can *extrapolate* information beyond the training domain. Therefore, you would be well advised to collect your training data carefully, invest your money cautiously, and make certain never to invest more than you can afford to lose.

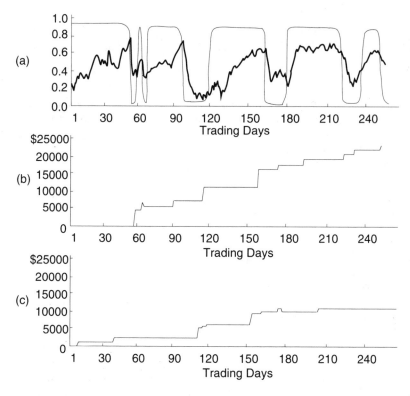

Figure 5.10 The graphs illustrating the performance of the commodity prediction network are shown. (a) This graph shows the relationship between the recommendations made by the neural network after training and the actual price curve for the selected commodity. (b) This graph illustrates the profit that the trained network would have realized if its recommendations had been followed, using the training data set as input. (c) This graph depicts the profit performance of the trained neural network when presented with out-year market data. Notice that in both profit graphs ((b) and (c)), the network never loses money. *Source:* A B–P ANN Commodity Trader [2]. *Copyright ©1991, Morgan Kaufmann Publishers. Used with permission.*

5.5 FINANCIAL-APPLICATIONS SUMMARY

In this chapter, we have investigated several different financial applications of neural networks. We have seen how the standard set of financial tools (e.g., mathematical performance indicators) have been used as input parameters to a neural network, and how the output from the network can be interpreted as an enhanced indicator of market performance. We have seen how others have successfully applied the technology to anticipate market performance, to independently evaluate the rating of bond offerings, and to forecast changes in commodity futures.

Undoubtedly, many readers will be disappointed that all of the applications described in this chapter were based on the BPN. The reasons for the pervasive use of this network in the financial industry are probably not related to a special characteristic of the BPN that makes it more appropriate for financial applications; rather, it is more likely due to the fact that the BPN is currently the most commonly used, and, therefore, the most easily accessible neural network, due to the commercial availability of BPN simulation software.

In the not-too-distant future, I expect that we will be reading about successful financial applications that employ other networks, such as the Hopfield memory or the Boltzmann network. In the meantime, we should continue exploring ways to use the information-fusing and pattern-recognition characteristics of neural networks to help anticipate market activity. Moreover, it is not unreasonable to expect smaller financial firms, and, yes, even private investors, to continue tinkering with the technology, uncovering new ways in which neural networks can be successfully applied to the problems of everyday business.

SUGGESTED READINGS

The financial world is an extremely competitive environment, with investors looking for any advantage that will enable them to increase earnings. With so many investors having access to large sums of money, it stands to reason that advanced technologies, such as neural networks, would be employed whenever possible to help investors evaluate opportunities. Indeed, the last five years have shown us that the financial-services industry has been the largest source of research funding in neural-network technology in the United States, apart from the federal government. Based on the number of recent papers published and articles written, it seems that neural networks have found a secure niche in this area.

Readers interested in investigating the financial and business applications of the technology further will be most interested in *Neural Networks in Finance and Investing* [10], a compendium of papers describing many different applications of neural networks in the financial industry.

The most current, and usually the most detailed, applications of advanced technologies in financial matters are described in the trade journal *Technical Analysis of* Stocks & Commodities. This monthly publication provides an in-depth analysis of the issues associated with trading stocks and bonds, and regularly presents articles written by financial people describing how neural networks, expert systems, fuzzy logic, and genetic algorithms have been successfully applied to financial issues.

Another good source of information describing financial applications of neural networks, as well as many other real applications of the technology, is the proceedings of the annual Neural Information Processing Systems (NIPS) conference. Unlike some of the other popular neural-network conferences, the NIPS conference emphasizes applications of the technology. While some of the papers published at this conference are highly technical, most address real-world applications that readers of this book would find most enlightening.

Finally, for those readers interested in understanding some of the problems associated with the traditional methods of understanding the dynamics of market prediction, the best reference we can provide is *Forecasting Economic Time Series* [5]. While highly mathematical, this book provides a solid foundation for understanding the subtleties of market prediction.

BIBLIOGRAPHY

1. Gerald Appel. *The Moving Average Convergence/Divergence Method*. SIGNALERT Corporation, 40 Middle Neck Road, Great Neck, NY, 1979.

2. Joseph E. Collard. A B-P ANN commodity trader. In Richard P. Lippman, John E. Moody, and David S. Touretsky, editors. *Advances in Neural Information Processing Systems 3*. Morgan Kaufmann Publishers, San Mateo, CA., pp. 551–556, 1991.

3. Soumitra Dutta and Shashi Shekhar. Bond rating: A non-conservative application of neural networks. In *Proceedings of the IEEE International Conference on Neural Networks*, San Diego, CA., pp. II(443–450), 1990.

4. Mark B. Fishman, Dean S. Barr, and Walter J. Loick. Using neural nets in market analysis. *Technical Analysis of* STOCKS & COMMODITIES, 9(April):18–21, 1991.

5. C. W. J. Granger and Paul Newbold. *Forecasting Economic Time Series*, second edition, Academic Press, Inc., 1986.

6. George C. Lane. Lane's stochastics. *Technical Analysis of* STOCKS & COMMODITIES, 4(May/June), 1984.

7. B. G. Malkiel. *A Random Walk Down Wall Street*, New York: Norton, 1985.

8. J. W. Peavy, III, and J. A. Scott. The AT&T divestiture: Effects of rating changes on bond returns. *Journal of Economics and Business*, 38:255–270, 1986.

9. Alvin J. Surkan and J. Clay Singleton. Neural networks for bond rating improved by multiple hidden layers. In *Proceedings of the IEEE International Conference on Neural Networks*, San Diego, CA., pp. II(163–168), 1990.

10. Robert R. Trippi and Efraim Turban, editors. *Neural Networks in Finance and Investing: Using Artificial Intelligence to Improve Real-World Performance*. Probos Publishing Company, Chicago, IL, 1993.

11. J. Welles Wilder. *New Concepts in Technical Trading Systems*, Trend Research, 1978.

Pattern Classification

*Experience is that marvelous thing that enables you to recognize a mistake
when you make it again.*

— *F. P. Jones*

In Chapter 4, we described applications of neural networks that perform a mapping from one multidimensional space to another. In that chapter, we called the mapping process an associative memory function; that is, the neural-network behavior was such that it could associate a specific output pattern with a particular input pattern, for all patterns in a training set. In this chapter, we shall investigate a special type of associative-memory called *pattern classifiers*. As we shall show, pattern classification differs from associative-memory applications primarily in our interpretation of the network behavior. In associative-memory applications, we interpreted the output state of the network as another multidimensional pattern. In pattern classification, we shall interpret the final state of the network in a manner that allows us to classify the input pattern as belonging to one of several categories. In essence, we shall allow the network to associate categories with the corresponding input patterns during training, then use the trained network to classify new input patterns.

Applications of this type are very appropriate for solution by neural network. As we have already seen, many neural networks adapt themselves to respond to certain combinations of input patterns to produce the desired output. We can conceptualize this behavior as **feature detection** within the network. In pattern-classification problems, we will use the response of the network to a new input pattern as an indication of the presence (or absence) of the feature combinations that the network learned to recognize.

As with associative memories, the input pattern space is usually very large, and there is no apparent mechanism for analytically determining the appropriate category for the input. This is not to say that there does not exist an analytical technique for classifying the input. Rather, the benefit of using a neural network for pattern classification is that the application can usually be created and tested without a significant investment in analysis of the problem domain.

In this chapter, we shall describe four pattern-classification applications of neural networks. As a part of that discussion, we shall emphasize the interpretation of the network response as it applies to the classification problem. We shall also show how the solution produced by the network provides a reasonable classification of the input.

6.1 NETTALK

The most famous example of a neural-network pattern classifier is the NETtalk system developed by Terry Sejnowski and Charles Rosenberg [11]. As shown in Figure 6.1, a BPN is trained to classify a character sequence as one of 26 possible phonemes[1] that are, in turn, used to generate synthetic speech. Obviously, the practical uses of such an application are somewhat limited. However, the NETtalk application is worthy of our study in that it demonstrates several subtle aspects of neural-network pattern classification that a novice should consider when developing new applications. The most important of these are

- The NETtalk system demonstrates the generalization characteristics of the BPN remarkably well. Specifically, once the network is trained to produce the correct phonemes in the 5,000-word training set, it performs quite reasonably when presented with words that it was not explicitly taught to recognize.

- The data-representation scheme employed by Sejnowski and Rosenberg is quite interesting. It allows a temporal pattern sequence to be represented spatially, while simultaneously providing the network with a means of easily extracting the important features of the input pattern.

We shall begin our investigation of the NETtalk application by first examining the data-representation scheme used by Sejnowski and Rosenberg. We shall then describe how the data were collected and used to train the network. Finally, we shall discuss some of the observations made by Sejnowski and Rosenberg with respect to the network's performance.

6.1.1 NETtalk Data Representation

It is acknowledged by many that English is among the most difficult languages to read, simply because there is so much diversity in the language. Anyone who has learned to read the English language knows that for every pronunciation rule, there is an exception. For example, consider the English pronunciation of the following words:

FIND   FIEND   FRIEND   FEINT

---

1. Phonemes are a standard representation of the sounds made during speech.

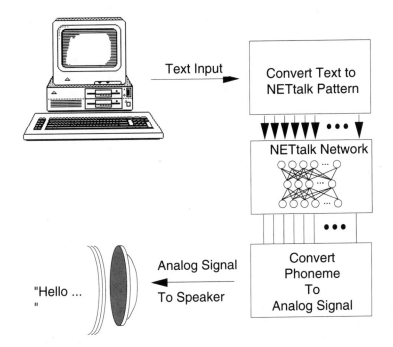

Figure 6.1 The system block diagram of the NETtalk application is shown. In this architecture, a front-end process converts the scanned text into the pattern representation for the BPN. The network, in turn, produces an output that is interpreted by a back-end process as the phoneme to be generated. The output of the system is therefore a synthetic pronunciation of written text.

While these four words are very similar in their form and structure, the pronunciation of each is vastly different. In each case, the pronunciation of the vowel(s) is dependent on a learned relationship between the vowel and its neighboring characters. Mastering these learned relationships is what makes English a difficult language to learn.

Obviously, the process of generating the correct phoneme sequence to synthetically pronounce these four words is much more complicated than simply mapping a phoneme to each character in a text string. Moreover, this example only touches on the complexities of the language. There are many other complex interrelationships between written text and spoken English, and any system constructed to perform this type of pattern classification must also be capable of capturing and encoding these interdependencies.

The NETtalk system constructed by Sejnowski and Rosenberg does just that—it captures the implicit relationship between text and sounds by using a BPN to learn these relationships through experience. However, to teach the network these relationships, Sejnowski and Rosenberg had to first develop a method

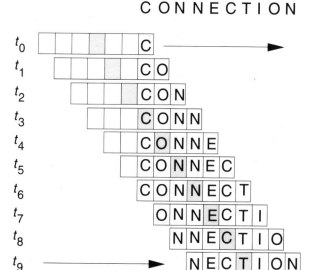

Figure 6.2 This diagram illustrates the sliding-window concept used to produce word patterns for the neural network. Initially, the window is padded with blanks to produce the silent phoneme. Characters from the word to be pronounced are then acquired by sliding the window over the word, one character at a time. This process continues until all of the characters in the word have passed by the focus position, with blank characters appended to the word to signal termination.

for converting the textual representation of the word into a pattern that the network could use, while preserving the positional influence of characters on each other in the textual representation.

To accomplish that goal, Sejnowski and Rosenberg adopted a *sliding-window* technique for representing words as spatial patterns. Essentially, the window is nothing more than a fixed-width representation of characters that form the complete input pattern for the network. The window "slides" across a word, from left to right, each time capturing (and simultaneously losing) one additional character. In order to allow both preceding and succeeding characters in each word to exert influence on the current character, the character in the middle of the window is interpreted as the focus character, with characters to the left and right of the center acting to influence the classification of the focus character. This process is illustrated in Figure 6.2.

In their article, Sejnowski and Rosenberg used a window of seven characters, with the third position designated as the focus character. This representation allows each character in a word to be influenced by its three preceding and three succeeding characters. According to the language studies performed prior to their experiments, three characters were adequate to exert the proper influence on the pronunciation of any one character in an English word.

One final transformation was necessary in order to cast the data in a form usable by the BPN. Because the network requires inputs that are numerical and continuous in the range of zero to one, it is necessary to convert each character into a pattern vector composed of numerical values. Sejnowski and Rosenberg chose to represent the input characters as pattern vectors composed of 29 binary elements—one for each of the 26 upper-case English alphabet characters, and one for each of the punctuation characters that influence pronunciation. Using this scheme, only one element in each character vector was "on" at any given time. This method of data representation also provided a side benefit for the neural network, in that it simplified the network's ability to distinguish different characters.

To see how this simplification occurs, consider the fact that, by using the data-representation scheme described above, the character pattern vectors are all orthonormal, which maximizes the distance between pattern vectors in Euclidian space. Because, as we described in Chapter 2, the BPN propagates signals by computing the inner product between input pattern vectors and corresponding connection-weight vectors, a natural extension of the processing performed by a neural-network processing element is the computation of the distance between these two vectors in Euclidian space. Thus, by ensuring pattern vectors are orthonormal, we enhance the ability of the neural network to distinguish important features from similar, but unimportant pattern components.

6.1.2   NETtalk Training

The training data for the NETtalk application consist of 5,000 common English words,[2] together with the corresponding phonetic sequence for each word. For each exemplar, a set of n input patterns was defined such that each input pattern contained one instance of the seven-character sliding window, with each character represented as a 29-element vector, where n represents the number of characters in the word. Using this scheme, the dimension of each input pattern was 203 elements (7 characters $\times$ 29 elements per character).

The output desired from the network for each input is an indication of the phoneme that should be applied to pronounce the current character. Sejnowski and Rosenberg chose to represent the output pattern as a 26-element vector, allocating one element for each phoneme classified by the network. The training data for the NETtalk application therefore contains 30,000 exemplars (assuming an average of six characters per word), with each exemplar composed of a 203-element input vector and a 26-element output vector. To perform the desired classification, Sejnowski and Rosenberg used a three-layer BPN, with 80 sigmoidal units on the hidden layer, completely interconnected with all elements on the input and output layers. This network is depicted schematically in Figure 6.3.

---

2. Many derivations of the NETtalk system use a much smaller training set, to reduce the training time.

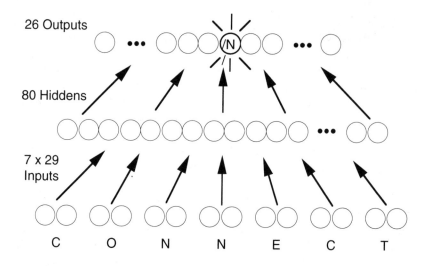

Figure 6.3 This diagram illustrates the architecture of the BPN used to perform the NETtalk application. The operation of the network is described in the text.

Exercise 6.1: Using the parameters given for the NETtalk application, estimate the number of computations needed to perform one training epoch in a software simulation of the network. Assume that the sigmoid activation function requires 30 calculations to perform, and that the momentum term (α) is not used. ∎

6.1.3 NETtalk Results

Sejnowski and Rosenberg constructed the training exemplars for the NETtalk application by first generating the input pattern vectors for the set of example words, then, for each of the input patterns, manually associating the proper phoneme with the focus character. The process was extremely tedious, and required several weeks to produce the final training set. Training the NETtalk BPN from the exemplar data was only marginally better, requiring 10 hours of computer time on a VAX 11/780 class computer system.

While the network was training, Sejnowski periodically stopped the process and allowed the network to simply produce whatever classifications it could, given a partial set of the training words as input. The classification produced by the network was then converted into the proper phoneme, and used to drive a speech synthesizer to produce an audible "snapshot" of the networks training state. The sounds produced by the network were recorded on audio tape. That recording captures the essence of the network's learning ability.

Before the training started, the network produced random sounds, freely mixing consonants and vowel sounds. After 100 epochs, the network had begun to separate words, recognizing the role of the blank character in text. After 500 epochs, the network was making clear distinctions between the consonant sounds and the vowel sounds. After 1,000 epochs, the words that the network were classi-fying had become distinguishable, although not phonetically correct. After 1,500 epochs, the network had clearly captured the phonetic rules, as the sounds produced by the BPN were nearly perfect, albeit somewhat mechanical. Training was stopped after epoch 1,500, and the network state was frozen.

At that point, the NETtalk system was asked to pronounce 2,000 words that it had not been explicitly trained to recognize. Using the relationships that the network had found during training, the NETtalk system had only minor problems "reading" these new words aloud. Virtually all of the words were recognizable to the researchers, and are also easily recognized by people not familiar with the system when they hear the audio tape recording. When the NETtalk system produces a "glitch," it is usually due to the existence of a phonetic relationship that the network was not exposed to while learning, and therefore represents a situation outside of the network's ability to classify.

Sejnowski and Rosenberg reported that NETtalk can read English text with an accuracy of "about 95%." This indicates that the NETtalk BPN did not simply memorize a set of words and their corresponding pronunciations—rather, it learned the general interrelations between English text and sounds, and can therefore apply those generalizations to read words it has never seen before.

At many of his public speaking engagements, Dr. Sejnowski replays portions of the NETtalk audio tape for his audience. Having heard that tape personally, I can attest to the fact that the NETtalk system has a very diverse vocabulary, and does remarkably well when presented with new words. In fact, listening to NETtalk learn to read is very much like listening to a child learning to read aloud. Words are often pronounced correctly, and, when errors occur, they are almost always due to very subtle structural differences between the misspoken word and other common words.

6.2   RADAR-SIGNATURE CLASSIFIER

Pulse Doppler radar technology has existed, in essentially its current form, since the 1940s. The primary application of pulse Doppler radar[3] is to detect an airborne target, and determine the *range* and *velocity* of the target relative to the radar station. Pulse Doppler radar operates on two very simple principles of physics: First, electromagnetic radiation (EMR) travels at a constant speed, and, second, EMR waves reflected from a moving body are *frequency shifted* in the direction of travel, much like sound waves are compressed in the direction of travel when emitted from a moving noise source. We illustrate these concepts in Figure 6.4.

Modern radar systems take advantage of these two principles to compute the range and velocity of any target that comes within the effective range of the radar transmitter. Usually, the radar system provides a digital readout of these

---

3. Traffic law enforcement notwithstanding.

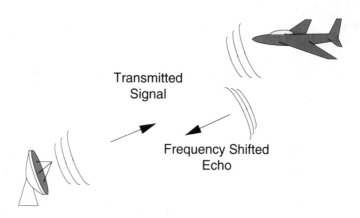

Transmitted
Signal

Frequency Shifted
Echo

Figure 6.4 This diagram illustrates the basic principles that govern the operation of pulse Doppler radar. A radar pulse, or *chirp*, is transmitted from the radar station. The EMR burst travels outward from the transmitter at the speed of light. When an EMR-reflective target is hit by the outgoing signal, some of the energy is reflected back to the radar receiver, which then determines the range and velocity of the target based on concepts described in the text.

parameters for each target acquired, leaving the chore of using the information to the radar operator. However, it has long been apparent that skilled radar operators are also able to ascertain the type of target acquired, even though the radar itself has no capability of making that same determination.[4] They make this determination based on the electronic *signature* of the radar return. Just as people have their own, personalized technique for signing their names, each radar target has its own, unique way of reflecting radar emissions. After observing several thousand returns, a radar technician can learn to recognize these signatures.

   As we indicated previously, radar-signature recognition is currently a strictly human phenomenon; there are no automatic means of identifying a target based on its radar-signature incorporated in radar systems. Let us now investigate how a neural network can be applied to the problem of automatic radar-signature recognition, an application that I helped develop while employed by Loral Space Information Systems. We shall begin with a brief discussion of the mathematics governing the operation of pulse Doppler radar, in order to describe the meaning of the electronic radar signature. We shall then show how different signatures were captured, and classified by a neural network.

---

4. Transponders can identify aircraft type, but we are concerned here with only radar systems.

6.2.1   Pulse Doppler Radar Theory

As indicated earlier in this section, pulse Doppler radar systems are designed to determine the distance, or range, and velocity of a target relative to a reference point (the radar station). Complicating matters is the fact that, quite often, the radar station is itself moving, as with on-board radar systems in airplanes, and must therefore correct any errors that may be induced by the movement of the platform.

On initial consideration of the problem of obtaining range and velocity of an EMR reflective target, you might think that the most straightforward method would be to use a fixed-frequency radar pulse, and then determine range as a function of the delay between transmission and echo reception, and velocity as a function of the phase shift in the return frequency. However, this simple technique is not practical, because it does not take into consideration the power loss of an EMR signal propagating through space.[5] If a target is much more than several hundred meters away, the returning echo will be lost in the EMR background noise.

The process of determining range and velocity in a reflected radar signal actually requires several steps, beginning with the transmission of the signal. Because we are interested in finding radar targets at very great distances, we must use a technique that will allow us to boost the signal-to-noise ratio (SNR) in the returning signal so that we can extract it from the background noise and analyze the echo. To help us boost the SNR in the echo, we begin by transmitting a *frequency-modulated* chirp, instead of a fixed-frequency pulse, so that we can correlate any returning signal with the original signal, and thus identify valid returns. Figure 6.5 illustrates the general form of the chirp signal.

Any signal detected by the receiver is processed by a series of filters, each designed to perform a special function for the radar system. For the sake of brevity, we shall ignore the initial stages of platform-motion compensation and stationary target removal. Instead, we shall focus on the process of extracting a valid Doppler return from the ambient EMR noise, because this is the process that produces the Doppler signature that we intend to classify.

A radar receiver is actually two separate receivers, one designed to detect the in-phase component of any EMR in the desired frequency range, the other to measure the quadrature, or phase-shift, component of the incoming signal. We shall refer to these signals as the real and imaginary components of a complex return signal. After compensating for platform motion and removing any stationary target information, both components of the incoming signal are fed to a matched filter to eliminate false returns and boost the SNR of a valid return. The matched filter is actually a three-step process, which we now describe and illustrate in Figure 6.6.

---

5. Recall from basic physics that power in a transmitted signal drops by the square of the distance traveled.

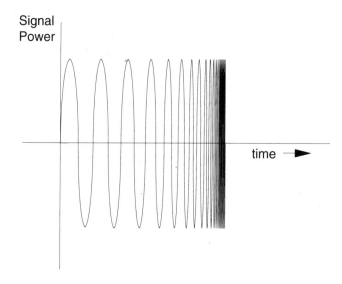

Figure 6.5 This figure illustrates the general form of a radar chirp. Notice that the frequency of the signal increases linearly with time. Since EMR waveforms of this type are non-existent in the natural world, we can detect a valid signal return by correlating the frequency of any return with the variable frequency of the original chirp, using the techniques described in the text.

1. The complex input signal from the receiver is sampled in discrete time, and converted from the time domain to the frequency domain using a fast Fourier transform (FFT). The size of the sample and the number of points used in the FFT are determined by the application, but we shall consider 512 samples and a 1,024 point FFT as nominal. To accommodate this processing, a single *pulse return interval* (PRI), which is the time period between transmitter chirps, is divided into separate sample periods, each comprised of 512 data points. Each of these samples is converted by the FFT, producing n, 1,024 complex vectors ($\mathbf{v}_i, i = 1, \ldots, n$), that collectively describe the PRI in the frequency domain.

2. A vector multiplication between each $\mathbf{v}_i$ and the complex conjugate, or *time-reversed* form of the initial chirp is performed. Because multiplication in the frequency domain is equivalent to convolution in the time domain, this operation has the effect of squelching any noncorrelated spectra, allowing only signals that are correctly correlated, and therefore valid echoes, to pass. The resulting vectors, $\mathbf{w}_i$, are a filtered representation of the return in the frequency domain.

3. The filtered return is converted back to the time domain by performing an inverse FFT (IFFT) on each $\mathbf{w}_i$. The resulting complex vectors, $\mathbf{x}_i$, represent

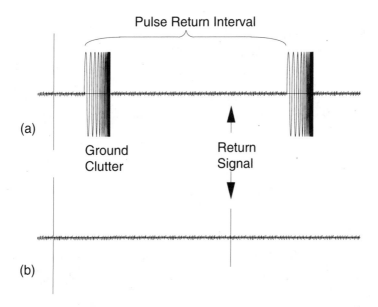

Figure 6.6 These graphs depict the waveforms during processing of a single PRI. The time scales are uniform throughout, and we only show the real, or in-phase component of the signal. (a) The spectra of the signal as measured at the radar receiver, prior to any processing. (b) After correlating, clutter is eliminated and the target becomes apparent.

the n, 512 sample points in the time domain, after filtering. The entire PRI is reconstructed by concatenating the n filtered vectors.[6] The resulting complex vector pinpoints the target return in the PRI.

As PRI data are processed, the radar system accumulates the results in a matrix form, where each row consists of one PRI of processed data and each column represents a discrete time interval, or *range bin*, within the PRI. After 32 successive returns are processed, the Doppler frequency information is extracted by filtering each return with a Blackman window, to minimize the effect of transient frequencies caused by performing an FFT on a finite series, transposing the matrix, and performing a 32-point FFT operation to extract the *Doppler profile* of each range bin.

The result is a complex, n-row, 32-column matrix, where each row indicates the magnitude of the Doppler shift occurring at the range represented by the row position. Small Doppler-shift magnitudes indicate no movement at that range. Large Doppler shifts indicate an EMR reflective target moving through the radar

---

6. This is actually a simplification of the actual process of recovering the signal. For more details, refer to the Suggested Readings section of this chapter.

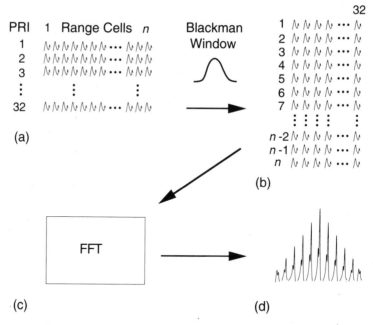

Figure 6.7 The process of converting 32 successive PRI returns into a Doppler signature is illustrated. (a) The PRI data are collected into a 32-row by n-column matrix, where each column represents a discrete time interval in the PRI, and each row contains the processed return data for the PRI. (b) The matrix is filtered and transposed to provide Blackman-weighted return data by column. (c) A 32-point FFT is applied to the Blackman-weighted matrix to obtain the Doppler profile of the return. (d) The Doppler matrix is concatenated by rows to form the Doppler signature of the return.

scan. If we concatenate the n rows of the Doppler matrix into a single vector, we produce the *Doppler signature* of the return. Figure 6.7 illustrates this process.

The Doppler signature of the return provides all of the information we need to determine range and velocity of a detected target. By considering the amplitude of the Doppler shift, and knowing that each bin represents a time slice of fixed duration and a known offset from the beginning of the PRI, we can determine the range of the target by simply interpolating between the two Doppler peaks. Similarly, target velocity can be determined by evaluating the difference in range between two successive returns.

6.2.2 Capturing the Radar Signature

All of the calculations described in the previous section are made automatically within any Doppler radar system. However, inspection of the Doppler signature reveals quite a bit more about the nature of the target. For instance, if the airframe of the target has no moving blades (indicative of a jet aircraft), the Doppler sig-

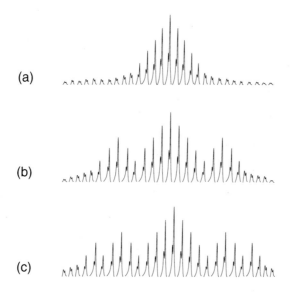

Figure 6.8   These diagrams illustrate Doppler signatures produced by different kinds of aircraft. (a) A jet (airframe only) produces a compact Doppler signature. (b) A two-bladed helicopter causes a spread in the signature, with side lobes forming on both sides of the peak, indicating rotation of the blades. (c) A four-bladed helicopter has a very wide signature, because blades rotate through the radar signal twice as often as with the two-bladed helicopter.

nature is fairly compact. If the target has blades rotating in the same plane as the radar signal (as with a helicopter), the signature will spread considerably. Other signatures will be obtained based on the type of aircraft, and any moving parts that may cause Doppler shift in the return. Figure 6.8 presents a representative sample of these different signatures.

Given that the radar system can produce these electronic signatures, we can use a neural network to address the pattern-classification problem. Specifically, we can train a network to mimic the pattern-recognition process performed by the radar technician and automate the classification of these different signatures as different types of aircraft. In order to do this, however, we must first decide on the type of network we shall require to perform the classification, then determine the best method for representing the electronic signatures and corresponding classifications for use by the neural network.

The most straightforward method for learning to classify these Doppler signatures is to create a network that learns to produce the correct output category for each signature. The BPN is the most logical choice for this type of application, because this network can generalize the characteristics of the input that lead to successful classification, and because it is designed to map input patterns to corresponding outputs. Furthermore, inspection of the radar-signature wave-

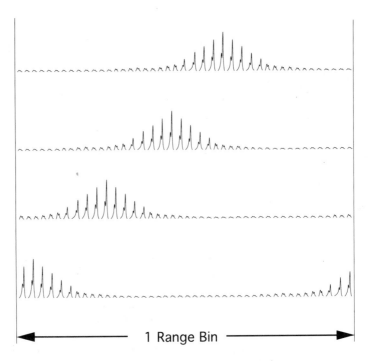

1 Range Bin

Figure 6.9   These graphs show how a Doppler signature shifts as a function of target range. Beginning at the top, the sequence shows a target approaching the radar station, with a corresponding left shift in the Doppler signature.

forms suggests an appropriate method for encoding the input patterns—we simply quantize each waveform, and scale the magnitude of each component of the pattern to a value in the appropriate range for the BPN. Similarly, the output of the network can be cast as m sigmoidal units, where each unit is considered to be an indicator of a specific aircraft type.

However, selecting the BPN will complicate the application somewhat, due to an easily overlooked detail in the input pattern representation scheme. From our discussion of how the radar signature is produced, consider that the signature will *shift* as the target moves through the range bins. As depicted in Figure 6.9, the Doppler signature moves horizontally in the pattern, as a function of the range of the target. If we simply train the BPN to recognize a single image of the Doppler signature, the network will not be able to correctly classify shifted signatures of the same target, due to the fact that the BPN is not a position-invariant pattern classifier.[7]

To compensate for the pattern shift, we must train the network using exemplars that account for the pattern shift. For example, the Doppler signature for

7. The behavior of the BPN was described in detail in Chapter 2.

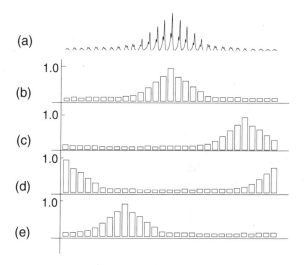

Figure 6.10   This diagram illustrates the exemplar encoding scheme used to capture the Doppler signature of various aircraft. (a) This diagram illustrates the general form of the radar return after extracting the signature. (b) The quantized form of the Doppler signature. (c) The quantized signature shifted right by ten range bins from the general form. (d) The quantized signature shifted by fifteen range bins. (e) The quantized signature shifted right by 26 range bins (or left by 6 range bins).

the airframe-only return, if quantized into 32 discrete samples, will become 32 training exemplars for the BPN—one for each possible shift of the input pattern. Similarly, the signature for the twin-bladed helicopter will become 32 different exemplars, each requiring a single output from the network unit that corresponds to the two-bladed helicopter classification. This exemplar encoding scheme is illustrated in Figure 6.10.

Exercise 6.2: As we shall describe, the BPN used in this application was able to correctly classify all of the signatures we asked it to learn. However, the same application developed using a feed-forward CPN failed miserably. Why? (Hint: Consider the input representation as a vector in 32 space.)   ■

6.2.3   Classifying Radar Returns

As a demonstration of the ability of a neural network to classify radar returns, we constructed a BPN in software on a multiprocessor neural-network accelerator board, and trained it using Doppler signatures of three different aircraft types: airframe only, a two-bladed helicopter with blades rotating at 300 RPM, and a four-bladed helicopter with blades rotating at 300 RPM. For each class of aircraft, a representative signature was computed using a radar signal-processing package developed for the application.

The network used to classify the Doppler signatures was a three-layer BPN, with 32 input units, eight units on a single, hidden layer, and three output units. The processing elements on the hidden and output layers were sigmoidal, and outputs were interpreted as a one-and-only-one indication of the class of the input signature. The use of sigmoidal activation functions at the output of the network had the effect of simplifying the classification process.

The exemplar data used to train the network consisted of 96 Doppler-signature aircraft-classification vector pairs. Using a learning rate (η) of 0.5 and a momentum term (α) of 0.6, the network converged to a solution after 1,700 training epochs, stabilizing with an absolute error magnitude less than 0.01. After training was completed, the configuration of the network (e.g., connection-weight values, number of units, and number of layers) was written to a file on the computer disk, to be used by an application that processed radar-return data in real time.

6.2.4 Radar Classification Results

In our test application, the radar signature of a target is extracted from synthetic radar data produced by a mathematical model of the target object. To ensure that we were evaluating the generalization capabilities of the BPN, the target model used in the test application was a different implementation of the target model used to generate the training data.

From the synthetic radar data, the Doppler signature of the object being modeled was extracted using conventional digital signal-processing techniques, then converted to a signature pattern for the network. The BPN was a software model of the network constructed from the information saved after training, and invoked by a simple function call from the top-level process. In this case, however, the network was used in the forward-propagation mode only, producing outputs that were interpreted as the class designation of the radar signature. Figure 6.11 illustrates a block diagram of the integrated-system architecture we used to evaluate the performance of the neural-network classifier.

The integrated system was constructed as a demonstration program to illustrate the power of neural-network pattern classifiers. The front-end process (the math model of the target) provided the radar data stream, which was filtered as described in this section. The output of the radar signal processor was the Doppler signature of the target, which was sent directly to the neural network for classification.

Prior to using the BPN to classify the Doppler signature, the processed returns were compared to the training signatures, to ensure that the target model was producing a reasonably accurate radar profile. Moreover, to test the tolerance of the classifier to "imperfect" signatures, the system allowed the user to interactively add noise to the radar data stream, prior to input to the filter processes. Our results indicate that, while the signatures produced by the math model, without noise, were similar to the training patterns, there was as much as a 15% difference between the signatures the network had learned to recognize and the signatures

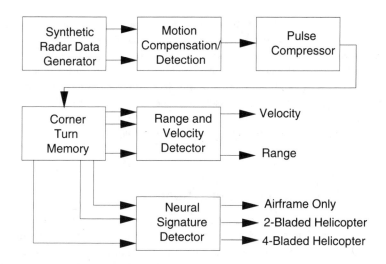

Figure 6.11   The block diagram of the integrated radar signal processor and neural-network classifier is shown. The operation of the system is described in the text.

produced by the model. When Doppler noise was added (such as might be produced by a tail rotor on a helicopter), the signature could vary from the training image by as much as 25%. Nevertheless, the BPN was able to correctly classify 100% of the radar signal returns produced by the model.

6.3   PROSTATE-CANCER DETECTION

Cancer of the prostate is a silent, but quite deadly disease that is rapidly becoming common in human males over the age of 45. In 1991, prostate cancer was estimated to be the most commonly diagnosed form of the disease, with the second-highest mortality rate of all forms of cancer in males [3]. If diagnosed in its early stages, however, prostate cancer is quite curable [9]. Unfortunately, early diagnosis is not always possible, because prostate cancer has no discernible symptoms in its early stages. Complicating matters is the fact that accurate diagnosis[8] usually requires an invasive procedure, meaning that the disease cannot be easily detected during routine health examinations.

Fortunately, public awareness concerning the nature of prostate cancer, and the danger inherent in delaying the diagnosis, has caused many individuals to have themselves proactively checked for prostate cancer. Also, recent advances in diagnostic technology have greatly simplified the process of detecting prostate cancer during its early stages.

---

8. At least in its early stages.

In this section, we shall examine one such diagnostic technology, made possible through the use of *ultrasound* inspection of the gland. In this application, developed by one of my graduate students, Mssr. Jean-Baptiste Enombo [5], the ultrasound image of the prostate is analyzed, texture features are extracted from the image, and the feature combinations are classified by a neural-network trained to recognize carcinoma in the ultrasound image. While this research is still very preliminary, the results indicate that neural-network technology might offer a very precise method for identifying prostate cancer using a safe, noninvasive detection procedure.

6.3.1 Ultrasound Data Collection

Medical research has shown that ultrasound examination of the prostate may provide a relatively safe method for identifying patients with active carcinoma. As with other ultrasound techniques, the patient is examined by passing an ultrasound transducer (in this case, a wand designed to be inserted into the rectum) along the area to be examined. An extremely high-frequency sound is emanated from the transducer into the body cavity, where the sound is absorbed (hyperechoic) or reflected (echoic) back to the transducer as a function of the viscosity of the tissue and the frequency of the transmitted ultrasound.

The transducer detects the returning echo pattern, and, after further processing, the pattern is electronically converted into a visual display of the surrounding tissue. To aid in the interpretation of the display, different echo levels are displayed using a graduated gray scale, with lighter pixels indicating echoic tissue, and darker pixels indicating hyperechoic tissue. Figure 6.12 illustrates a typical prostate ultrasound image.

Prostate cancer is currently identified by visual interpretation of the ultrasound image. Studies [4, 10] have shown that cancerous lesions tend to be more hyperechoic than normal glandular tissue. Unfortunately, hyperechoic tissue is not, by itself, a precise indication of cancer. Other studies have shown that while 96% of all prostate cancer lesions are hyperechoic, only 40% to 50% of hyperechoic regions are cancerous [8, 1]. Examples of normal tissue structure that exhibit hyperechoic echo patterns include muscle surrounding the prostatic urethra, the ejaculatory ducts, atrophic glands, and benign hypertrophy [7].

There are also biological limitations in diagnosing cancerous tissue from ultrasound images, due primarily to noise in the resulting image and the limited ability of the human visual system to distinguish subtle variations in gray levels. As an illustration of these limitations, consider the image in Figure 6.13, which is an ultrasound image of the prostate shown without clarification.[9] On initial inspection, it is difficult to discern the boundary of the prostate from the surrounding tissue, let alone identify possible cancerous tissue. Even when the

---

9. Figure 6.13 is, in fact, identical to the image shown in Figure 6.12, with only the clarification details removed.

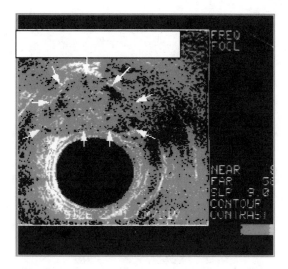

Figure 6.12   This figure illustrates a typical ultrasound image of the prostate gland. For clarity, we have indicated the perimeter of the gland in the image. The dark circle in the center of the image is the rectum, and the surrounding tissue is illustrated in levels of gray that indicate variations in tissue density. Notice the level of noise in the image. *Source:* Feature analysis and neural network classificationof prostate ultrasound images [5]. *Copyright ©1994, by Jean-Baptiste Enombo. Used with permission.*

prostate has been isolated visually, separating hyperechoic regions from the noise is a challenging task.

6.3.2   Ultrasound Texture Analysis

In order to assist in the interpretation of ultrasound image analysis, the image data can be enhanced through the use of spectral, textural, and contextual image-processing techniques. These techniques are employed to filter the noisy data into representations that more closely resemble the type of information the human visual system is designed to process. In his investigation, Mssr. Enombo used a textural analysis of the prostate ultrasound to extract information regarding the structure of the gland in terms of its texture. Specifically, 13 textural features were extracted for each resolvable point in the ultrasound image, and these features were then used to construct the training exemplars for the classification network.

The textural features used by Mssr. Enombo, which were originally derived by Robert Haralick et al. [6], assume that the image to be analyzed is represented as a spatial-dependence matrix, $\mathbf{P}$, where each point P_{ij} is a normalized gray tone with N_g discrete gradations. To simplify the notation in the textural analysis, we adopt the following four identity relations:

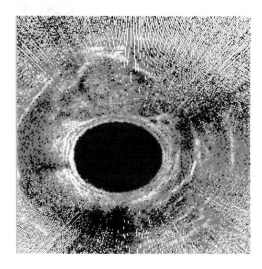

Figure 6.13 This figure illustrates a typical ultrasound image of the prostate and surrounding tissue as a doctor or clinician might see the image during an examination. The regularly occurring white dots are data dropouts, or *holidays*, and occur because of the implementation of the transducer. Given this noisy image, how quickly can you find the prostate, and identify the hyper-echoic, or potentially cancerous regions? *Source:* Feature analysis and neural network classificationof prostate ultrasound images [5]. *Copyright ©1994, by Jean-Baptiste Enombo. Used with permission.*

$$P_x(i) = \sum_{j=1}^{N_g} P_{ij} \qquad (6.1)$$

$$P_y(j) = \sum_{i=1}^{N_g} P_{ij} \qquad (6.2)$$

$$P_{x+y}(k) = \sum_{i=1}^{N_g} \sum_{j=1}^{N_g} P_{ij} \qquad (6.3)$$

$$P_{x-y}(k) = \sum_{i=1}^{N_g} \sum_{j=1}^{N_g} P_{ij} \qquad (6.4)$$

where $k = i + j$ in Eq. (6.3) and $k = |i - j|$ in Eq. (6.4).

Prior to the experiment, four patients diagnosed with clinically organ-confined prostate cancer were examined using the ultrasound equipment, and the images were recorded on broadcast-quality videotapes. The patients then underwent radical prostatectomy procedures, and the removed organs were subjected to 4-mm whole-mount serial cross-sectioning, as shown in Figure 6.14. Pathol-

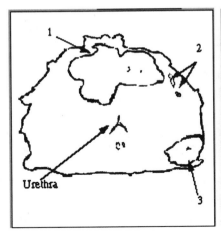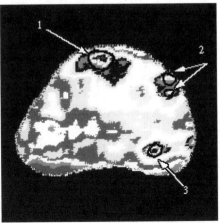

Figure 6.14   This diagram illustrates the whole-mount cross-section pathology of the prostate specimens. Initially, 1.0 to 1.5 cm of tissue at the apex and anterior portions of the organ are excised. The remainder of the organ is sliced horizontally at 4 mm intervals, and a thin slice from each cross section is mounted on a slide. These specimens are then subjected to a microscopic examination by a pathologist to determine exact regions of the gland containing the prostatic andenocarcinoma. *Source:* Feature analysis and neural network classificationof prostate ultrasound images [5]. *Copyright ©1994, by Jean-Baptiste Enombo. Used with permission.*

ogy reports were obtained for each specimen, so that the cancerous tissue could be located as precisely as possible.

While the pathology investigation was being conducted, the video images from the ultrasound examinations were digitized in color at the NASA Johnson Space Center (JSC). The three bands of color were converted to hue, saturation, and intensity images, and the intensity band was further transformed into a 512×512 pixel matrix in 64 gray shades. Thirteen textural features were then extracted for every 9×9 pixel window in the vertical direction, using the texture analysis algorithms developed by Haralick et al. For the reader's convenience, we recreate these algorithms as follows:

- The angular second moment, given by

$$f_1 = \sum_i \sum_j P_{ij}^2 \qquad (6.5)$$

- Contrast between points, given by

$$f_2 = \sum_{n=0}^{N_g-1} n^2 \sum_{i=1}^{N_g} \sum_{j=1}^{N_g} P_{ij} \tag{6.6}$$

- The correlation between points, given by

$$f_3 = \frac{\sum_i \sum_j ij \, P_{ij} - \mu_x \mu_y}{\sigma_x \sigma_y} \tag{6.7}$$

where μ_x, μ_y, σ_x, and σ_y are the mean and standard deviations of $P_x(i)$ and $P_y(j)$.

- The variance between points, given as

$$f_4 = \sum_i \sum_j (i - \mu)^2 P_{ij} \tag{6.8}$$

- The inverse difference moment, given by

$$f_5 = \sum_i \sum_j \frac{1}{1 + (i - j)^2} P_{ij} \tag{6.9}$$

- The sum average of each point, given by

$$f_6 = \sum_{i=2}^{2N_g} i \, P_{x+y}(i) \tag{6.10}$$

- The sum variance of each point, given as

$$f_7 = \sum_{i=2}^{2N_g} (i - f_8)^2 P_{x+y}(i) \tag{6.11}$$

- The sum entropy of each point, given by

$$f_8 = -\sum_{i=2} 2N_g P_{x+y}(i) \log(P_{x+y}(i)) \tag{6.12}$$

- The entropy, given by

$$f_9 = -\sum_i \sum_j P_{ij} \log(P_{ij}) \tag{6.13}$$

- The difference variance, given by

$$f_{10} = \sum_i (i - \mu)^2 P_{x-y}(i) \tag{6.14}$$

- The difference entropy, given as

$$f_{11} = -\sum_{i=0}^{N_g-1} P_{x-y}(i) \log(P_{x-y}(i)) \tag{6.15}$$

- The information measures of correlation, given by

$$f_{12} = \frac{HXY - HXY_1}{\max(HX, HY)} \tag{6.16}$$

$$f_{13} = \sqrt{1 - e^{-2HXY_2 - HXY}} \tag{6.17}$$

where

$$HXY = -\sum_i \sum_j P_{ij} \log(P_{ij})$$

$$HXY_1 = -\sum_i \sum_j P_{ij} \log(P_x(i) P_y(j))$$

$$HXY_2 = -\sum_i \sum_j P_x(i) P_y(j) \log(P_x(i) P_y(j))$$

and HX and HY are entropies of $P_x(i)$ and $P_y(j)$, respectively.

In Figure 6.15, we illustrate several textural images of the prostate ultra-sound, so that the reader may compare the information derived from the analysis of the images with the original ultrasound image.

6.3.3   Cancer-Classification Exemplars

Mssr. Enombo computed the 13 texture features for each pixel in the digitized ultrasound image of the prostate. The values obtained for each pixel were then individually normalized, and concatenated into a 13-component pattern vector that became the input exemplar for a BPN classifier. The desired output for each pixel was the cancer/noncancer indication obtained by correlating the pathology report for the specimen with the ultrasound image pixel position.

There were several difficulties that had to be overcome in order to construct these training patterns. First, the pathology report could not be directly correlated to the ultrasound image data for several reasons, including the following:

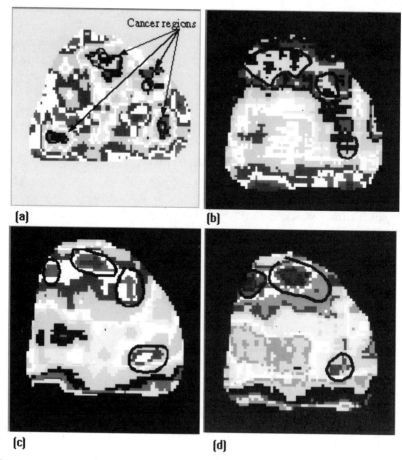

Figure 6.15   These figures illustrate the information derived from a textural analysis of the prostate ultrasound data. (a) The angular second moment of the image. (b) The contrast in the image. (c) The variance of the image. (d) The inverse difference moment. *Source:* Feature analysis and neural network classificationof prostate ultrasound images [5]. *Copyright ©1994, by Jean-Baptiste Enombo. Used with permission.*

- The ultrasound-image data had been obtained from views of the prostate within the body, taken at 2-mm vertical increments. The pathology, however, had used 4-mm vertical increments in the dissection of the specimen. Because there was no guarantee that the pathologist had dissected the gland at the same vertical points as the ultrasound images, there was a ±2-mm margin of error in the data.

- When the specimen was dissected and mounted for examination, tissue dispersal occurred horizontally, altering the view of the cross section. To correct for this "squashing" effect, the ultrasound image was initially *warped*, or stretched, to match the cross-section area of the pathology. However, digitally warping the image tended to distort the texture features of the images, so the pathology report was warped to match the ultrasound image. Using this technique, the pixels indicating cancerous cells in the ultrasound were classified from the warped pathology data.

Furthermore, the ultrasound image of the prostate had data dropouts, or *holidays*, where the ultrasound echo was corrupted. These holidays occur at precisely the same position in any display, and increase in frequency in images further from the transducer. To minimize the effect of the holidays in the texture analysis, only the ultrasound data from the peripheral region, closest to the probe, was considered. This was not judged to be a severe constraint on the application, because most cancers begin in the peripheral zone, and spread to other locations in the prostate.

Nevertheless, Mssr. Enombo developed more than 63,000 exemplars, using visual inspection of the texture displays to locate the lesions. Once the cancerous regions had been manually located, a computer program was used to construct the exemplar data using the normalized texture features that had already been extracted for the cross section. The corresponding cancer/noncancer designation for that point was determined based on whether the pixel in question fell within the region that had been designated as cancerous. In Figure 6.16, we illustrate the form of the exemplar data, and how it was constructed for the application.

6.3.4   Cancer-Detection Results

Initially, a BPN containing 13 input units, eight units on a single hidden layer, and two output units was trained to recognize textures that indicated a high likelihood of cancer. In this experiment, all 13 of the texture features were used as input, and the output layer used sigmoidal activation functions to produce binary cancer/noncancer indications. After training was completed, tests were run to evaluate the network's ability to generalize. Initially, the network was asked to classify the textural features of a different cross section within the same specimen. Then, the network was used to classify the ultrasound images from the three patients that the network had not been trained to recognize. Several interesting results were determined during this phase of the experiment.

First, using different ultrasound layers from the patient on which the network was trained, the BPN successfully recognized noncancerous regions in the test images 98.9% of the time. The network produced false-positive indications in only 1.08% of the tests. Similarly, the network correctly classified texture features as cancerous in 88.7% of the trials, and produced false-negative indications in the other 11.3% of the tests. When the tests were conducted on patients other than the one on whom the network had been trained, the results fell somewhat. While noncancerous regions were correctly recognized in 98% of the tests, cancerous regions were correctly identified in only 60% of the trials.

A more interesting result was obtained after examining the state of the trained network, however. By looking at the feature combinations that the hidden

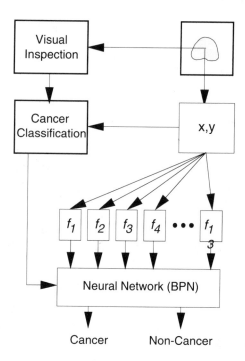

Figure 6.16 This diagram illustrates the process of developing exemplar patterns for the prostate-cancer detection network. The texture features are extracted for each pixel in the peripheral range of the image, normalized, and then associated with a cancer/noncancer designator assigned by a program that determines whether the pixel falls within a region designated as cancerous. *Source:* Feature analysis and neural network classificationof prostate ultrasound images [5]. *Copyright ©1994, by Jean-Baptiste Enombo. Used with permission.*

layer of the network responded to in order to produce the correct output indications, it was found that only five of the 13 texture features actively contributed to a successful diagnosis of cancer. Based on this result, another network was constructed and trained, this time having only the five input elements that had previously been identified as being instrumental in successful recognition. After training had been completed, the tests were performed as before. This time, however, the BPN improved its classification accuracy noticeably. Using different ultrasound layers from the training specimen, the network accurately identified cancer 94.8% of the time, and with data taken from the other patients, the network accuracy improved to 75%. These results are summarized in Table 6.1.

Overall, the neural network did an excellent job of classifying prostate cancer from ultrasound-image textures. The one set of images that were the most difficult to classify (Patient D) are explainable in that the image data for that patient were extremely noisy. Statistically, if we combine the performance of each network across all four test suites, we find that, the neural-network classifier ex-

Test	Network	Non-Cancer	Cancer	False-Positive	False-Negative
Patient A	13–8–2	98.92	88.71	1.08	11.29
Patient A	5–7–2	98.87	94.80	1.08	5.20
Patient B	13–8–2	99.72	58.78	0.28	41.22
Patient B	5–7–2	99.78	71.92	0.28	28.08
Patient C	13–8–2	99.20	61.33	0.80	38.67
Patient C	5–7–2	99.18	77.27	0.82	22.73
Patient D	13–8–2	99.97	8.54	0.03	91.46
Patient D	5–7–2	99.97	51.34	0.03	48.66

Table 6.1 This table presents the statistical results of the BPN cancer classifier network. Numerical entries in the table represent the percentage score of the network in each category. False-positives are those instances where the network classified the pixel texture as cancerous when the pathology indicated it was not. Likewise, false-negatives are those instances where the network classified the texture pattern as noncancerous, which again contradicts the pathology.

hibited a 98.3% accuracy rate in classifying pixel data. However, it must be stated that these results are very preliminary, and that much work remains before neural networks can be used to classify ultrasound images without additional interpretation by the physician.

6.4   PATTERN-CLASSIFICATION SUMMARY

In this chapter, we have examined applications of neural networks where the network was used to classify an input pattern into one of several categories. In one application, the categories were defined dynamically, while in others, the categories were determined before the network was constructed. We have examined a fairly diverse set of applications in this chapter, in order to convey to the reader the idea that the power of the technology is not solely in the processing of information, but rather in the *representation* of that information. As we have seen, pattern-classification networks are fundamentally identical to associative-memory (or other *mapping*) networks. We can surmise, then, that the pattern-matching ability of the neural network can be a powerful tool when used to extract meaningful relationships between (apparently) unrelated data elements, to assist in the classification of those patterns.

SUGGESTED READINGS

There are many excellent texts describing the theoretical foundations of the basic technologies addressed in this chapter. Readers interested in learning more about radar from a rigorous mathematical perspective are referred to M. Skolnik's classic work *Introduction to Radar Systems* [12]. For readers interested in a more applications-oriented discussion of radar and its related technologies, Raymond Berkowitz's *Modern Radar: Analysis, Evaluation, and System Design* [2] provides a good, broad-based discussion of radar theory and practical applications of the technology.

With regard to medical and diagnostic applications, there has been a plethora of excellent papers published describing how neural networks have been successfully applied to recognizing and identifying medical problems. Many of these papers have been published in the proceedings of the Neural Information Processing Systems (NIPS) conferences, held annually and sponsored by the International Neural Network Society.

Finally, NASA sponsors more than a dozen excellent conferences on advanced automation technologies, with an emphasis on space-related applications, and publishes proceedings from most of these meetings. Johnson Space Center (JSC) and the Jet Propulsion Laboratory (JPL) are the two NASA facilities most actively involved in advanced automation research. Specifically, the proceedings of the Space Operations Automation Research (SOAR) conference, held annually and sponsored by JSC provide a good overview of the research being conducted in neural network applications with respect to aerospace and control systems.

BIBLIOGRAPHY

1. R. J. Babaian, H. Miyashita, R. B. Evans, A. C. von Eshenbach, and E. I. Ramirez. Early detection program for prostate cancer: Results and identification of high-risk patient population. *Urology,* 37(3):193–197, 1991.

2. Raymond S. Berkowitz, editor. *Modern Radar: Analysis, Evaluation, and System Design.* John Wiley & Sons, New York, 1965.

3. C. C. Boring, T. S. Squires, and T. Tong. Cancer statistics. *CA—A Cancer Journal for Clinicians,* 41(1), 19, 1991.

4. W. F. Dåhnert, U. M. Hamper, and J. C. Eggleston. Prostatic evaluation by transrectal sonography and prostate specific antigen in the search for prostate cancer. *Journal of Urology,* 139:758–761, 1986.

5. Jean-Baptiste Enombo. *Feature Analysis and Neural Network Classification of Prostate Ultrasound Images,* Master's Thesis, The University of Houston–Clear Lake, Houston, TX, 1994.

6. R. M. Haralick, K. Shanmugam, and I. Dinstein. Textural features for image classification. *IEEE Transactions on Systems, Man, and Cybernetics,* Vol. SMC–3(6), pp. 269–285, 1973.

7. A. Glen Houston, S. B. Premkumar, David E. Pitts, and R. J. Babaian. Statistical interpretation of texture for medical applications, *Biomedical Image Processing and Three-Dimensional Microscopy,* 1660, pp. 576–582, 1992.

8. R. P. Huben. The USA experience: Diagnosis and follow-up of prostate malignancy by transrectal ultrasound. *Progress in Clinical and Biological Research,* 237:153–159, 1987.

9. F. Lee. Transrectal ultrasound in the diagnosis, staging, guided needle biopsy, and screening for prostate cancer. *Progress in Clinical and Biological Research,* 237:73–109, 1987.

10. F. Lee, P. J. Littrup, and S. T. Torp-Pederson. Prostate cancer: Comparison of transrectal ultrasound and digital rectal examination for screening. *Radiology,* 178:389–394, 1988.

11. Terrence J. Sejnowski and Charles R. Rosenberg. Parallel networks that learn to pronounce English text. *Complex Systems,* 1:145–168, 1987.

12. M. I. Skolnik. *Introduction to Radar Systems,* McGraw-Hill, New York, 1962.

C H A P T E R

Image Processing

Where is the screen upon which the eyes display the scenes of life?

— Source unknown

Image processing, as we shall use the term in this chapter, is any process that extracts meaningful information from image data. Using this definition, we could say that we have seen several examples of neural networks performing image-processing application in previous chapters. For instance, consider the prostate-cancer classification system, discussed in Chapter 6. The input to the classifier was, in a sense, raw image data, and the output produced by the classifier was information extracted from the image-texture analysis.

In this chapter, however, we shall concern ourselves with applications that extract information in order to determine the *scene content* of an image, using the entire picture matrix as input. To put this idea in perspective, consider how a human perceives television. The screen image is really nothing more than a collection of dots, each a different color, intensity, and brightness. Individually, those dots are meaningless. Collectively, however, the arrangement of dots on the screen provides enough information for the human viewer to recognize the physical objects contained in the image data. The only problem is that we do not completely understand how the brain is able to convert the image from a set of discrete picture elements to an internal representation of an object that makes sense in the context of the real world.

We do know, however, that people see images on a television screen because when the visual imagery data is processed by the brain, the visual cortex[1] is somehow able to extract information about the scene content, and then relate the information to other, familiar objects that we have already internalized. This process is commonly referred to as *recognition,* and has historically been one of the most complicated aspects of image processing.

---

1. The visual cortex is the region in the brain where sight is implemented.

In this chapter, we shall explore the application of neural networks in image-recognition tasks. We shall conduct this investigation in a manner that is slightly different from the survey approach we have taken in previous chapters. Specifically, we shall begin our discussion with an overview of a very special neural-network paradigm that has been developed specifically to perform image-recognition processes. We do so to illustrate how special-purpose networks can be constructed to address niche-application areas. After completing this overview, we shall begin our discussion of image-processing applications of neural networks.

7.1   IMAGE-PROCESSING NETWORKS

In this section, we shall briefly describe the operation of the **neocognitron** [6], the model of **selective attention,** and the **internal-representation** [11] network paradigms. We have deferred our discussion of these networks until now, because, unlike the more general network models described in Chapter 2, these networks do not learn to perform an application through repeated exposure to training exemplars. Rather, the networks are *constructed* specifically for an application. Moreover, connection weights are determined through a special form of unsupervised learning, and then *shared* by many processing elements.

7.1.1   The Neocognitron

As it was originally defined by Kunihiko Fukuschima in "A Neural Network for Visual Pattern Recognition," [5] the neocognitron was designed to perform a single function: position independent, optical character recognition. The power of the network comes from its architecture, which, as we indicated earlier, is constructed specifically for the application. This is not to say that the network is only useful in this one application—actually, it could have many. However, modifying the neocognitron to perform other applications usually involves modifying the interconnections between processing elements, not in the sense that connection weights are modified to learn new information, but in the physical sense, where connections between units are implemented selectively. As we shall show in later sections, however, there are exceptions to this rule. In fact, since its development in 1983, the neocognitron has been improved in many ways to perform a variety of image-processing functions, and, hence, is worthy of our study.

As shown in Figure 7.1, the neocognitron is a hierarchical structure of processing layers, with internal layers organized as pairs of sublayers. Each sublayer is composed of a series of two-dimensional (2D) processing planes, with each plane containing an array of network processing elements. The behavior of each processing element is defined in essentially the same manner as the processing elements that we discussed in Chapter 1. However, we shall not concern ourselves with the low-level operation of the units in this network, as we are primarily interested in the conceptual processing that occurs at the level of the plane.

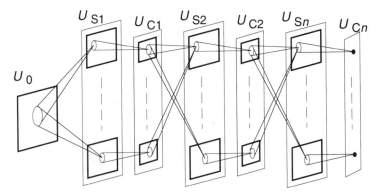

Figure 7.1   This diagram illustrates the architecture of the neocognitron as described by its inventors. The input layer, designated here as U_0, is arranged in a 2D matrix and serves to hold the image data for the rest of the network. Each internal layer is organized as a collection of *planes*, or 2D matrices, that successively integrate abstract information from the input layers that feed it. The output consists of a single layer of processing elements that, in the character-recognition application, classify the input image as one of ten digits.

Fukushima and his colleagues developed this structure, in part to mimic the observed behavior of the human visual cortex, but also to illustrate the ability of a neural network to extract meaningful information from images. Although not biologically accurate, the structure of the neocognitron lends itself to extracting information contained in images through a process of successive integration of features.

For the character-recognition application, the neocognitron is organized into nine layers, alternating **simple cell**, or S-cell, layers with **complex cell**, or C-cell layers. The S-cell layers are defined such that each S-cell is essentially a feature detector, responding only to the presence of a specific feature[2] in the input. Different S-cells in the same layer are sensitive to the same feature, at different locations in the input space, with locations being determined by the interconnection between the input and S-cell layer.

It is important to recognize that the neocognitron is not a fully connected network, in the same sense that the BPN is fully connected between layers. Rather, connections in the neocognitron are established selectively to define the **receptive field**, or the region in the input to which the S-cell is responsive, for the plane. This selective connectivity is the mechanism that enables the neocognitron to respond to its predefined features, regardless of position.

Associated with each S-cell layer is a corresponding C-cell layer, although the number of planes in the C-cell layer does not have to match the number of planes on the corresponding S-cell layer. The C-cell planes integrate the response

---

2. For the character-recognition task, input features were defined as line segments at different orientations on the retina.

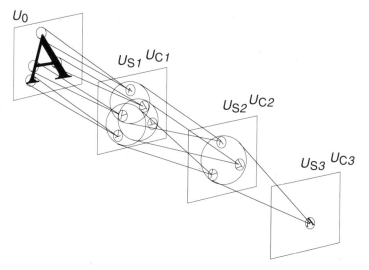

Figure 7.2   This diagram illustrates the process of character recognition within the neocognitron network. For clarity, we have omitted many of the planes on each layer, and collapsed the network somewhat. The operation of the network is described in the text. *Source:* Neocognitron: A neural network model for a mechanismof visual pattern recognition [6]. *Used with permission. Copyright ©1983 IEEE.*

of the S-cell layers that feed them, responding if at least one of the S-cell input planes has activated.

From an information-processing perspective, this structure allows the neocognitron to recognize and respond to shapes in the input image that represent abstract concepts at successively higher levels. Interestingly, this process of successive abstraction led one researcher to compare the operation of the neocognitron with biological models that advocate the existence of *grandmother cells*[3] in the brain.

In Figure 7.2, we illustrate the ideas underlying the operation of the neocognitron. Essentially, the input layer serves as a 2D *retina*, holding the image data for propagation through the network. Each subsequent S-cell–C-cell layer combination acts to detect and integrate the feature combinations from the receptive field on the previous layer, until finally the network responds by classifying the image as a specific character. At that point, we can say that the neocognitron has recognized the input-character image.

We shall forego a detailed discussion of the internal operation of the neocognitron, because, as we mentioned earlier, the implementation of the network is specific to the character-recognition application. For our purposes, it is sufficient

---

3. The term *grandmother cell* is an allusion to a single neuron that will only activate when you see a picture of your grandmother.

to convey an appreciation of how the network operates, not the specifics of its implementation.

7.1.2 The Selective-Attention Model

The model of selective attention [4] is actually a network that is composed of two identical neocognitrons, arranged so that the output of the first network feeds the input of the second. Do not be misled, however. We have not reversed the position of the second network. Rather, we allow information to propagate from the higher layers down to the layer that was considered to be the input in the original network. Bear in mind that we do not alter the connectivity of the original network at all. The only modification we must make to the second neocognitron is in the implementation of the processing that occurs in the processing element— we must invert the behavior of the unit so that the information being sent down from the higher layers is decomposed into its component parts before being sent to the subsequent layer. Thus, when information is propagated from the top of the network, the C-cell layers *specify* the abstract concept from the higher layers, while the S-cells locate the position of the specific object in the subsequent layer.

This behavior is illustrated in Figure 7.3. As you can see, the *bottom-up* neocognitron extracts the scene content from the input image data to produce a "recognized" representation of the object in the image, while the *top-down* network acts to reconstruct the memory of the prototype, or *ideal*, image of the object. This scheme of producing a "memorized" version of the object is mindful of the operation of the ART networks, although the ART models use the recalled pattern to reinforce the memory.

One significant advantage of the selective-attention model is that it locates the position of the recognized object in the input image. This behavior can be conceptualized as focused attention, because the top-down network produces an output that appears to focus on the image of the recognized object in the scene. It is this characteristic of the network that inspired Fukushima to name the network as he did.

7.1.3 Internal-Representation Networks

In a paper published in 1989, Takashi Omori and Taku Nagase [11] described a novel enhancement to the model of selective attention that allows the network to recognize multiple objects in a single image. Their approach is based on an iterative process, where each recognition cycle extracts a single object from the input image and *masks* it out of the input. The resulting image is then repropagated through the networks, which extract the next image, and so on.

The network model described by Omori and Nagase is illustrated in Figure 7.4. To illustrate the operation of this network, consider an application where the selective-attention network had been constructed to recognize four geometric shapes in the input image: a square, a triangle, an inverted triangle, and a diamond. Initially, the network is in a quiescent state, and the mask layer is empty. If

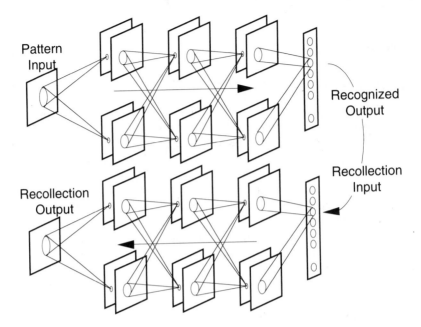

Figure 7.3 This diagram illustrates the architecture of the model of selective attention. As described in the text, the two networks operate concurrently, the bottom-up network acting to recognize objects in the input image, and the top-down network serving to recall an idealized image of the recognized object, and to locate the position of the recognized object in the original image. *Source: Adapted from* Image understanding by neural networks [11]. *Used with permission. Copyright ©1989 IEEE.*

we then apply an input image to the network that contains some combination of the recognizable images, Omori and Nagase assert that:

1. The network will extract the image of one of the objects by first propagating the input to the output of the bottom-up network. The result is a pattern that classifies one of the objects.

2. The classified pattern is then propagated through the top-down network, which reconstructs the image of the recognized object, and locates it in the image.

3. The reconstructed image of the recognized object is then applied to the mask layer, which holds the restored image.

4. The mask layer is connected to the first layer of S-cells in the bottom-up network through inhibiting connections that mirror the connections to the neocognitron retina. Thus, activation of the mask units eliminates the image of the recognized object from the image applied to the selective-attention network.

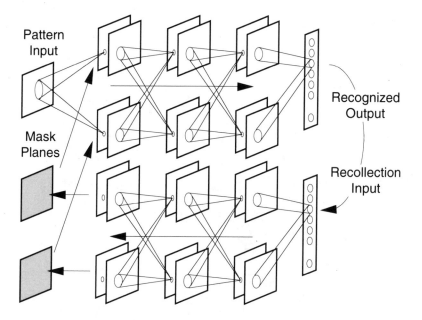

Figure 7.4   This diagram illustrates the structure of the internal representation of images (IRI) network. The operation of the network is described in the text. *Source: Adapted from Image understanding by neural networks* [11]. *Used with permission. Copyright ©1989 IEEE.*

5.   The entire process then repeats, this time eliminating one of the remaining, unrecognized objects from the image.

6.   The process continues until all of the objects have been recognized. This condition is indicated when the state of the mask layer duplicates the state of the input image. In this situation, the input applied to the selective-attention network is a null image.

In Figure 7.5 we illustrate a slightly more practical application of the internal representation of images (IRI) network. In this example, the network has been constructed to recognize the common symbols used to represent electronic components in a circuit diagram. Omori and Nagase assert that the IRI can successfully identify each of the symbols in the image, and that the recognition of these symbols is the first step toward machine interpretation of similar diagrams.

This concludes our (rather brief) discussion of the neocognitron and its derivative networks. Readers interested in a more thorough discussion of the theory of these paradigms are referred to the publications previously cited, or any of the texts described in the Suggested Readings section of this chapter.

Image Input

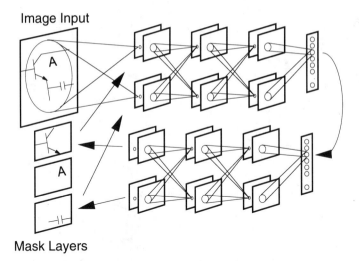

Mask Layers

Figure 7.5   This diagram illustrates how the IRI network could be used to "read" an electronic schematic diagram. As each symbol is recognized, an external process could establish the function represented by the symbol, and determine the behavior of the resulting circuit. *Source: Reprinted with permission from* Image understanding by neuron network. *In* Proceedings of the International Joint Conference on Neural Networks, *June 1989. Copyright ©1989 IEEE.*

7.2   GENDER RECOGNITION FROM FACIAL IMAGES

The BPN is not commonly used for image-processing applications, because that network tends to be overly sensitive to the position of the object in the image. To illustrate this point, consider the operation of a BPN similar to the character-recognition network described in Chapter 4. To successfully use a BPN in this application, we must ensure that the character image is properly framed in the input pattern vector prior to presentation to the network. If the image is off by a single pixel in any direction, the pattern vector applied to the network will be significantly different from the pattern vector that the network learned to recognize, resulting in a likely misclassification of the character. This is illustrated in Figure 7.6.

In a paper published in 1991, B. A. Golomb, et al. [7] described a novel approach using multiple BPNs to determine a person's gender based only on the image of the face of that person. While it does not solve the pattern-framing issue described above, it does illustrate how multiple BPNs can be used to perform feature extraction from image data, a precursor to position-independent pattern recognition. For that reason, we shall now investigate the implementation of that system.

(a)

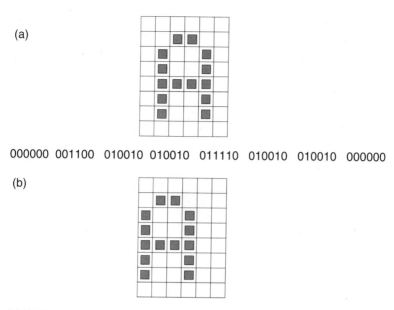

000000 001100 010010 010010 011110 010010 010010 000000

(b)

000000 011000 100100 100100 111100 100100 10010 0 000000

Figure 7.6   This figure shows why a BPN can be "confused" by an improperly framed character image. In both examples, the character image is contained inside a larger window. Notice the differences between the two patterns, and consider how a BPN trained to recognize the first pattern might fail to recognize the second image. (a) This diagram shows the form of the pattern vector for a properly framed A. (b) This diagram illustrates an improperly framed A, offset from its "proper" position by a single horizontal pixel.

7.2.1   Multiple-Network Architecture

The scheme employed by Golomb et al. uses a standard three-layer BPN trained to reproduce an output pattern identical to the input pattern as the means for extracting the visual features from the facial image. The twist is that the hidden layer contains significantly fewer processing elements than either the input or output layers, and it is the activation pattern produced by the hidden layer that represents the extracted feature vector for the input image. Once extracted from the first BPN, the feature vector is then used as the input to another BPN that learns to classify gender from the extracted features.

As shown in Figure 7.7, the first BPN compresses the image from 900 pixels (representing the 30×30 pixel matrix) to 40 features. The compressed form of the image is then used as input to another BPN, which classifies the gender of the subject represented by the feature vector. Using the combination of BPNs in this manner has two benefits in this application: First, the compression network serves to reduce the dimension of the pattern to be classified from 900 to 40 (a reduction of approximately 96%), thus simplifying the classification process; and, second,

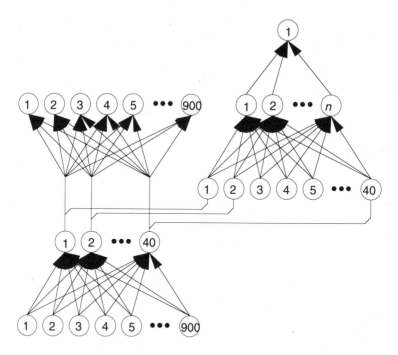

Figure 7.7   This diagram shows the architecture of the multiple network system developed to determine gender from facial images. The operation of the system is described in the text. *Source:* SEXNET: A neural network identifies sex from human faces [7]. *Copyright ©1991, Morgan Kaufmann Publishers. Used with permission.*

by training the compression network to reproduce the input at the output, we have forced it to extract the features from the input that lead to successful restoration of the image. In effect, the hidden layer in the image-compression BPN is performing a principle component analysis [1] on the image data, encoding the eigenvectors for the image patterns.

7.2.2   Facial-Image Representation

To collect training information for the networks, photographs were taken of 45 male and 45 female subjects. In an attempt to remove visual cues or distractions from the images, the subjects were photographed with no apparent jewelry, makeup, facial hair, or other visual indications of gender. Each subject was also draped with cloth from the neck down, to ensure that the image data focused on the facial features of each subject. Each subject was photographed from a full-face perspective, although there was no attempt to ensure consistent head position in all the photographs.

Once the training photographs had been obtained, the images were digitized into 256 gray-shade images. Each image was then preprocessed, using conventional image-processing techniques, to scale and translate each image to a uniform size, specifically 12 horizontal pixels between the center of the eyes, and eight vertical pixels from the eyes to the mouth. If necessary, the image was then rotated to move the head to the vertical. Finally, each image was adjusted using a pixel block-averaging technique to guarantee the same average brightness, and cropped to a 30×30 pixel image to minimize any reference to hair or background.

After preprocessing, the resulting images were converted into a pattern vector form for use by the BPN by first concatenating each row of the pixel matrix to form a 900-element vector. Next, each pixel in the vector was scaled into a numerical value in the range from zero to one, using a simple linear technique expressed by

$$x_i' = \frac{x_i}{255} \tag{7.1}$$

where x_i represents the integer gray value assigned to the pixel, and the denominator reflects the fact that the pixels can take on any one of 256 gray-shade values, ranging between zero and 255, inclusive.

Finally, the researchers assigned a gender status to each image by correlating the image to the subject. Thus, for the *SexNet*[4] application, the training exemplars consisted of 90 image-gender patterns. Had this been a standard BPN application, the network would have been trained using the conventional BPN training algorithm on the exemplar set. As we indicated earlier, however, the SexNet researchers went a step further in their application by using a BPN to extract the important features of the image prior to classification. We shall now investigate the implementation of that system.

7.2.3 SexNet Training

The first step in creating the SexNet application was to train the image-compression network. This network was constructed as a standard, three-layer BPN, with 900 inputs, 40 units on the hidden layer, and 900 outputs. The hidden units used the sigmoidal activation function, arguably to improve the network's ability to compress the image data, while the output units were linear. Next, the exemplar data constructed to train the SexNet application was separated into input and output patterns. The input image patterns were then duplicated, and organized into a set of 90 image-image exemplars. It was these data that were then used to train the data-compression BPN.

Exercise 7.1: Describe why the linear activation function was the appropriate choice for the output units in the compression network in the SexNet application. ∎

---

4. SexNet was the name used in the original paper to describe this application.

The image-compression network was trained for 2,000 epochs, during which time the network learned to generate an "adequate" reconstruction of the input image. According to the original authors, "adequate" image reconstruction was a subjective measure indicating that the 90 images produced by the network were "distinct and discriminable, although not identical" to the original images. Unfortunately, no indication of the global error produced by the trained network is provided in the original paper, so we must assume that the training was sufficient to maximize the image reconstruction from the extracted features.

Once the image-compression network had completed training, the connection weights in that network were frozen, and the 90 images were then propagated through the network, one at a time. After each pattern had been propagated through the network, the activation of each of the units on the hidden layer was recorded as a 40-element vector, producing 90, 40-element feature vectors. These feature vectors were then paired with the gender classification for the image that they represented, and these feature-gender pairings became the training set for the gender-classification network.

The gender-classification network contained 40 input units, one sigmoidal output unit, and different numbers of units on the hidden layer in different training trials. The output of the network was interpreted as an indication of "male" if the single output unit had an output value greater than 0.5, and "female" otherwise.

The reason for using different numbers of hidden-layer units was to determine the effect of the hidden-layer units on the successful classification of the input-feature vector. Five different versions of the gender-classification network were constructed and tested, using 2, 5, 10, 20, and 40 hidden-layer units as the number of units in each trial. In each trial, training occurred normally, using 80 randomly selected feature-gender pairs of the 90 available as the training set. The remaining 10 were held out until after training was completed, to determine how well the gender-classification network had generalized its solution.

7.2.4   Gender-Recognition Results

The performance of the SexNet was evaluated, after training had been completed, by asking the system to classify the gender of all 90 faces. Because, for any given trial, the system had only learned 80 of the 90 possible faces, accurate results were expected for 72% of the images (the training images) while the remaining 28% provided an indication of how successful the system had been at extracting appropriate features from the image and classifying the feature patterns.

The results were then compared to the ability of five humans, who were unfamiliar with the subjects, to correctly identify the gender of the people in the images. In addition, each human was asked to provide a binary indication of certainty for each of their gender classifications.

In their paper, Golomb et al. report that the SexNet with 10 units in the gender-classification network correctly classified 77, 90, 72, 90, 81, 90, and 90 of the images in seven trials, each trial using a different subset of the 90 images for training, for an overall accuracy of 93.7%. In comparison, the five human subjects classified 82, 80, 78, 82, and 76 of the 90 images correctly, for an average accuracy of 88.4%.

Interestingly, there were other correlations between the behavior of the SexNet and the human subjects. In particular, one of the male images gave the SexNet numerous problems, being misclassified as "female" when used as a test image, and slowing the training of the gender-classification network when used as a training pattern. The same image was misclassified as "Female," "Sure" by all five human subjects. In another instance, the SexNet repeatedly misclassified one of the male images as female any time that image was not included in the training set. Further analysis of the problem revealed that the error was not with the operation of the SexNet—the image that was being misclassified was, in fact, clearly a female that had been erroneously labeled a male in the exemplar set.

While these results suggest that, although not necessarily a biological model for image processing, the BPN can correctly extract the attributes of an image that lead to the correct classification of the object in the image. More significantly, however, is the notion that the BPN can be used to determine the correct set of attributes needed to encode the image with no *a priori* knowledge of the characteristics of the image. As evidenced by the SexNet application, the process of training a BPN can provide an automatic means of determining, and extracting, the information contained in raw data.

7.3   IMAGERY FEATURE DISCOVERY

In the previous sections of this chapter, we have shown how the neocognitron and its derivative networks have been used to identify, and locate, objects contained in image data, and how multiple networks have been combined to solve a complex problem in image processing. In this section, we shall investigate how a team of researchers at Sandia National Laboratory combined both aspects of these applications to identify the images of military targets in synthetic aperture radar (SAR) imagery [2]. Specifically, the developers used a neocognitron network to extract the information content from the SAR image data, and then allowed an ART2 network to classify the resulting feature pattern.

7.3.1   SAR Image Representation

Synthetic aperture radar is, quite simply, a process of mapping terrain, and any manmade objects on the terrain, by applying knowledge about the reflectivity of materials to an EMR signal return.[5] Conceptually, SAR operates by assigning an intensity value to each resolvable point in the electronic signal produced by an EMR pulse bouncing off of terrestrial objects and returning to the SAR receiver.

---

5. Readers who have skipped chapters in this book may find it helpful to review the section on pulse Doppler radar signature classification, in Chapter 6, before progressing further in this section.

Figure 7.8   This diagram depicts the SAR imagery of a tank. Notice how, even though the image is obviously not representative of the appearance of the tanks in the human visual spectrum, we are still able to discern the object in the SAR image. *Source: Adapted from* Feature discovery via neural networks for object recognition in SAR imagery [2]. *Used with permission. Copyright ©1992 IEEE.*

The resulting image is therefore a representation of the electronic return after it has been mapped into the visual spectrum. In Figure 7.8, we illustrate a typical SAR return after it has been processed.

The primary benefit of using SAR instead of relying strictly on visual imagery is that manmade objects tend to reflect EMR signals more readily than visible radiation, thus making those objects more difficult to disguise. A corollary effect is that SAR imagery tends to reduce the disruptive effect of background clutter in a scene. The problem, however, is that the human visual system has evolved over the millennia so as to optimize the performance of that system in the visible light frequencies. When we artificially map nonvisible EMR frequencies into the visible spectrum, our biologically tuned system can become confused, and we can easily overlook, or misclassify, objects in the SAR images.

However, we have already seen many examples of neural networks that have been constructed to process information outside of the sensory range of humans. We shall now investigate how the Sandia research team developed a neural architecture to identify objects in SAR imagery.

7.3.2   SAR Network Architectures

The scheme employed by Fogler and colleagues was to use a partially implemented neocognitron to extract the important features from the SAR imagery, and then allow a modified ART2 network to classify the resultant feature vector as a

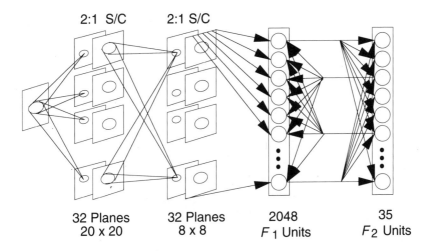

2:1 S/C   2:1 S/C

| 32 Planes | 32 Planes | 2048 | 35 |
| 20 x 20 | 8 x 8 | F_1 Units | F_2 Units |

Figure 7.9 This figure illustrates the network combination used to process the SAR imagery. The neocognitron has the effect of extracting the feature vector represented in the SAR image data, while the ART2 network classifies the feature combination. In this application, only one class of patterns was interesting, even though there may have been many feature patterns that represented the interesting category. The technique used to determine the classification of the pattern by the ART2 network is described in the text.

recognized target or a noninteresting object. As shown in Figure 7.9, the neocognitron processes the SAR imagery as presented on the retina. The connections between the retina and the first layer of S-cells consist of connections that are adapted using the unsupervised learning technique described by Fukushima [5], then shared by units on the other planes within the layer.

As described in Section 7.1, each successive layer in the neocognitron allows the network to more narrowly classify the object in the input image. Rather than extend the architecture of the neocognitron developed for this application to the point that the network could perform the classification of the SAR imagery, the investigators instead chose to use the neocognitron to extract the general feature combinations of the input, then allow a modified ART2 network to complete the classification process.

The advantage to this approach lies in the extensibility of the ART2 network structure. To put this notion in perspective, recall that most of the classification networks we have examined up to this point require the user to *prespecify* the total number of categories into which the input pattern can be classified. While useful in many applications, this *fixed-class* method of classification is not very practical when we are considering a system that must account for an unknown number of categories. Because we are interested in classifying military tanks in SAR imagery, this is analogous to building a system that can only recognize a certain

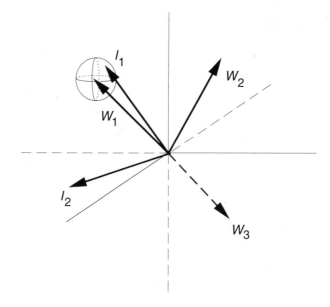

Figure 7.10 This diagram illustrates how hyperspheres can be implemented in an ART network in order to solve the one-class problem. Each hypersphere is located in n-space by an eigenvector of the pattern class, and is sized by the radius of the hypersphere. In the ART network, the eigenvector can be considered to be the memory pattern stored in the top-down connections from the F_2 layer. The radius of the hypersphere is then determined by the value of the vigilance parameter, which describes the maximum distance any pattern vector can be from the characteristic vector, and still be associated with the memory pattern.

number of tanks. What happens, then, if the opposition creates a new class of tank that appears significantly different than any other class of tank previously known? In a fixed-class system, the system (probably) fails by either misclassifying the type of the tank, or by classifying it as a noninteresting target.

The twist in this application, however, is that, even though the number and type of objects that have to be classified may change over time, we are still only interested in a *one-class* determination: Is the object in the SAR image a potential target, or is it not? One method for creating a system that can perform one-class classification is to use a *hyperspherical-distance* classifier to separate the classes. A hyperspherical-distance classifier is one that surrounds the member elements of the target class with hyperspheres in the n-dimensional pattern space. As illustrated in Figure 7.10, a member of the target class is any point that is contained by the hyperspheres defined in the space. In theory, the ART network provides this type of pattern classification as an inherent part of its structure. To see how this happens, let us now consider the operation of the ART network in a little more detail.

In the ART2 network, the F_1 layer acts as a pattern preprocessor that simultaneously performs noise elimination and contrast enhancement on the input pattern. It also has the effect of normalizing the input pattern vector to allow the competitive F_2 layer to compare the input pattern vector with the vectors stored in the bottom-up connection weights in an inner-product sense. Thus, the first phase of pattern propagation in the ART2 removes noise from the input, and finds the best match of previously learned patterns to activate the memory.

Similarly, the F_2 layer serves to encode the memory of all of the input patterns previously encountered. Another way to conceptualize this process is to think of the stored memories in the top-down connection weights in the ART2 network as the set of target classes that the network can identify. If all of the target classes stored in the network were, in fact, members of the one class the network is being asked to classify, then membership in the one class is indicated by the network's acceptance of the current input. If the ART2 *recognizes* the current input pattern, it is considered to be a member of the target class.

7.3.3 SAR Exemplars

For the tank-recognition application, simulated SAR imagery data was developed using a software package that allowed the Sandia researchers to model several different tanks in a variety of backgrounds. For training purposes, one tank model was used, with SAR imagery for each model being produced at 5-degree azimuthal rotations. This process produced 72 SAR images of the tank, of which 36 became the training set, and 36 were held out to test the tolerance of the system to the image aspect.

Additionally, two other sets of image data were collected during this phase. The first set, which represented a *near-target* class, consisted of 50 SAR images of another tank class, which might be representative of nonhostile tank, at various azimuthal rotations. The second set was comprised of 600 randomly selected clutter images, taken from actual SAR returns.

Unfortunately, the original authors do not elaborate on the resolution of the SAR image produced, nor do they mention the gray-scale scheme used to represent the image data. They do, however, mention that the retina in the neocognitron was a 2D array organized as 48×48 processing elements. We can surmise, then, that the SAR data mapped directly to this representation. Moreover, it does not really matter how many gray-scale gradations were used to represent the SAR imagery. We can apply Eq. (7.1) to scale any gray-scale representation by merely substituting the maximum number of gradations in the imagery for the denominator. Thus, we now have a method for converting the SAR imagery data into a form usable by the neural networks.

7.3.4 Training the SAR Networks

Training the networks to perform the SAR image target classification occurs in two distinct steps. First, the neocognitron was repeatedly presented with all of the SAR exemplars collected from the target class. During this time, the neocognitron was allowed to self-adapt, but learning in the ART2 was disabled. Exemplars for the ART2 network were collected after training of the neocognitron was completed. This delay was necessary, to allow the neocognitron to discover its own method for representing the image features. Once the neocognitron had adequately encoded the SAR image features,[6] learning was disabled, and the ART2 was allowed to learn the feature vectors produced by the neocognitron. These feature vectors were produced by additional presentation of the SAR training patterns to the neocognitron with learning disabled. The activity patterns on the top layer were then presented directly to the ART2 for encoding, and the entire process was repeated until the ART2 had learned to recognize all of the features present in the training patterns.

After the ART2 had learned to classify all of the feature vectors produced by the neocognitron, learning was turned off, and the system was tested to determine if it could accurately distinguish targets from near-targets in noisy SAR images. When operated in this mode, the neocognitron was presented with an arbitrary SAR image, either from the set of 36 target images that had been withheld from training, or from one of the other two image classes (near-target and clutter). After it completed the process of extracting the feature components from the input image, the resulting feature vector was given to the ART2 for classification. If the ART2 found a matching pattern in its memory, the image was classified as a target. Conversely, if the ART2 fails to recall the feature vector, a condition indicated when the winning F_2 unit produces a memory that is less than the vigilance parameter, the image is classified as a nontarget.

7.3.5   SAR Target-Identification Results

The Sandia researchers found that the system they developed to classify SAR imagery was, overall, very successful. In Figure 7.11, we present the results of these experiments as they were reported in the original paper. Of particular interest is the relationship between the value of the vigilance parameter used in the ART2 network and the ability of the system to operate correctly. If the vigilance parameter were set below 0.88, the system misclassifies some of the near-target test set as targets. Conversely, when the vigilance parameter goes above 0.94, the system begins to misclassify true targets, as it loses the ability to generalize to the target aspect. The ideal value for the vigilance parameter was found to be 0.91. At that value, the system correctly classified 34 of 36 targets and misclassified 2 of 50 near-targets. In all cases, the system appears to do extremely well when presented only with clutter.

---

6. The criteria for making this determination are described in [5].

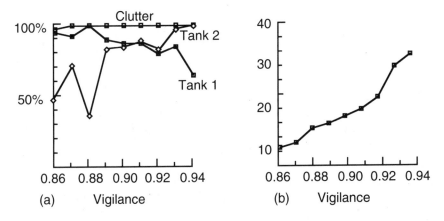

Figure 7.11   These graphs illustrate the results of the SAR image classification system. (a) This graph depicts the relationship between the vigilance parameter in the ART2 network and the accuracy of the system. (b) This graph shows the relationship between the number of F_2 layer units needed to completely classify the target class and the vigilance parameter in the network. *Source: Adapted from* Feature discovery via neural networks for object recognition in SAR imagery [2]. *Used with permission. Copyright ©1992 IEEE.*

7.4   AIRCRAFT TRACKING IN VIDEO IMAGERY

The final application we shall describe in this chapter is a relatively simple image-processing application where the neural network is used to extract the image of an aircraft from a 2D video image and locate the center of the aircraft in the image. This application is interesting for several reasons: It shows how a standard BPN architecture can be constructed to use time-dependent information to improve the network's tolerance to noise and background distractions; it shows how neural networks can be quickly developed to solve problems that were previously intractable or cost prohibitive; and it shows how neural networks can be successfully integrated (or retrofit) with other information-processing technologies.

7.4.1   Tracking-System Requirements

The U.S. Air Force (USAF) does routine ordnance testing to evaluate the performance of its aircraft and munitions. Most of the tests are performed over specially designated test areas on government-owned land. The test sites are typically arranged so that the target area is surrounded by *cinetheolodites*, which is nothing more than a special-purpose *video-tracking station*. Each station is situated such that an operator positioned inside the station can videotape the flight of the incoming test aircraft, and record the deployment of the ordnance under test.

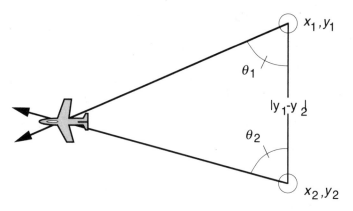

Figure 7.12   This diagram shows how the position of an aircraft can be determined by triangulation. For clarity, we are only concerned here with terrestrial positioning. Each video station has a fixed position, indicated by the latitude and longitude coordinates next to each station. Further, the azimuthal rotation of the siting device (the video camera) is known with respect to a horizontal reference angle. The position of the aircraft can then be precisely determined by a simple trigonometric calculation to find the intersection of the two siting lines.

Each video station has a fixed reference in its latitude, longitude, and altitude. Furthermore, the videotape recorded at each station is electronically tagged with the azimuthal orientation of the camera as the videotape is recorded, to reference the physical position of the recording camera. However, the cameras are manually aimed and controlled, meaning that, quite often, the image of the test aircraft tends to move around in the recording. Because these recordings are used to evaluate the performance of the deployed ordnance, it is imperative that the exact position of the aircraft be known at the point of release, so that the flight of the ordnance can be accurately measured.

The basic approach to locating the position of the aircraft is to use triangulation—that is, to correlate the position and directional information associated with the recorded images from two (or more) video stations. In two dimensions, this can be done by finding the intersection of the two lines formed by the position of the recording stations and the azimuthal rotation of each camera at the time the video was recorded. This process is illustrated in Figure 7.12.

Unfortunately, the process is complicated somewhat, because, as we mentioned earlier, the video cameras are manually aimed at the incoming aircraft. As anyone who has used a hand-held video camera with a telephoto lens will know,[7] even slight movements in the camera will cause the image of the target to *jitter.* This jittering effect is actually the local manifestation of the positioning

---

7. This discussion precludes the use of automatic picture-stabilization controls.

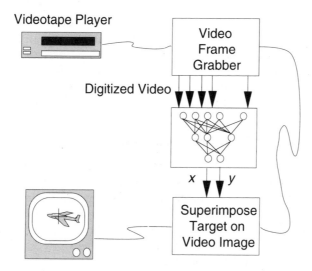

Figure 7.13 This block diagram illustrates the architecture of the system developed to track aircraft images in an input video stream. In this application, the BPN was simulated on the multiprocessor neural emulation tool (NET) computer system developed by the author. The neural-network coprocessor provided an effective means of off-loading much of the computation from the host processor. As a result, the system was able to process the input video stream at near real-time rates.

problem—if the camera is not pointed *directly* at the aircraft, there is an error in the rotation of the platform, which will induce a more significant error in the positioning calculation.

To correct the *jitter* effect, the USAF has previously used enlisted personnel to manually inspect *each frame* of video after a test to determine the offset of the aircraft from the center of the image. That offset is then used to correct the positioning calculation, which, in turn, is used to evaluate the performance of the ordnance. As you can imagine, manual inspection of several videotapes after each ordnance test is a very time-consuming, labor-intensive process.

7.4.2 Tracking-System Architecture

In an attempt to determine if a computer could be used to automate the video-analysis process, we developed a system that used a BPN to locate the center of mass of the airplane in the input imagery. Once we knew where the plane was in each frame, it was a simple matter to correct the azimuthal rotation angle for that video frame.

As shown in Figure 7.13, the architecture of the system we developed incorporated a number of subsystems besides the neural network. The playback from the recorded video was initially digitized by running the video stream through a video *frame-grabber* device. The output from the frame grabber was a 64×64

pixel matrix, with each pixel encoded in a 256 gray-shade integer format. The video image was then converted into a form usable by the BPN, which had learned to identify the image of an aircraft and provide, as output, the x and y pixel coordinates of the center of the plane in the image. For demonstration purposes, we then superimposed a cross-hair at the coordinates indicated by the BPN on the digitized video, so that we could assess the accuracy of the network.

7.4.3   Tracking-Network Architecture

Initially, a standard BPN was used to try to locate the aircraft in the input image. To train the network, a program was created that captured 250 randomly selected digitized images from the recorded video. For each image, the pixel coordinates (x, y) of the center of the airplane image were manually determined. The training exemplars were then constructed by applying Eq. (7.1) to each pixel value in each of the 250 digitized images. Similarly, the target x and y pixel coordinates were scaled to values between zero and one.

The first network trained had 4,097 input units, organized such that one unit was allocated to each input pixel, with an additional bias element. The hidden layer contained 50 sigmoidal units, and the output consisted of 2 linear units. This network gave good results, but had quite a bit of difficulty dealing with background clutter. For instance, the network would track the aircraft through a clear or overcast sky without difficulty, but when the plane dropped low enough to include mountains in the background of the image, the network immediately became confused. Apparently, the network had not learned to recognize airplanes so much as it had learned to find the darkest section in the image. As a result, the network would usually indicate a position halfway between the image of the plane and the mountains as its targeting position.

To overcome this difficulty, another network was constructed that contained 8,193 input elements, 50 units on the hidden layer, and two linear outputs. As shown in Figure 7.14, this network was trained with image data from the current frame, together with the imagery from the preceding frame. This modification had the effect of keeping the network from making drastic targeting changes when there were multiple dark areas in the image simultaneously. This scheme worked extremely well, keeping the aircraft correctly targeted in 95% of the imagery. The other 5% were video frames that contained multiple distractions, or occurred shortly after a sequence where the network had lost focus on the airplane.

7.4.4   Tracking-System Issues

There are several aspects of this application that warrant further study. In this section, we shall review some of these issues, to illustrate how they arise, and to show how they may be overcome when creating applications of your own design.

First, there is the issue of performance. Because the targeting process in this application occurred after the video information had been recorded, it was not

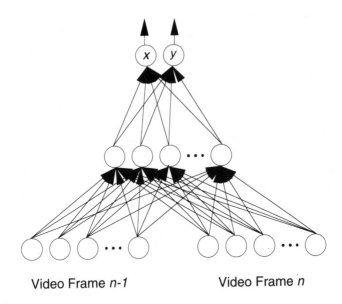

Figure 7.14   This diagram illustrates the architecture of the BPN constructed to perform the aircraft-tracking application. The first 4,096 input elements encoded the scaled, digitized imagery from the current video frame, while the next 4,096 units encoded the imagery from the previous video frame. This architecture allowed the BPN to track the aircraft in the video frame, while simultaneously minimizing the effect of other objects in the image.

necessary that the system had to be able to process the imagery in real time. However, in many applications, especially in image processing, it is imperative that the data be processed at, or very near to real-time rates.

To illustrate why this might pose a problem here, consider the computational requirements necessary to perform this application. Each image must first be digitized, then scaled, then propagated through the BPN before we have extracted the required information from the image data. In this sequence of events, the propagation through the neural network will be the most computationally expensive. We can see why this is so if we analyze the process of simulating the BPN described in this section.

The second network contains 404,950 connections, 100 between the hidden layer and the output, and the remainder between the input layer and the hidden layer. To propagate a pattern through the network, each connection requires two floating-point calculations: A multiply followed by an addition operation. Furthermore, the sigmoid activation function is a transcendental computation, requiring anywhere between 10 and 100 floating-point operations each time it is computed, depending on the implementation of the function. Even if we assume that only 10 calculations are required for the sigmoid, we are still faced with performing 810,400 floating-point computations every time one image pattern is propagated through the network.[8]

Because real-time video is nominally 30 image frames per second, we require a computer that can perform at least 24.3 million floating-point operations every second just to simulate the network. Scaling each input image requires additional CPU time, as does acquiring the digitized video image. Increasing the image resolution quickly compounds the problem, especially if the network must process the raw imagery. Obviously, performance can pose a significant constraint on any neural network application.

Another concern was the accuracy of the network. Because it was necessary to ensure that the system was providing an accurate measure of how far the image of the airplane was from the center of the image frame in order to exactly locate the position of the aircraft, it was necessary (in this case) to postprocess the output of the system to identify any images that had been incorrectly targeted. However, the inclusion of the postprocess is not indicative of a failure of the BPN to perform its function in this application. In this case, no other automatic solution existed, and the cost of developing a perfect system was deemed excessive. Therefore, as in many other practical applications of neural-network technology, it was decided that a reasonable solution was preferable to no solution.

7.5   IMAGE-PROCESSING SUMMARY

In this chapter, we have seen how neural networks have been used to identify objects contained in imagery data, in and outside of the visual spectrum. We have investigated another neural-network architecture that is both powerful and useful for performing rotational and translational invariant feature extraction. We have also examined two applications that use a combination of neural networks, each to perform a different aspect of information processing for the complete application. While these applications exhibit only rudimentary skills when compared to the processing that goes on in the human visual cortex, they nevertheless illustrate the natural ability of the inherently parallel networks to process a great deal of information in parallel, and fuse the image data into a meaningful interpretation.

SUGGESTED READINGS

The literature abounds with image-processing applications of neural networks. It seems that the parallel architectures inherent in neural-network structures are particularly suited to processing the distributed representation of information in an image. Readers interested in exploring a more detailed (albeit complex) treatment of the biological implications of neural networks with respect to vision and image

---

8. During learning, this number can easily triple.

processing are referred to *Visual Perceptions: The Neurophysiological Foundations* [12].

For a more complete description of the operation of the neocognitron, one of the most thorough treatments is provided in *Neural Networks: Algorithms, Applications, and Programming Techniques* [3]. Furthermore, Kunihiko Fukushima has published numerous papers describing the implementation of the neocognitron, the model of selective attention [4], and other networks based on the neocognitron processing model.

There are also several special-purpose networks that have been developed specifically for image-processing applications. Many of these network paradigms are based on Stephen Grossberg's boundary contour system [8] or feature contour system [9]. Still others use a spatiotemporal architecture to detect motion in a preferred direction [10]. I have deliberately chosen to omit applications based on these networks from this chapter, because it would not have been fair to the reader to introduce a specialized network architecture for each application discussed, although many would have been appropriate. Readers are encouraged, however, to explore these network paradigms and their applications on their own.

BIBLIOGRAPHY

1. G. W. Cottrell, P. Munro, and D. Zipser. Image compression by back propagation: An example of extensional programming. *UCSD Institute for Cognitive Science Technical Report* ICS-8702, 1987.

2. R. J. Fogler, M. W. Koch, M. M. Moya, L. D. Hostetler, and D. R. Hush. Feature discovery via neural networks for object recognition in SAR imagery. *Proceedings of the International Joint Conference on Neural Networks*, Baltimore, MD, pp. IV(408–413), 1992.

3. James A. Freeman and David M. Skapura. *Neural Networks: Algorithms, Applications, and Programming Techniques.* Addison-Wesley Publishing Company, Reading, MA, 1991.

4. Kunihiko Fukushima. Neural network model for selective attention in visual pattern recognition and associative recall. *Applied Optics,* 26(23):4985–4992, December 1987.

5. Kunihiko Fukushima. A neural network for visual pattern recognition. *Computer,* 21(3):65–75, March 1988.

6. Kunihiko Fukushima, Sei Miyake, and Takayuki Ito. Neocognitron: A neural network model for a mechanism of visual pattern recognition. *IEEE Transactions on Systems, Man, and Cybernetics,* SMC-13(5)826–834, September–October 1983.

7. B. A. Golomb, D. T. Lawrence, and T. J. Sejnowski. SEXNET: A neural network identifies sex from human faces. In Richard P. Lippman, John E. Moody, and David S. Touretsky, editors, *Advances in Neural Information Processing Systems 3,* Morgan-Kaufmann Publishers, Inc., San Mateo, CA, pp. 573–577, 1991.

8. S. Grossberg and E. Mingolla. Neural dynamics of form perception: Boundary completion, illusory figures, and neon color spreading. *Psychological Review,* 92:173–211, 1985.

9. S. Grossberg and E. Mingolla. Neural dynamics of perceptual grouping: Textures, boundaries, and emergent segmentations. *Perception and Psychophysics,* 38:141–171, 1985.

10. Jim-Shih Liaw and Michael A. Arbib. A biologically inspired neural network model for 3-D motion detection. *Proceedings of the International Joint Conference on Neural Networks,* Seattle, WA, pp. I(661–665), July 1991.

11. Takashi Omori and Taku Nagase. Image understanding by neuron network. *Proceedings of the International Joint Conference on Neural Networks,* Washington DC, pp. II(235–240), 1989.

12. L. Spillman and J. S. Werner, editors. *Visual Perceptions: The Neurophysiological Foundations,* Academic Press, San Diego, CA, 1990.

C H A P T E R

Process Control and Robotics

The dynamic principle of fantasy is play, which . . . appears to be inconsistent
with the principle of serious work. But without this playing with fantasy, no
creative work has ever yet come to birth.

— Carl Jung

Process control can be loosely defined as any activity performed to maintain a
dynamic system in a stable condition. In its most general sense, process control
is a function that we perform every minute of the day without even being aware
of the intricacies of the task. Virtually every action performed by a human being, or any other sentient creature, for that matter, requires some form of process
control. As an illustration, consider the simple act of eating: There is a process to
be performed (e.g., transporting the food to the mouth), and the *plant*, or system
that performs the process, cannot operate without guidance (e.g., the hand cannot
manipulate the eating implements, nor can it guide the food to the mouth without
receiving the proper control signals from the brain). Moreover, the system controller (the brain) receives a constant stream of data from peripheral sensors (e.g.,
the eyes and the sense of body awareness) that allow it to interactively assess the
state of the system. Based on the sensory input, the controller is able to constantly
induce small corrective actions that keep the system under control at all times.

It is one thing for living creatures, with an innate sense of being and all of the
sensory systems provided by nature, to perform complex tasks; it is quite another
thing, however, to automate the performance of these tasks. Machines have no
sense of awareness, and no explicit memory of previous attempts to complete
an assigned task; nor do they have the memories of the failures associated with
those attempts. Without these memories, and without the capability of rational
thought, machines have no innate ability to alter their behavior, and are thus
doomed to forever repeat errors. Even machines designed to operate in dynamic
environments are unable to adapt beyond certain limits.

Robotics is a special form of process control, in that the system to be controlled is a mechanical implementation of a biological process. Robotics also provides us with an interesting application environment to study the application of neural networks to tasks that are typically classified as "process-control" tasks, because either the dynamics of the process are often not well understood or the control mechanism needed to manage the process is computationally prohibitive.

In this chapter, we shall examine several applications of robotic process control, and show how these complex tasks were successfully addressed by using a neural network as the process controller. We shall show how these networks were able to *learn* the dynamics of the application, and, by extension, were able to address problems that were deemed intractable when using more conventional control methods.

We shall begin our discussion with a brief summary of classic control theory, in order to illustrate the underlying principles of that discipline. Once we have established this foundation, we shall then begin our investigation of neural-network control applications, emphasizing the details of how the networks learned to perform the desired function, and illustrating how the applications were modeled for the neural-network controller. Readers already comfortable with the theoretical concepts of process control may skip directly to the applications discussion, which begins in Section 8.2.

8.1 CONTROL THEORY

Control theory, the body of mathematics that describes the interactions between a controllable process and the mechanisms used to monitor and correct errors in the process, is one of the oldest disciplines in automation technology. In fact, one of the earliest known applications of an automatic control system dates back to ancient Greece. In 250 B.C. [7], a man named Philon developed a float-regulator mechanism to maintain a constant level of fuel oil in an oil lamp. Philon's system, which is depicted in Figure 8.1 was fairly simple by today's standards. Nevertheless, it illustrates some of the fundamental ideas of modern control theory, including the notion of *feedback*, in which the actual system output is compared to the desired response, and the difference between the two is used to alter the input to the system.

In Figure 8.2, we illustrate block diagrams of the two basic types of automatic control systems in common use today: These are referred to as *open-loop* and *closed-loop* systems. The primary difference between the two is the use of feedback signals in the closed-loop system. Feedback allows the controller to determine if, and by how much, the output is in error. After assessing the state of the system via the feedback signal(s), the controller can make corrective adjustments at the input of the system, thus causing the output to stay within some predetermined tolerance level.

Because open-loop systems are not nearly as interesting, or as sophisticated, as their closed-loop counterparts, we will focus our attention on the implemen-

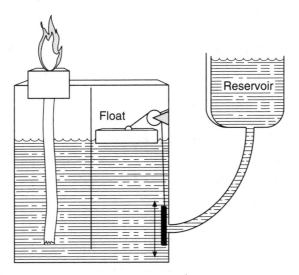

Figure 8.1 This diagram illustrates the operation of Philon's fuel-regulation system. As the oil in the lamp decreases, a float moves in proportion to the amount of fuel that had been depleted. The movement of the float causes a valve to open, which allows additional fuel oil to enter from a reservoir. With the influx of new oil, the float rises, causing the valve to close. This system contains all of the aspects of a modern control system: There is a process to be controlled (the level of the fuel in the lamp); a sensor (the float), which provides feedback (control of the valve); and a cause-effect relationship between system input and output (fuel input causes the amount of fuel in the lamp to increase). Because of the process control, this dynamic system maintains equilibrium.

tation of closed-loop systems in the ensuing discussion. Bear in mind, however, that many of the concepts we shall develop to describe closed-loop systems can also be successfully applied to the analysis of open-loop systems.

8.1.1 Closed-Loop Systems

Many processes, ranging from the simple to the complex, have been successfully automated because there is a well-understood, causal relationship between the process and the inputs to that process. Furthermore, if one of the inputs to the system is actually a signal indicating an error at the output, and the system operates in a manner that attempts to minimize the error signal, the system is said to be *closed-loop* or *self-adjusting*. As a simple example, consider the automatic fine tuning (AFT) circuitry incorporated into virtually every FM radio receiver built today. This circuitry satisfies the definition of a closed-loop control system: It monitors the output of the primary tuning circuits in the receiver, detects when the tuning circuitry has drifted from the carrier frequency of the incoming signal, and initiates a corrective action in the tuner circuits to dynamically realign the tuner. The AFT system operates automatically, and,

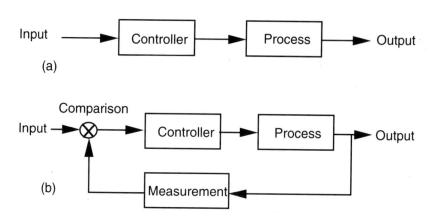

Figure 8.2   These diagrams illustrate the structure of the two basic control system types. (a) Open-loop systems are constructed such that the system controller has no direct access to the output of the system, and hence has no direct mechanism for assessing the error of the system. (b) Closed-loop systems incorporate a measurement subsystem that provides the system controller with a direct indication of the output of the system, thereby allowing the controller to determine the changes at the input to correct any error at the system output.

perhaps more importantly, is able to correct signal drift errors that have been induced by temperature changes within the receiver, to characteristic changes in performance of circuit components due to aging, or to any of several other factors.

The AFT example also serves to introduce the important concept of *positive* and *negative* feedback control systems. In most control applications, feedback is negative; that is, an error signal, which is usually the difference between the actual output of the system and its desired response, is developed and has the effect of altering the behavior of the system controller to reduce the output of the system. There are, however, many applications requiring positive feedback, where a feedback signal has the effect of increasing the output from the system. In the AFT example, the feedback signal is actually dual purpose: A large positive error has the effect of reducing the resonant frequency of the radio tuner, while a large negative error has the opposite effect. Thus, the system behaves in a manner that strives to keep a zero feedback error, thereby keeping the radio tuned to the desired frequency.

Using the principles of feedback and correction, it is possible to construct models of extremely complex processes. From these models, we can apply mathematical tools that enable us to understand the behavior of the models, and, hence, the nature of the systems we are trying to control. In the sections that follow, we shall briefly describe how control-system models can enable us to understand, and automate, a wide variety of tasks.

8.1.2 Mathematical Models

Because most of the applications of control systems involve complex interrelationships between input and output, we must develop a set of mathematical tools that we can use to analyze the relationships between the outputs produced by a system and the *system variables*, or the controllable parameters, of the system. Moreover, most of the systems we will want to control are *dynamic,* meaning that we must use *differential equations* to construct the system model.

In any real application, it is not practical, and certainly not possible, to know everything about the system being considered. In many cases, we can greatly simplify the task of constructing a system model by making some assumptions about the nature of the system, and then *linearizing* the differential equations we will use to model the system. In so doing, we are, in effect, reducing the scope of the problem to that region of the variable space where the system response is linear, thus simplifying the analysis of the system.

For example, consider the electrical system depicted in Figure 8.3. To understand how this system will behave for different values of *resistance, inductance, capacitance, current,* and *voltage,* we can construct a mathematical model of the circuit and test its response for different values of R, L, C, $i(t)$, and $v(t)$. One method for constructing the mathematical model of this system is to use Kirchoff's current law, which states that the electrical current into any node in an electrical circuit is exactly equal to the current out of the node at any time t.[1] Thus, the mathematical model for this system is given by the equation

$$\frac{v(t)}{R} + C\frac{dv(t)}{dt} + \frac{1}{L}\int_0^t v(t)dt = i(t) \qquad (8.1)$$

where the parameters R, L, and C refer to the electrical resistance, inductance, and capacitance of the component, respectively. Because we are dealing with a system that exhibits a dynamic behavior through time, we use the terms $v(t)$ and $i(t)$ to refer to the instantaneous voltage across, and current through, the circuit at any time t.

If we assume that the current through the given circuit is constant, that is $i(t) = I$, we can determine the voltage in the circuit across all components as a function of time by the equation

$$v(t) = \frac{1}{L}e^{-\alpha t}\cos(\beta t + \theta) \qquad (8.2)$$

where L is again the electrical inductance of the circuit and the terms α, β, and θ are used to indicate the *time constant* of the circuit, the *period* of the voltage oscillation, and the *phase angle* between the voltage and current signals. Figure 8.4 illustrates the typical voltage curve for an underdamped RLC circuit.

---

1. Current through an electrical component can be expressed as a function of the instantaneous voltage across the device, a technique we employ here.

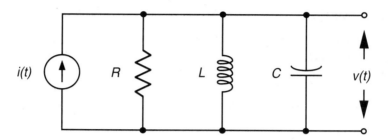

Figure 8.3   A dynamic electrical system is shown. The equation describing the behavior of this system is developed in the text.

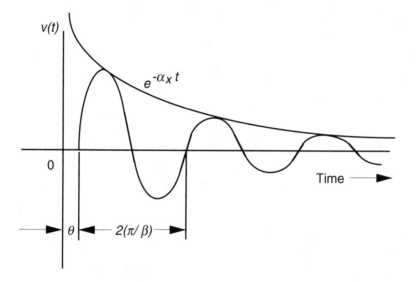

Figure 8.4   The voltage curve for an underdamped RLC circuit is shown. Notice the relationship between the dynamics of the curve and the parameters α, β, and θ, which are described in the text.

Inspection of this graph indicates that the system undergoes a dynamic transition period, beginning at time t_0, which is the instant that current is first applied to the circuit. The voltage (and, hence, current) dynamics tend to die out after approximately five time periods (β), leaving the system in its steady state.

8.1.3   Linear Approximations of Dynamic Systems

Most real-world dynamic systems are linear within some range of their variables. If, however, we allow system variables to increase without limit, all systems will eventually become nonlinear. In the *RLC* circuit example, if we were to allow the input current to increase indefinitely, the components would eventually overheat and fail, perhaps catastrophically.

Fortunately, we can limit our analysis of most systems to specific operating ranges of the input variables, within which, the response of most dynamic systems can be modeled using a *linear approximation* technique. As we have already indicated, the benefit of linearizing a dynamic system is that the analysis of a linear system is much less computationally taxing than the analysis of the corresponding dynamic system.

A linear system is one in which two conditions are satisfied. First, it must satisfy the principle of *superposition*, which states that, if the response of the system to any stimulus, $x_n(t)$, is $y_n(t)$, then the response of the system to multiple excitations must be equal to the sum of the system responses to each of those excitations. Second, it must satisfy the condition of *homogeneity*, which states that the system must preserve any magnitude scale factor between input and output. Stated more precisely, for excitation $x_n(t)$ and response $y_n(t)$, a linear system must satisfy the conditions

$$x_1(t) + x_2(t) \Rightarrow y_1(t) + y_2(t) \qquad (8.3)$$

$$\beta x_1(t) \Rightarrow \beta y_1(t) \qquad (8.4)$$

where Eq. (8.3) specifies the condition of superposition, and Eq. (8.4) describes the condition of homogeneity.

By this definition, a system characterized by the equation $y = x^2$ is not linear, because it does not satisfy the condition of superposition. Similarly, a system characterized by the equation $y = mx + b$ is not linear, as it does not satisfy the condition of homogeneity. However, we could use this system to *approximate* a linear system if we consider only small changes to x and y, which we shall call Δx and Δy, about a specific operating point, (x_0, y_0). Thus,

$$y_0 + \Delta y = mx_0 + m\Delta x + b$$

from which we can conclude that $\Delta y = m\Delta x$. Given these constraints, the system satisfies the homogeneity requirement.

The process of approximating a linear system from a more complex dynamic system is merely an extension of this basic idea. If we consider a multivariable system characterized by the relation

$$y = g(x_1, x_2, x_3, \ldots, x_n) \qquad (8.5)$$

we can construct a linear approximation of the system using a Taylor series expansion about the operating point $(x_{1_0}, x_{2_0}, x_{3_0}, \ldots, x_{n_0})$. Neglecting the higher-order terms, we can then write

$$y = g(x_{1_0}, x_{2_0}, x_{3_0}, \ldots, x_{n_0}) \tag{8.6}$$

$$+ \left. \frac{\partial g}{\partial x_1} \right|_{x_1 = x_{1_0}} (x_1 - x_{1_0})$$

$$+ \left. \frac{\partial g}{\partial x_2} \right|_{x_2 = x_{2_0}} (x_2 - x_{2_0})$$

$$+ \left. \frac{\partial g}{\partial x_3} \right|_{x_3 = x_{3_0}} (x_3 - x_{3_0})$$

$$+ \ldots$$

$$+ \left. \frac{\partial g}{\partial x_n} \right|_{x_n = x_{n_0}} (x_n - x_{n_0})$$

to construct the linear approximation of the system.

8.1.4   The Laplace Transform

The Laplace transform is a mathematical tool that enables us to convert differential equations in the time domain into much easier to solve algebraic equations in the frequency domain. Once the system equations have been transformed, we then merely solve for the variables of interest, and convert the system back into the time domain by applying the inverse Laplace transform.

We can see how the Laplace transform works by considering the Laplace operator, s. In the time domain, we let s be equivalent to the differential operator. Similarly, we let the inverse Laplace operator be equivalent to the integral operator in the time domain. Specifically, let

$$s \equiv \frac{d}{dt} \tag{8.7}$$

$$\frac{1}{s} \equiv \int_{0+}^{t} dt \tag{8.8}$$

The Laplace transform for a function of time, $f(t)$, is defined as the function $F(s)$ by the equation

$$F(s) = \int_0^\infty f(t) e^{-st} dt \tag{8.9}$$

$$= \mathcal{L}(f(t)) \tag{8.10}$$

To find the Laplace transform for a function of time, we simply write the Laplace function using the specific time-domain function in place of $f(t)$, and evaluate the integral at its limits. For example, the Laplace transform of the function $f(t) = t, t > 0$ is found by

$$F(s) = \int_0^\infty e^{-st} t\, dt$$

$$= \frac{e^{-st}(-st - 1)}{s^2}\Big|_0^\infty$$

$$= \frac{1}{s^2}$$

Exercise 8.1: Find the Laplace transform for the time-domain function $f(t) = \cos a\omega t$, $t > 0$, where a is a constant value. ■

It follows that the inverse Laplace transform can be used to convert a frequency-domain function, $F(s)$, into its time-domain equivalent form. The inverse Laplace transform is defined as

$$f(t) = \frac{1}{2\pi j} \int_{\sigma-j\infty}^{\sigma+j\infty} F(s) e^{st}\, ds \tag{8.11}$$

The Laplace transform exists for any linear differential system for which the transformation integral converges. Fortunately, this requirement holds for any physically realizable system, greatly simplifying the analysis of practical control systems. Also simplifying the situation is the fact that many common time-domain functions have their corresponding Laplace transforms listed in tabular form in reference publications, such as any of the *CRC* handbooks [9]. Thus, the use of Laplace transforms is not restricted to mathematicians; indeed, mere mortals regularly use Laplace transforms to analyze control-system performance.

As an illustration of the power of the Laplace transform, let us consider again the electrical system described at the beginning of this section. The differential equation describing the response of that system is given in the time domain by

$$x(t) = C\frac{d^2v(t)}{dt^2} + \frac{1}{R}\frac{dv(t)}{dt} + \frac{1}{L}v(t) \tag{8.12}$$

We can transform Eq. (8.12) into the frequency domain by applying the Laplace transform for each of the differential components of the system. The transformed equation is thus

$$X(s) = C\left(s^2 Y(s) - s y(0^+) - \frac{dy(0)}{dt}\right) + \frac{1}{R}\left(sY(s) - y(0^+)\right) + \frac{1}{L}Y(s) \tag{8.13}$$

If we then let $x(t) = 0$, $y(0^+) = y_0$, and $\frac{dy}{dt}\big|_{t=0} = 0$, we can reduce Eq. (8.13) to

$$0 = Cs^2 Y(s) - Cs y_0 + \frac{1}{R}sY(s) - \frac{1}{R}y_0 + \frac{1}{L}Y(s) \tag{8.14}$$

Solving for Y(s) yields

$$Y(s) = \frac{(Cs + \frac{1}{R})y_0}{Cs^2 + \frac{1}{R}s + \frac{1}{L}} \tag{8.15}$$

$$= \frac{p(s)}{q(s)} \tag{8.16}$$

Equations (8.15) and (8.16) tell us quite a bit about the nature of this system. If we set $q(s) = 0$, we will have determined the situations under which the frequency response of the system is infinite. These situations are called the *singularities* of the system. Conversely, the roots of the polynomial $p(s)$ are called *zeros* of the system, because under the conditions that satisfy $p(s) = 0$, the response of the system is also zero.

Exercise 8.2: Find the poles and zeros of the electrical system modeled by Eq. (8.15) when $R = 33$ ohms, $L = 50$ mH, and $C = 10\mu$F. ■

Finally, in most control-system applications, it is desirable to know the final, or *steady-state* response of the system to a specific stimulation. We can use the Laplace transform to determine the steady-state response of such a system by evaluating the relation

$$\lim_{t \to \infty} y(t) = \lim_{s \to 0} sY(s) \tag{8.17}$$

where poles on the imaginary axis and in the right half-plane and higher-order poles at the origin are not considered.

8.1.5   Transfer Functions

The *transfer function* of a linear system is defined as the ratio of the Laplace transform of the output to the Laplace transform of the input variable, subject to the condition that the initial state of the system is quiescent. It is useful to know the transfer function of a system, because once that ratio has been determined, the system may then be treated as a "black box," which can be connected to other "black boxes" to construct even more complex systems.

Again using the electrical circuit example, we can write the transfer function of that system as

$$G(s) = \frac{Y(s)}{X(s)} = \frac{1}{Cs^2 + \frac{1}{R}s + \frac{1}{L}} \tag{8.18}$$

We can then build models of larger systems using the building block we have just created by using graphing techniques to represent the connectivity between subsystems. By knowing the transfer function of every component (or subsystem) in a system, we can determine the behavior of the complete system by evaluating the response of each component to its respective input signal(s). We illustrate this concept in Figure 8.5.

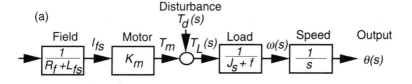

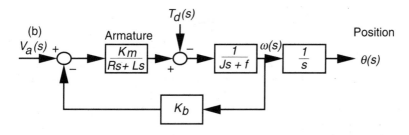

Figure 8.5 These diagrams illustrate the relationship between system-transfer functions and the building-block model of complex systems. (a) This figure represents the *RLC* circuit model we have been evaluating in this section. Using this diagramming scheme, inputs to the system are shown by incoming arrows, outputs as outgoing arrows. The label on each arc in the diagram represents the output of the system with respect to its input. (b) A more complicated system model is shown, this time providing for external perturbations in the system.

We could continue this discussion of control theory and analysis techniques for several more chapters without even beginning to scratch the surface of the topic. Rather than doing that, we shall now turn our attention to the neural-network control applications that we earlier promised to address, and trust that the reader can now better appreciate the capabilities of that technology to perform complex control functions.

8.2 CART/POLE BALANCER

In the previous section, we examined some of the analysis techniques that a control-systems engineer could use to model, and then analyze, the behavior of a complex control system. However, throughout that discussion, we assumed that the systems to be evaluated had easily derived mathematical models that could be used as the basis for the system analysis. Beginning in this section, we shall look at applications of control systems where the process to be controlled is not apparent, thus making the application of the traditional control-theory tools difficult.

The first of these control problems is referred to as the *cart/pole-balancer* application. As the name suggests, the problem is to come up with an automatic

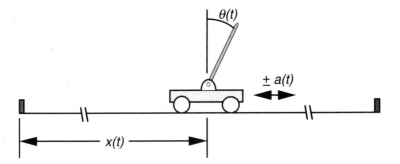

Figure 8.6 This diagram depicts the constraints on the cart/pole-balancer system. The cart is free to move in only one plane, but it may move in either direction, and as quickly or as slowly as is needed to maintain the position of the pole. The pole is mounted to the cart on a hinge that allows 180 degrees of angular rotation in the same plane as the cart movement. The goal is to develop a control system that can be used to maintain the vertical position of the pole while keeping the cart as close to the center of the system as possible.

means of controlling the back-and-forth movement of a cart in order to balance a vertical pole attached at its base to the cart. To simplify the problem, we shall consider the movement of the cart and the pole in only one plane. We can therefore assume that the cart runs on a rail, in order to prevent any lateral movement, and that the pole is attached to the cart by a hinge that allows movement only in the same plane as the movement of the cart.

We shall complicate the problem somewhat by insisting that the length of the rail is finite, and that the cart may not move beyond the end of the rail in either direction. Further, we shall require our control system to balance the pole, and maintain the balanced state, with the cart ideally positioned as close to the center of the track as possible. Figure 8.6 illustrates the physical arrangement of this system.

8.2.1 Conventional Controller Design

For this application, we can denote the position of the cart as $x(t)$, where $x = 0$ is assumed to be the position of the cart at the center of the track. Negative values of $x(t)$ will indicate the cart is to the left of center, while positive values of $x(t)$ position the cart to the right of center. A sensor provides a measurement of the angular position of the pole with respect to the vertical, $\theta(t)$. Acting on the cart is a force that controls its acceleration, denoted as $f(t)$, with positive values indicating acceleration toward the right. Two other parameters of the system are monitored: the time rate of change in the position of the cart, $\dot{x}(t)$, and the angular velocity of the falling pole, given by $\dot{\theta}(t)$.

We can model the dynamics of this system by writing the equations that describe the effect of the acceleration force on the position of the pole, and then developing a control model to maintain the system such that $\theta(t)$ and $\dot{\theta}(t)$ are zero. The dynamic equation that describes this system is given by

$$f(t) = ax(t) + b\dot{x}(t) + c\theta(t) + d\dot{\theta}(t) \qquad (8.19)$$

where the terms a, b, c, and d are constant coefficients that represent the physical characteristics of the system, which are found empirically.

For the given system, the force needed to balance the pole can be assumed to be constant and of fixed magnitude for each movement of the cart. Further, because the cart can move in only two directions, we can surmise that the required force will vary only in its sign, depending on the direction of the cart. We can therefore rewrite Eq. (8.19) to account for the effects of the force on the position of the pole as

$$f(t) \cong \alpha\,\mathrm{sgn}\left(ax(t) + b\dot{x}(t) + c\theta(t) + d\dot{\theta}(t)\right) \qquad (8.20)$$

where α is used to represent the magnitude of the force applied.

Equation (8.20) embodies the dynamics of the system, but from a practical point of view, creating a controller to maintain the desired stable state of the system would be difficult due to the problem of obtaining accurate sensor measurements for each of the four required parameters. We can overcome this difficulty by rewriting Eq. (8.20) as a difference equation that approximates the required balancing force by using state measurements taken at the current time, and at the time step immediately prior to the current time. Thus,

$$f(t) \cong \alpha\,\mathrm{sgn}\left((a+b)x(t) - bx(t-1) + (c+d)\theta(t) - d\theta(t-1)\right) \qquad (8.21)$$

This is as far as we can take the design of a conventional process controller, because we have no *a priori* knowledge of the values of the coefficients a, b, c, and d. If we did, we could continue the design by solving the differential equation using the techniques described in Section 8.1, and by constructing a feedback control system to achieve the desired results. However, the design we would create would be application specific; that is, we could not reuse the system to solve a similar problem without again going through the analysis process.

Let us now investigate how a neural network can be used to solve this control problem. In the process, we shall explore some of the advantages the neural-network solution has over the conventional controller design.

8.2.2   Neurocontroller Design

The application of a *neurocontroller* to the problem of pole balancing was first described by Professor Bernard Widrow, of Stanford University, in 1962 [11]. Professor Widrow revisited the problem in 1987, when, with graduate student Viral Tolat, the problem was recast from a simply mechanical application to one that relied on human visual perception to provide the necessary feedback to

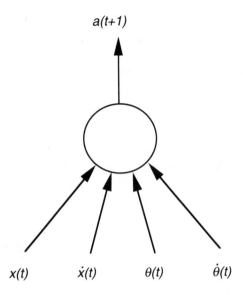

Figure 8.7   The Adaline network used by Professor Widrow to control the cart/pole-balancer system is shown. The adaline is essentially a single unit BPN. The inputs and output of the device are described in the text.

control the cart. We shall begin with Professor Widrow's original solution, and then show how the application was revised to utilize the visual feedback.

Professor Widrow's original approach was based on the use of an Adaline[2] that took the four monitored signals ($x(t)$, $\dot{x}(t)$, θ, and $\dot{\theta}(t)$) as input, and learned to produce a signal indicating the required acceleration needed to maintain the pole near the vertical. The architecture of this control network is illustrated in Figure 8.7.

The exemplar data used to train the Adaline was collected from an operational, closed-loop proportional controller that was designed specifically for the experiment.[3] For training purposes, all four sensor parameters were scaled prior to presentation to the Adaline to values that ranged between -1 and 1. Similarly, the force applied to the cart, which is the target output for the Adaline, was recorded and scaled for each set of input parameters. Widrow reported that the Adaline required less than 100 presentations of the 250 training exemplars collected from the conventional controller to learn to keep the pole balanced.

In another discussion of the application, Robert Hecht-Nielsen [3] describes

---

2. An ADAptive LINear Element, which is essentially a single-unit network with connections adapted using the LMS algorithm.

3. You may note the irony here, in that a classical controller had to be developed to train the neurocontroller.

how the neurocontroller developed by Widrow is able to keep the cart in the center of the track. In essence, a false bias signal, which is linearly dependent on the position of the cart ($x(t)$), is added to the $\theta(t)$ indicator supplied to the neurocontroller after training. Thus, the neurocontroller receives inputs that indicate that the pole is leaning slightly toward the center of the track, and initiates the corrective force needed to center the pole. As a side effect, the cart moves toward the center of the track.

8.2.3   Vision-Based Neurocontroller

In a paper published in 1988, Viral Tolat and Professor Widrow [10] described an experiment conducted to determine if it were possible to construct a neuro-pole balancer that could be trained using subjective visual assessments of the situation, rather than purely objective measurements. It is interesting that, while a child can quite easily balance a broomstick in her hand, most people cannot balance a two-dimensional broomstick if forced to rely only on vision. It seems that when we manually balance a pole, we receive most of the information about the state of the pole through our sense of touch.[4] Without tactile feedback, balancing the computer-generated simulation of a pole attached to a cart is virtually impossible for a human in real time.

Tolat and Widrow overcame this difficulty by slowing the simulation to $1/30^{\text{th}}$ of real time, and by allowing the human trainer to compare two images of the system side-by-side: one to represent the current state of the system, and, next to it, the image representing the state of the system at the time step immediately prior to the current time step.

As illustrated in Figure 8.8, the network used to perform this experiment was again an Adaline, this time having 111 input connections instead of the four used in the earlier experiment. The dimension of the input pattern was determined by the pixel image used to represent the state of the pole (a 5×11 binary image), which was doubled in order to allow simultaneous presentation of the current and last state images. Tolat and Widrow also used a *bias* input to the Adaline, for reasons described in Chapter 2. The concatenation of these two, 55 pixel image patterns with the bias signal comprise the 111 input elements needed to represent the state of the system.

The output of the Adaline is interpreted as a simple indicator of the direction of the force needed to maintain the pole in an upright position. Because it was assumed that the force applied to the cart would be a constant value, the linear output of the Adaline was converted into a bipolar value by taking the sign of the linear output and using that as the output value. This conversion is equivalent to running the linear output of the Adaline through a binary threshold unit before allowing the output to be used externally.

---

4. You can prove this to yourself by trying a simple experiment. Close your eyes and try to balance a pole in your hand. Chances are that you will have no problem.

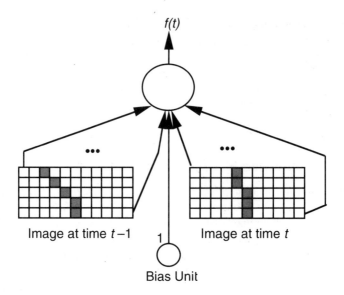

f(t)

Image at time *t* −1   1   Image at time *t*

Bias Unit

Figure 8.8   The architecture of the Adaline used to solve the cart/pole-balancing problem using visual supervision is shown. The operation of this device is described in the text. *Source: Adapted from* An adaptive 'broom balancer' with visual inputs [10]. *Used with permission. Copyright ©1988 IEEE.*

The Adaline was trained by collecting all combinations of five cart positions (far left, near left, center, near right, far right) with 13 different pole angles. These 65 images were then shown to a human trainer sequentially, with the computer determining the next image to be shown based on the current state of the system and the user's response to the situation. As the images were presented, the computer displayed for the user the current and last state images, and recorded these displays as the input pattern for the exemplar. The output associated with the input pattern was the user's action: a −1 to indicate an application of the control force to move the cart to the left, and a +1 to indicate the user's desire to move to the right.

Tolat and Widrow collected one training exemplar for each of the 4,225 possible situations (65^2 image combinations), and used this information to train the Adaline. They found that the Adaline could solve the problem, maintaining the pole in an upright position, after fewer than 50 complete training cycles.[5] Figure 8.9 illustrates the results of training as described by Tolat and Widrow.

---

5. A training cycle is the presentation of each input pattern in the training set, along with the update cycle to adjust the connection weights after every pattern presentation. In most network simulations, this is also referred to as a training *epoch*, a term derived from the geological analogy to the amount of computer time needed to perform the training cycle.

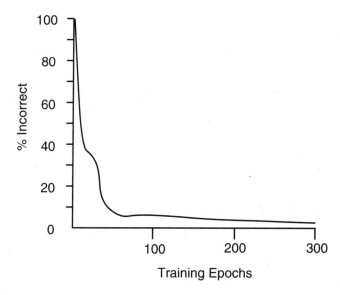

Figure 8.9   This graph shows the error of the Adaline during training to learn the visual pole-balancing application. In this diagram, the vertical axis represents the percentage of errors made by the adaline during a training cycle, and the horizontal axis represents the training cycle progression. Note that the final error of the network was not zero, but was an acceptably low value for the number of patterns it was being asked to learn ($\frac{4}{4,225} = 0.094\%$ error).

8.2.4   Conventional and Neurocontroller Comparison

Let us now compare the neural-network solution developed by Tolat and Widrow with the conventional control solution. From inspection of Eq. (8.21), which we present again for convenience, we can see remarkable similarity between the analytical model represented by the difference equation model and the implementation of the Adaline network.

$$f(t) \cong \alpha \operatorname{sgn}\big((a + b)x(t) - bx(t - 1) + (c + d)\theta(t) - d\theta(t - 1)\big)$$

In each model, the output is a simple, bipolar indication of the direction of the force needed to keep the pole balanced. If we let $\alpha = 1$, Eq. (8.21) tells us that the direction of the force needed to keep the pole balanced is dictated by the current and previous states of the system, as indicated by the position of the cart ($x(t)$) and the angular position of the pole ($\theta(t)$).

Given that we can adequately describe all potential configurations of the system in 4,225 current and last-state images, and represent each of the two state images as a 111-element input pattern, the network solution is equivalent to a best-fit solution to 4,225 simultaneous, linear equations having 111 unknowns. Moreover, the Adaline finds a solution to the problem without having to know in advance the empirical values of the difference equation coefficients. This observation suggests that the neural-network controller is readily modified to other, similar applications without requiring a time-consuming analysis of the system, a benefit not found in the conventional controller solution.

Another interesting aspect of this neurocontroller application is that the Adaline finds a solution to the problem without requiring any sensory input, other than the image information representing the state of the system. This suggests that the visual representation of the state of the system contains a wealth of information that can be used to infer the explicit parameters required by a conventional controller, such as the exact position of the cart and pole.

8.3   BIPEDAL-LOCOMOTION CONTROL

Another interesting application of neural-network control was developed by D. M. A. Lee and Professor W. H. ElMaraghy [5] of the University of Western Ontario, in Canada. In this application, Mssr. Lee and Dr. ElMaraghy created a dynamic model of a bipedal walking device, and then developed a scheme to use two BPNs to control the application of torque to the hip joints, thus enabling the biped system to "walk."

While the walking device described in their paper was never actually built, Lee and ElMaraghy simulated the dynamic model of the walker on a computer. Their results show how an adaptive neurocontroller can provide a more robust control response than conventional control techniques. Indeed, the ability of the neurocontroller to generate the control response needed to keep the system stable, even when presented with situations that were not anticipated in the training scenarios, is quite impressive.

8.3.1   Biped Dynamic Model

Modeling all of the dynamics associated with bipedal locomotion in three dimensions is an awesome problem. Even a simple model must account for any roll, pitch, or yaw induced in the body mass, the interaction between the application of torque at the hip joint and the response of the legs at the knees and foot, the interaction between the mass of the foot and contact with the ground, and the weight transfer between the legs as the biped strides. To simplify the dynamics of the model, and hence the control system for their experiment, Lee and ElMaraghy limited their investigation to a biped walker constrained to the sagittal plane. They further simplified their dynamic model by

- Considering the legs to be kneeless.
- Lumping the head, arms, and trunk of the walker into a single body mass.
- Considering the feet to be massless.
- Assuming instantaneous support exchange between the right and left legs.
- Traversing only level terrain.

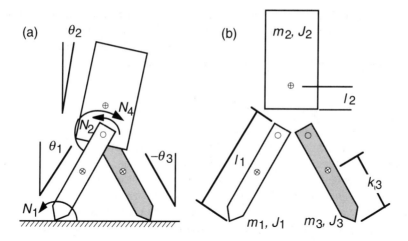

Figure 8.10 The bipedal walker model described in the text is illustrated in these figures. (a) This figure shows the interpretation of the forces and angles utilized by the model from a system perspective. (b) An exploded view of the model, illustrating the details of each mass and the parameters used to construct the model. *Source: Adapted from* A neural network solution for bipedalgait synthesis [5]. *Used with permission. Copyright ©1992 IEEE.*

Mass	Mass Moment of Inertia	Length
		$l_1 = 0.933\,\text{m}$
$m_1 = 12.2\,\text{kg}$	$J_1 = 0.697\,\text{kg}\cdot m^2$	$k_1 = 0.546\,\text{m}$
$m_2 = 49.0\,\text{kg}$	$J_2 = 2.350\,\text{kg}\cdot m^2$	$l_2 = 0.280\,\text{m}$
$m_3 = 12.2\,\text{kg}$	$J_3 = 0.697\,\text{kg}\cdot m^2$	$l_3 = 0.933\,\text{m}$
		$k_3 = 0.546\,\text{m}$

Table 8.1 This table contains the physical parameters used to model the biped walker. The interpretation of these data is in the text.

The model of the walker used by Lee and ElMaraghy is depicted in Figure 8.10, and the values used to describe the physical characteristics of the model are presented in Table 8.1. The equations describing the dynamics of the model are derived in Mssr. Lee's master's thesis [4], which we shall not replicate here, for brevity.

The biped walker described by this model propels itself forward by applying a torque to the legs in alternating hip joints. The leg in contact with the ground supports the weight of the walker while the other leg swings into position for the next stride. When the swinging leg contacts the ground surface, two things happen simultaneously: The velocity of the moving leg is instantly reduced to zero, which induces a reactive force in the body mass, and the weight of the biped is transferred from the rearward leg to the forward leg. After completing one forward stride, control switches to the forward leg, allowing the biped to mirror its actions, which results in another forward stride. The entire process repeats indefinitely, halting only when the walker stumbles and falls.

8.3.2   Controlling the Biped

From the previous description of a bipedal walking device, let us now consider the strategy employed by Lee and ElMaraghy to control the gait of the biped. They assumed that the biped was initially provided with a "kick-start" impetus to initiate its gait. Once started, the momentum from the previous step, coupled with the torque provided by the system controller was used to sustain the gait and balance of the biped. Using conventional linear control methods, a controller was developed to generate the torques required to sustain a *specific* gait; however, because the biped is an inherently unstable dynamic model and the controller was designed using a linear approximation of the system, the conventional controller could only sustain the gait for a few seconds.

At this point, Lee and ElMaraghy modified the architecture of the control system to incorporate two BPN neural networks as adaptive control elements. As shown in Figure 8.11, each network learned to control the application of torque to a specific leg by observing the output of the linear controller and correlating that output to the state of the system.

For training purposes, the system state was sampled at 10 millisecond intervals. At each discrete time step, the state of the system was captured and represented as a six-element vector, $\mathbf{x}(t)$, of the form

$$\mathbf{x}(t) = \theta_1(t), \dot{\theta}_1(t), \theta_2(t), \dot{\theta}_2(t), \theta_3(t), \dot{\theta}_3(t) \tag{8.22}$$

where $\theta_1(t)$ represents the angle of the left leg with respect to the vertical, $\theta_2(t)$ indicates the angle of the body mass, $\theta_3(t)$ represents the angular position of the right leg, and the time rate of change for each measurement is indicated by the derivative notation. For each input state pattern, the corresponding output from the two conventional controllers (N_2, N_4) was captured and stored as the target output vector.

8.3.3   Control-State Representation

In their paper, Lee and ElMaraghy do not discuss how they chose to represent the state information for the neurocontroller. They allude to the use of one unit for each parameter, but, as we shall now describe, that simple representation poses a slight problem. Let us diverge from our architecture discussion for a moment, then, and consider the problem of data representation for the neural network. Please note that the scheme we suggest here is most likely different from the technique employed by the original authors.

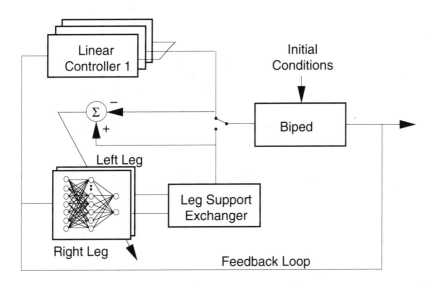

Figure 8.11 The architecture developed to train the neural-network gait controllers is shown. In this diagram, the output of the linear controller is used as the target output for the neural network. The state of the system, indicated by the feedback loop, is simultaneously fed to the linear controller and the neurocontrollers. Thus, the neural networks "learned" to mimic the response of the linear controller for a variety of situations. *Source: Adapted from* A neural network solution for bipedalgait synthesis [5]. *Used with permission. Copyright ©1992 IEEE.*

Because we have elected to represent the state of the biped as a set of specific measurements, we must find a way of representing that information in a form usable by the BPN we have selected. For this application, each parameter was measured in degrees from the vertical, while the velocity parameters are indicated in degrees per second. Thus, each measurement could legally take on a value between zero and 359.

Practically, however, angles larger than 90 degrees are never encountered, unless the biped toppled over. Because the vertical axis was chosen as the reference, we can use the scheme suggested by Lee and ElMaraghy, which is to represent as positive those angles that are to the right of vertical, and as negative those angles to the left of vertical.

To convert these data into a format suitable for use by the neural network, we could simply scale the parameter to a value between zero and one. This approach is complicated by the fact that we cannot know beforehand the maximum or minimum values for each parameter. For example, during normal operation, the angle of the leg may vary between −20 degrees and +20 degrees. Using the by-now familiar scaling technique, we would call the positive 20-degree measurement the +1 limit, and the negative 20-degree measurement the 0 limit.

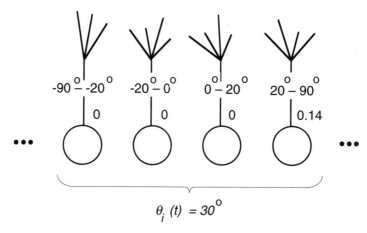

Figure 8.12 This diagram illustrates the use of multiple input units to represent different ranges of input values. Using this scheme, each input parameter (e.g., $\theta_i(t)$) would be represented by four input elements.

However, when the biped stumbles, the angle of the leg may jump to 70 degrees or more. Using our scaled representation, that measurement would produce a scaled input of $+3.5$. Because we must maintain input values between zero and one, however, we must come up with another scheme.

One method for overcoming the scaling difficulty is to use multiple input units to represent different ranges of input values, and scale the inputs to each of these units between the minimum and maximum values of the ranges. This idea is illustrated in Figure 8.12. Using this scheme, we could use four input units to represent all possible values for the leg angle: The first unit would represent angles between -90 degrees and -20 degrees; the second unit would encode angles between -20 degrees and 0 degrees; the third unit would indicate angles between 0 degrees and $+20$ degrees, and the fourth unit would indicate angles between $+20$ degrees and $+90$ degrees. Note that there is no requirement that the range of values represented by the four units be uniform.

8.3.4 Training the Neurocontroller

Lee and ElMaraghy reported collecting 7,584 training exemplars for each network. At the sampling rate cited, this represents almost 76 seconds of data produced by the conventional controllers. From this, we can deduce that the training data must have been collected over many simulations, as the authors indicate that the conventional controller could not maintain the gait for more than two seconds before the biped became unstable and fell.

The two neurocontrollers (again, one for each leg) were trained simultaneously on a Sun Sparcstation computer system. Training required 50 hours of computer time for the networks to converge on a solution.

8.3.5 Results of the Experiment

Once trained, the neurocontrollers were enabled and the output from the conventional controller was disabled. The biped simulation was then initiated by applying the initial impetus vector,

$$\mathbf{x}_0(t) = 17.0°, 70.2°/\text{sec}, 0°, 0°/\text{sec}, 17.6°, 75.8°/\text{sec} \qquad (8.23)$$

which corresponds to a leg stride of 0.544 meters and an average forward speed of 0.853 meters/second.

The neurocontroller was able to sustain the gait consistently for more than 25 seconds. Even more fascinating is the observed response of the neurocontrollers in periods of high instability. Lee and ElMaraghy report that, approximately seven seconds into the simulation, the biped slows and the upper-body mass begins to topple backward. However, the neurocontroller is able to avert the unstable condition by applying the leg torque needed to compensate for the situation. As a result, the biped continues walking for another 19 seconds before it fails.

In this simple experiment, the neurocontroller-based biped simulation consistently outperformed the conventional controller by a wide margin. Figure 8.13

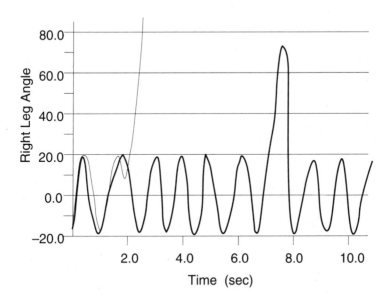

Figure 8.13 This graph illustrates the observed performance of the right leg controller for the biped simulation. The heavy line represents the response of the leg to the neurocontroller, and the thin line indicates the performance of the conventional controller. Notice the stability of the neurocontroller and its ability to compensate in an unstable situation. *Source: Adapted from* A neural network solution for bipedal gait synthesis [5]. *Used with permission. Copyright ©1992 IEEE.*

illustrates the performance graphs for the neurocontroller and the conventional controller for the first 10 seconds of the simulation.

Perhaps even more intriguing is the visible image of the walking biped. Given the static nature of paper and ink, it is difficult to convey the subtleties of the interaction between legs and body, each working together to maintain a stable gait. However, watching such a simulation as it is running, when the image of the biped appears on the video screen in animated form, is remarkably similar to the experience of watching a child take its first steps.[6] In Figure 8.14 we illustrate the dynamics of the walking biped.

8.4   ROBOTIC MANIPULATOR CONTROL

In the previous section, we saw how a neural network could be used to control the application of a control force to a robotic device to maintain the stability of the robot. We shall now investigate the use of a neurocontroller to solve the **inverse-kinematics** problem in a simple robotic manipulator. We shall begin with a description of the problem domain, describing the mathematical models of the robotic system that we seek to control. Then, we shall describe how researchers Jenhwa Guo and Vladimir Cherkassky [2] of the University of Minnesota developed a neurocontroller based on the Hopfield memory model to implement an effective control strategy.

8.4.1   Kinematics Model

Kinematics is the study of the geometry of a manipulator arm as it relates to the position of the arm with respect to the movement of the manipulator linkages, or joints. In most robotic arm models, the position and orientation of the manipulator is directly controlled by the movement of the joints. Yet, a typical control model for such a manipulator, such as the one illustrated in Figure 8.15, has no means of assessing the position of the arm in space. Rather, the control is based on movement commands provided to the controller in the form of desired velocity parameters for the controllable joints.

To construct a controller of this type, we must begin by describing our reference points for the manipulator. First, let $\mathbf{q}$ be the n-dimensional vector describing the desired movement parameters for a controllable joint with n degrees of freedom, and $\mathbf{x}$ be the m-dimensional vector describing the position of the manipulator in m space. The general form of the kinematics equation describing the relationship between $\mathbf{q}$ and $\mathbf{x}$ is given by

$$\mathbf{x} = f(\mathbf{q}) \tag{8.24}$$

---

6. I know my daughter will forgive me for the comparison, but I think the biped is significantly more stable than she was when she took her first few steps.

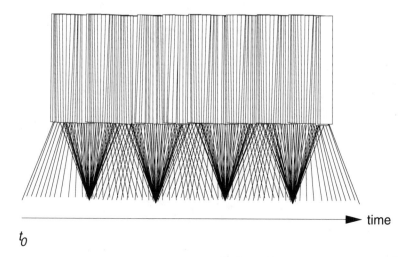

Figure 8.14   This diagram illustrates the gait of the biped as it "learns" to walk. for brevity, we have only illustrated the first five seconds of the simulation. *Source: Adapted from* A neural network solution for bipedal gait synthesis [5]. *Used with permission. Copyright ©1992 IEEE.*

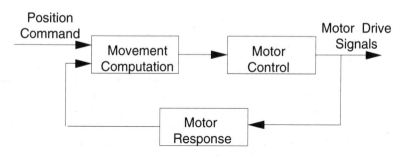

Figure 8.15   A block diagram illustrating a typical control model for a robotic manipulator system is shown. The response of the model is described in the text.

We assume here that the **mapping function**, $f(\mathbf{q})$, is a continuous, nonlinear function with a well-understood structure. The inverse-kinematics equation, given by

$$\mathbf{q} = f^{-1}(\mathbf{x}) \tag{8.25}$$

is then simply the inverse mapping function from Cartesian space position to joint movement command.

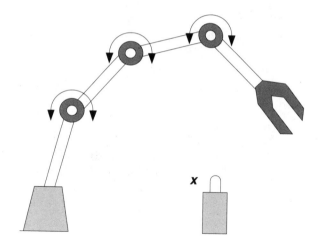

Figure 8.16 This diagram illustrates the inverse-kinematics problem in robotic arm control. The joint shown in this diagram has three degrees of freedom. We want to move the manipulator at the end of the arm from its current position in two-dimensional space to point x. Because the arm has more degrees of freedom than the dimension of the movement space, we have several alternative control vectors that we could use to cause the arm to move to the desired position. This means that the proper control vector must be determined numerically, because there is no *closed-form* method to determine the best alternative.

Considering the nature of the problem, it is easy to see the difficulty in determining the appropriate command vector $\mathbf{q}(t)$ needed to move an arm to an arbitrary position, x: While the target position of the manipulator is fixed in Cartesian space, there are cases where there are many different movement commands that produce the desired end position. As shown in Figure 8.16, the problem for the system controller is how to determine *beforehand* the command vector that is going to produce the best results with minimal wasted motion.

For those cases where a closed-form solution to Eq. (8.24) does not exist, Guo and Cherkessky suggest using a technique based on the differential motion between the joint displacements and the target location. Specifically, they let

$$\dot{\mathbf{x}} = \mathbf{J}(\mathbf{q})\dot{\mathbf{q}} \qquad (8.26)$$

where $\dot{\mathbf{q}}$ and $\dot{\mathbf{x}}$ are joint and Cartesian velocities, respectively, and $\mathbf{J}(\mathbf{q})$ is the $m \times n$ Jacobian matrix determined by $\partial \mathbf{f}/\partial \mathbf{q}$.

Using this formulation, for cases where $\mathbf{J}$ is square and nonsingular,[7] the actuator velocity vector, $\dot{\mathbf{q}}$, can be determined by

---

7. When the manipulator is nonredundant, meaning $m = n$, and the system has no closed-form solution, the Jacobian matrix will be square and nonsingular.

$$\dot{\mathbf{q}} = \mathbf{J}^{-1}\dot{\mathbf{x}} \qquad (8.27)$$

Similarly, when the manipulator is overcompensated,[8] Eq. (8.26) can be inverted as

$$\dot{\mathbf{q}} = \mathbf{J}^{+}(\mathbf{q})\dot{\mathbf{x}} \qquad (8.28)$$

where $\mathbf{J}^{+}$ is the Moore-Penrose pseudo-inverse of the Jacobian matrix, and is given by

$$\mathbf{J}^{+} = \mathbf{J}^{T}(\mathbf{J}\mathbf{J}^{T})^{-1} \qquad (8.29)$$

From these relationships, Guo and Cherkassky develop an energy equation similar to Hopfield's traveling salesperson energy equation. Specifically, they begin by formulating an energy equation that minimizes least-mean squared error in the Cartesian velocity vector, given as

$$E = \frac{1}{2}\sum_{i=1}^{m}(\dot{x}_i^{d} - \dot{x}_i)^2 \qquad (8.30)$$

where $\dot{x}_i^{d}$ is the desired Cartesian velocity component. Then, from Eq. (8.26),

$$\dot{x}_i = \sum_{j=1}^{n} J_{ij}\dot{q}_j \qquad (8.31)$$

where J_{ij} is a function of joint displacements. By combining Eqs. (8.30) and (8.31), Guo and Cherkassky derive the energy function for the system as

$$E = -\frac{1}{2}\sum_{\substack{j=1 \\ i=1}}^{n} T_{ij}\dot{q}_i\dot{q}_j - \frac{1}{2}\sum_{j=1}^{n} I_j\dot{q}_j + \frac{1}{2}\sum_{i=1}^{m}\dot{x} \qquad (8.32)$$

where

$$T_{ij} = -\sum_{l=1}^{m} J_{li}J_{lj}$$

and

$$I_j = \sum_{i=1}^{m} J_{ij}\dot{x}_i^{d}$$

---

8. An overcompensated manipulator is characterized by the conditions $m < n$ and $\mathrm{rank}(\mathbf{J}) = m$.

Guo and Cherkassky then implement a novel version of the Hopfield memory by defining a method of adapting the connection weights of the network over time. They accomplish this feat by taking the derivative with respect to time of Eq. (8.32) and simplifying, to produce a dynamic equation that can be used to describe the temporal evolution of the network connection weight matrix. Specifically, they define the energy function for the network as a function of time, given by

$$\frac{d\mathrm{E}}{dt} = -\sum_{i=1}^{n} \frac{d\dot{q}_i}{dt} \left(\sum_{j=1}^{n} T_{ij}\dot{q}_j + I_i \right) \qquad (8.33)$$

If we further assume that k_i is an arbitrary, positive value, Guo and Cherkassky assert that the equation governing the time evolution of each network unit is given by the equation

$$\frac{d\dot{q}_i}{dt} = k_i \left(\sum_{j=1}^{n} T_{ij}\dot{q}_j + I_i \right) \qquad (8.34)$$

Inspection of Eqs. (8.33) and (8.34) reveals that the energy function for the system is always negative; hence, the energy in the system will always decrease as time progresses. This observation confirms that the mathematical control model suggested by Guo and Cherkassky can indeed by implemented as a Hopfield memory. We shall now investigate this method of implementation.

8.4.2   Neurocontroller Design

As you recall from Chapter 2, the Hopfield memory is a neural-network structure comprised of a single layer of processing elements with connections that feed back into all other units in the network. External inputs are supplied, one to each unit, and the network is then iterated until the units achieve a stable state. Once stabilized, the output values from each unit are interpreted in a manner indicated by the particular application.

To design a Hopfield model neurocontroller for the inverse-kinematics problem, we shall consider an arm that has n degrees of freedom; that is, the arm shall contain n joints, each of which has the ability to rotate in at least one direction. From the original statement of the problem, we know the desired end position of the manipulator, and we need to know the command vector for the arm that will produce the desired end position. Because we have chosen to cast the problem with respect to velocity parameters for each robotic joint, we shall model the Hopfield memory such that the steady-state output from each unit in the network is interpreted as the appropriate velocity indicator for a corresponding joint. This neurocontrol model is illustrated in Figure 8.17.

From Eq. (8.34), we can see that the state of each Hopfield unit is determined by the external input, I_i, and the sum of the outputs from all units, $\dot{q}_j$, through

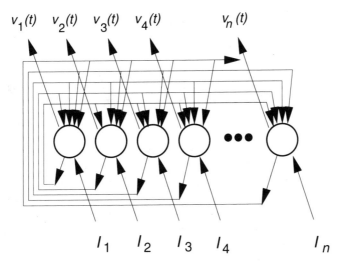

Figure 8.17 This diagram illustrates the use of a Hopfield memory to control an *n*-degree-of-freedom robotic arm. The output from each unit in the network is interpreted as the velocity parameter for its corresponding joint, after the network has achieved its stable condition.

their corresponding connection weights, T_{ij}. From our earlier definition of T_{ij}, we know that the connection weights in the network are determined by the Jacobian matrix from the energy equation. Thus, at every discrete time step in the simulation of the network, we simply update the connection weights and input parameters based on the state of the controller, and perform one signal propagation through the network. We repeat this process for each time step until the network stabilizes. At that point, the energy function, and hence the controller error, has been minimized, and the output values from the processing elements can be used to control the movement of the arm joints.

Guo and Cherkassky provide no indication of how input and output values should be scaled to provide the appropriate control signal. However, this is not a critical issue for our purposes, because the range of values needed to control the arm will depend on the physical implementation of the controller. We need only recognize that it may be necessary to scale input and output values to values between -1 and $+1$, to limit the magnitude of the signals propagated through the Hopfield network.

8.4.3 Neurocontroller Results

In order to understand the performance of the neurocontroller developed in the previous section, Guo and Cherkassky compare the Hopfield formulation of the control equations with the model of a closed-loop dynamic system. Specifically, they rewrite Eq. (8.34) as

$$\frac{d\dot{\mathbf{q}}}{dt} = \mathbf{k}(-\mathbf{J}^{\mathrm{T}}\mathbf{J}\dot{\mathbf{q}} + \mathbf{J}^{\mathrm{T}}\dot{\mathbf{x}}^d) \tag{8.35}$$

$$= -\mathbf{k}\mathbf{J}^{\mathrm{T}}(\dot{\mathbf{x}} - \dot{\mathbf{x}}^d)$$

by substituting the definitions for T_{ij} and I_i in Eq. (8.34) and simplifying. By then substituting the formulation of Eq (8.35) into the energy equation for the system, they obtain

$$\frac{d\mathrm{E}}{dt} = -(\dot{\mathbf{x}} - \dot{\mathbf{x}}^d)^{\mathrm{T}}\mathbf{J}\mathbf{K}\mathbf{J}^{\mathrm{T}}(\dot{\mathbf{x}} - \dot{\mathbf{x}}^d) \tag{8.36}$$

$$\leq -\sigma_J\lambda_K|\dot{\mathbf{x}} - \dot{\mathbf{x}}^d|^2 \tag{8.37}$$

where σ_J is the minimum eigenvalue of $\mathbf{J}\mathbf{J}^{\mathrm{T}}$ and λ_K is the minimum eigenvalue of **K**. Inspection of Eq. (8.37) indicates that as λ_K increases, network convergence time decreases, thus producing a very rapid solution with the neurocontroller.

    The operation of the controller was tested using a four-degree-of-freedom ($n = 4$) robotic arm simulation moving in a planar environment ($m = 2$). For $K_j = 10$, the Hopfield network converged on a solution in 20 milliseconds, and, for $K_j = 20$, a solution was achieved in 10 milliseconds. In both cases, the error produced by the neurocontroller was less than 0.05 degrees/second. Also, as you might expect, the solution obtained was independent of the degrees of freedom in the arm, a distinct advantage over conventional numerical techniques.

8.5   CONTROL-APPLICATION SUMMARY

In this chapter, we have examined several process-control applications that use neural networks in place of the conventional, analytical models. We have seen how neural networks offer a means of rapidly developing applications that solve the desired control functions without requiring a major investment in time and effort, as would be required to develop the equivalent analytical system models. Furthermore, we have shown how neural networks have been used successfully to address control problems that were previously viewed as intractable, either from an analytical perspective, or from an implementation point of view.

    This is not to say that neurocontrollers will make all conventional control applications obsolete. They will not. However, in many applications it is prudent to develop models of a system that can be rapidly, and cost effectively, evaluated. Under such circumstances, neurocontrollers may offer a good prototyping tool.

    Even in those applications that require extensive analysis in order to develop precision control systems, the use of neural networks to model an application prior to analysis can provide insights to the system designer that might otherwise be overlooked. Adaptive networks tend to find their own methods for encoding relationships between system input and output during learning. If we invest a little time and effort to "dissect" a trained network, we may discover that the internal representation scheme developed by a trained network is not far removed from the method that a detailed system analysis would indicate as the optimal method for controlling a system. If so, the use of neural networks could save quite a bit of time in the early stages of process-control system design.

SUGGESTED READINGS

The literature contains many papers describing control-systems applications of neural networks. We have only touched on the topic in this chapter. Readers interested in learning more about conventional control methods are referred to two excellent texts on the subject: *Industrial Process Control Systems*, by Dale R. Patrick and Stephen W. Fardo [8], presents a solid theoretical foundation of the technology; and *Understanding Electronic Control of Energy Systems*, by Don L. Cannon and Gerald Lueke [1], provides a thorough examination of the practical issues of the technology.

Readers interested in investigating the fundamentals of robotics and robotic control systems are referred to the text by Matthew T. Mason and J. Kenneth Salisbury [6], which describes the foundations of robotic manipulators. With regard to neurocontrol applications, the best texts currently available are the annual proceedings of the Neural Information Processing Systems, Natural and Synthetic (NIPS) conferences sponsored by the IEEE. Each year, approximately one dozen excellent papers are published in those proceedings describing practical applications of robotic neurocontrol. Another good source for technical papers pertaining to robotic neurocontrol is the proceedings of the IEEE Conference on Neural Networks, published annually by the IEEE press.

BIBLIOGRAPHY

1. Don L. Cannon and Gerald Lueke. *Understanding Electronic Control of Energy Systems*, Charles W. Battle, editor. Texas Instruments, Dallas, TX, 1982.

2. Jenhwa Guo and Vladimir Cherkassky. A solution to the inverse kinematics problem in robotics using neural network processing. In *Proceedings of the International Joint Conference on Neural Networks*, Washington, DC, pp. II(299–304), June 1989.

3. Robert Hecht-Nielsen. *Neurocomputing*, Addison-Wesley, Reading, MA, pp. 342–344, 1990.

4. D. M. A. Lee. *A Neural Network Approach to Biped Locomotion and Postural Stability*. M.E.Sc. Thesis, The University of Western Ontario, London, Ontario, Canada, May 1991.

5. D. M. A. Lee and W. H. ElMaraghy. A neural network solution for bipedal gait synthesis. In *Proceedings of the International Joint Conference on Neural Networks*, Baltimore, MD, pp. II(763–768), July 1992.

6. Matthew T. Mason and J. Kenneth Salisbury, Jr. *Robot Hands and the Mechanics of Manipulation*. MIT Press, Cambridge, MA, 1985.

7. O. Mayer. *The Origins of Feedback Control*. MIT Press, Cambridge, MA, 1970.

8. Dale R. Patrick and Stephen W. Fardo. *Industrial Process Control Systems*. H. W. Sams Publishing Company, Indianapolis, IN, 1979.

9. Lennart Räde and Bertil Westergren. *Beta Mathematics Handbook*, second edition. CRC Press, Boca Raton, FL, 1989.

10. Viral V. Tolat and Bernard Widrow. An adaptive 'broom balancer' with Visual Inputs. In *Proceedings of the International Conference on Neural Networks*, IEEE Press, New York, NY, pp. II(641–647), July 1988.

11. Bernard Widrow. The original adaptive neural net broom balancer. In *Proceedings of the International Symposium on Circuits and Systems,* pp. 351–357, May 1987.

Fuzzy Neural Systems

In this world, nothing is certain but death and taxes.
— Benjamin Franklin

Life is replete with ambiguity. We all make countless daily decisions that are based on incomplete, or inexact information, unconsciously acknowledging the fact that life experiences are rarely black or white, on or off, or yes or no. Often, our judgment is influenced by our own situation. For example, if asked to describe my physical appearance, I would probably use any (or all) of the following phrases:

Medium build, *average* height, *dark* hair.

From these phrases, you have likely constructed a mental image of my appearance. But how does your imagined image compare to my true appearance? What, exactly, constitutes *average* height? If you are an American, the phrase *average height* probably means that I am somewhere between 170 and 180 centimeters (cm) tall. If you are Japanese, however, *average height* probably means that I stand somewhere between 160 and 170 cm tall. Because you (probably) do not know my heritage, it is very likely that each reader will have a slightly different impression of my appearance. This example only touches on the diversity of life in the real world.

Yet, almost paradoxically, we have insisted on creating computing systems that operate on *binary* information, systems that interpret and manipulate objects in the real world based on decisions that can only be cast as *true* or *false*. Obviously, we have excluded, or at least *complicated*, the automatic processing of many real-world applications, simply because the information is difficult to represent in a binary form. This is not to say that computing systems cannot be programmed to address these applications—many such systems have already been created. However, when building any system, it always makes sense to use the proper tool for the job.

243

In previous chapters, we have shown how neural networks have provided an alternative technology in many real-world applications. In several of the examples we have studied, the neural network was used to perform a subfunction in the overall system operation. The particular service performed by the network was the piece of the application that was best suited to interpretation, in that the information to be processed by the network was imprecise, incomplete, or otherwise imperfect. In this chapter, we shall explore the integration of neural networks and **fuzzy logic,** two complementary technologies that are designed to process non-binary information. In so doing, we shall show how the combination of these two technologies can provide system solutions that are much more appropriate in many real world applications, and, hence, much less complex.

We shall begin with an overview of fuzzy logic, to introduce the concepts underlying that discipline, and to show how fuzzy systems are constructed and used in real applications. Following that, we shall begin our investigation into the integration of fuzzy logic and neural networks, showing how the combination of these technologies can produce synergistic results.

9.1   FUZZY LOGIC

How many grains constitute a *pile* of sand? One hundred? One thousand? From another perspective, if we start with a pile of sand, how many individual grains can we remove before it ceases to be a pile? Obviously, there is no exact answer to any of these questions. This implies that there is no exact truth in the concept of a pile of sand. There are, however, *varying* degrees of truth. A half-depleted pile of sand is still a pile, just not as big as it was before we started removing sand. This is the essence of fuzzy theory: All things are a matter of degree.

Fuzzy logic, however, is a mathematical technique for understanding, and controlling, specific manifestations of fuzzy theory. It is based on the logical manipulation of continuously variable truth values. As first described by Jan Lukasiewicz [7] in the 1930s, the truth in any assertion can be indicated by a real number in the range [0, 1]. More precisely,

$$t : \{\text{Assertions}\} \longrightarrow [0, 1] \qquad (9.1)$$

where $t : \{x\}$ is the function that indicates the truth of the assertion x [5].

In 1965, Lofti Zadeh [10] published a paper that formally developed the multivalue set theory that has come to be known as fuzzy logic. In that paper, Zadeh showed how the *bivalent indicator function*, I_A of nonfuzzy subset A of X, which is given by

$$I_A(x) = \begin{cases} 1 & \text{if } x \in A \\ 0 & \text{otherwise} \end{cases} \qquad (9.2)$$

could be extended to the multivalued indicator function, μ_A of fuzzy subset A of X, given by

$$\mu_A(x) : X \longrightarrow [0, 1]. \tag{9.3}$$

The significance of the multivalued indicator function, which is also known as the *membership function* for fuzzy sets, is that it allows us to combine fuzzy sets using the standard logic operators, and to measure the degree to which any fuzzy element x belongs to set A. For example,

$$\mu_{A \cap B}(x) = \min(I_A(x), I_B(x)) \tag{9.4}$$

$$\mu_{A \cup B}(x) = \max(I_A(x), I_B(x)) \tag{9.5}$$

$$\mu_{\overline{A}}(x) = 1 - \mu_A(x) \tag{9.6}$$

$$A \subset B \text{ iff } \mu_A(x) < \mu_B(x), \quad \forall x \text{ in } X \tag{9.7}$$

$$\mu_A(x) = \text{Degree}(x \in A) \tag{9.8}$$

9.1.1   A Fuzzy Example

The relationships described in Eqs. (9.4 through 9.8) tell us how we can logically manipulate objects contained in fuzzy sets to evaluate the certainty in any assertion. Before we can apply any of these rules, we must establish a specific *context* for the application. The context of the application defines the **universe of discourse** for the fuzzy set, which ensures that any meaning that we might assign to the **hedges**, or fuzzy subsets, used in classifying the fuzzy set are consistent throughout the analysis.

For example, consider the fuzzy set describing ambient temperature. The hedges we shall use to develop a fuzzy set for this application are *Low, Medium,* and *High.* As shown by the graph in Figure 9.1, these three fuzzy categories overlap each other, such that, within certain ranges of temperature, a specific temperature could simultaneously be considered *Low* and *Medium,* or *Medium* and *High.*

9.1.2   Possibility Theory

In statistics, the **probability** of an event describes the likelihood that a specific event will occur, all other factors being equal. It is an exact method, appropriately applied when all possible situations that can occur in a given event can be uniquely identified. For example, the probability that an evenly balanced coin will turn up *heads* on any given coin toss is exactly 50%. Similarly, the probability that any specific play, denoted by x_i, will win the Texas State Lotto, where a player must match six different numbers between 1 and 50 with six numbers from the same range selected randomly, in any order, is given by

$$p(x_i) = \frac{6!}{(50!/44!)} \tag{9.9}$$

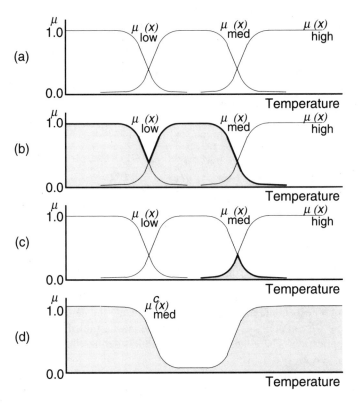

Figure 9.1 These graphs show the relationship between ambient temperature values and the fuzzy categories called *Low, Medium,* and *High.* In all of these graphs, notice the relationship between the fuzzy set operators defined by Eqs. (9.2 through 9.6) and the membership curve as x varies. (a) This graph illustrates the temperature distributions with respect to the fuzzy categories. (b) This graph shows the *union,* or logical disjunction, between the *Low* and *Medium* fuzzy categories. (c) This graph shows the *intersection,* or logical conjunction between the *Medium* and *High* fuzzy categories. (d) This graph shows the *negation,* or logical complement, of the *Medium* category.

This equation says that there are exactly 15,890,700 different combinations of six integers in the range from 1 to 50. The chance that one specific combination chosen on a particular play will match the six randomly selected digits is therefore exactly one in 15,890,700.

There are other constraints on probability theory, all grounded in statistics. One such constraint is that the probabilities associated with each unique situation in a random event must sum to one; otherwise, the event is not truly random. This constraint also ensures a specific, and well-defined **probability distribution** for that event.

However, *possibility* theory describes an elastic constraint on fuzzy variables. A possibility distribution differs from a probability distribution in that it is nonstatistical. Moreover, a possibility distribution is usually derived empirically, because it is often quite difficult to measure the truth content in any practical assertion.

There are, however, relationships between probability and possibility. One intuitive relationship is that impossibility implies improbability. Obviously, if an event x_i on the variable Y is *impossible*, then the probability of event x_i is zero. Another relationship is that a possibility distribution of a variable, Y, forms an upper bound on the probability distribution of Y. These relationships are embodied in the equations

$$\pi_Y(x_i) = 0 \Rightarrow p_Y(x_i) = 0 \qquad \textbf{(9.10)}$$

$$p_Y(x_i) \leq \pi_Y(x_i) \qquad \textbf{(9.11)}$$

where the function $\pi_Y(x_i)$ denotes the *possibility* of event x_i on variable Y, and the function $p_Y(x_i)$ indicates the *probability* of event x_i on variable Y.

Possibility theory also has its own set of constraints. As with probability, where

$$\sum_i p(x_i) = 1 \qquad \textbf{(9.12)}$$

possibility is constrained by the requirement that no value in the distribution can ever be greater than one. In equation form,

$$\max_i \pi(x_i) \leq 1 \qquad \textbf{(9.13)}$$

An example will help clarify the distinction between these two concepts. Suppose you sit down for breakfast one morning and find that eggs are being served. Issues regarding health and cholesterol intake aside, the *probability* that you will eat n eggs at that one meal is given by a Poisson distribution, as shown in Figure 9.2(a). This graph says that it is quite likely that you will eat one egg, and not very likely that you will eat more than three. Figure 9.2(b) illustrates the *possibility* distribution for the same situation. This graph indicates, however, that there is a very good possibility that you could eat as many as three eggs before becoming sated. After that, the possibility quickly abates as it becomes physically impossible to consume additional eggs.

In fuzzy systems, we use these possibility distributions on fuzzy variables, which are also called **measure of belief functions,** to define the hedges in the context of the fuzzy set. As an illustration, recall our earlier example of ambient temperature. The three fuzzy hedges we had defined—*Low, Medium,* and *High*—were actually the possibility distributions for each of these categories. If, for example, the ambient temperature is 20° C, then, according to our hedges, there is a 90% possibility that we would call the temperature *Medium*, a 60% possibility that we would call the same temperature *Hot,* and a virtual impossibility that we would call it *Cold.*

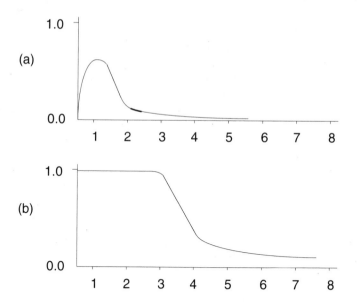

Figure 9.2 These graphs illustrate the differences between probability and possibility. (a) The probability distribution with respect to number of eggs consumed at one meal. (b) The possibility distribution for the same scenario.

9.1.3 Fuzzy Reasoning

Fuzzy reasoning is usually performed in a three-step process. First, the **crisp** variables, which are the precise measurements describing the current state of the system, are acquired and **fuzzified.** Second, knowledge, usually in the form of **fuzzy rules,** is applied to the fuzzified variables, in order to determine the proper course of action. Finally, the outputs from the reasoning logic are **defuzzified,** and are used to control the response of the system.

The reasoning logic, which is performed in the second step of the process described above, is the heart of a fuzzy system. Because we are concerned with systems that measure the truth of the situation as a matter of degree, we shall apply a generalized form of the *modus ponens* [8, 9] reasoning to infer the relationships between the fuzzy variables and control the application of rules in our fuzzy system.

The *modus ponens* rule of inference says that if we are given a truth relationship between two facts and that one fact is known to be true, then we may deduce the second fact. This rule is usually written as

$$
\begin{array}{ll}
\text{Given} & A \rightarrow B \\
& A \\
\hline
\text{Deduce} & B
\end{array}
$$

(9.14)

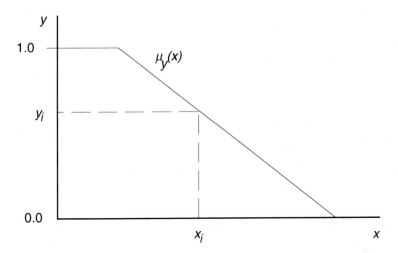

Figure 9.3 This graph illustrates the process of determining the truth content in a fuzzy assertion. The vertical axis on the graph represents the belief in the assertion, while the horizontal axis indicates the values the assertion may take on. The possibility function is shown as the curve on the graph. Given this possibility function, for the specific assertion x_i, the truth value is determined by evaluating the possibility function at x_i. as shown in the graph, the result is y_i.

In fuzzy logic, we generalize the *modus ponens* rule of inference to allow us to deal with continuously variable degrees of truth. Specifically,

$$\begin{array}{ll} \text{Given} & A \rightarrow B \\ & A' \end{array}$$

$$\overline{\qquad\qquad\qquad\qquad}$$

$$\begin{array}{ll} \text{Deduce} & B' \end{array} \qquad\qquad \textbf{(9.15)}$$

where A' is a fuzzy variable that partially matches A. In this case, if we know that A is partially true, then we can infer that B is also partially true. But this inference begs the question: How true is *partially* true?

The most common, and general-purpose, technique for determining the truth content in a fuzzy inference is, quite simply, to use the possibility function for each variable as the truth index for an assertion. Assuming that the possibility function provides a reasonable approximation of the belief in an assertion, we can quantify the truth value for a specific assertion by evaluating the possibility function at the specified value. This process is illustrated in Figure 9.3.

Now that we have established the mechanism of inference in our fuzzy system, let us consider how we might use that mechanism to implement a form of fuzzy reasoning. As we indicated earlier, fuzzy rules embody the knowledge that governs the action of the system. These rules are usually constructed as self-contained *IF-THEN* modules, where the *IF* clause captures the conditions under which the rule is valid, while the statements following the *THEN* indicator control the resulting action. For example, consider the following fuzzy rules:

Rule	1:	Rule	2:
IF	Temperature is *High*	IF	Temperature is *High*
AND	Fan Speed is *Slow*	OR	Fan Speed is *Fast*
THEN	Fan Speed = *Medium*	THEN	Fan Speed = *Medium*

What makes these rules useful in controlling a fuzzy system is that each rule describes the course of action to be taken under a certain set of circumstances. But how do we determine when the prescribed circumstances are satisfied? To do so, we must have a means for *combining* fuzzy indicators to determine our belief in the assertions that define each rule.

9.1.4   Combining Fuzzy Indicators

Inferring responses based on a single indicator, as described by the generalized *modus ponens* rule of inference, is a very straightforward method of reasoning, albeit very simplistic. The most significant problem with this approach is that it does not allow for interrelationships between fuzzy indicators. We shall correct that deficiency by taking advantage of the fuzzy-membership rules described by Eqs. (9.4 through 9.6). Before we can apply these rules, however, we must decide how we shall determine the truth content in multiple fuzzy indicators. As shown in Figure 9.4, there are three methods for accomplishing that goal:

- **Max-Min** inference clips the output of each of the membership functions at the truth level of the assertion.

- **Max-Av** inference averages the level of membership with the belief level in the assertion.

- **Max-Dot** inference scales the output memberships by the belief value for the assertion.

In the ensuing discussion, we shall focus on the max-min technique, although the processes that we shall develop would be appropriate for all three inference methods.

To determine the truth value of Rule 1, the possibility functions for each assertion are *clipped* at the value indicated by the crisp variable. The resulting belief functions are then combined through application of the appropriate logic rule. In this case, we apply Eq. (9.4) because of the conjunctive relationship between the assertions. This process is illustrated in Figure 9.5.

9.1.5   Fuzzy Inference Across Multiple Rules

The technique just described for fuzzy inference is adequate when there is only one rule in the system. To allow multiple rules to exist in a fuzzy environment, we shall modify our inference technique slightly, to allow us to combine the belief

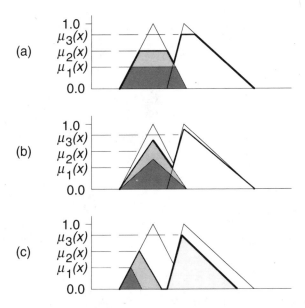

Figure 9.4 These diagrams illustrate the process of determining the truth content across multiple fuzzy assertions. (a) The max-min technique clips the output of each membership function. (b) The max-av method averages the membership values. (c) The max-dot approach scales the membership values.

values obtained across multiple rules. Be aware, however, that a fuzzy system may contain many rules dealing with different aspects of the system operation. In this discussion, we are only concerned with combining rules that operate on the same fuzzy output parameters.

The approach we shall take for combining fuzzy inferences is to geometrically average the belief functions obtained from each inference. We perform the averaging function by disjunctively combining the two-dimensional shapes of the inferred belief functions, then by finding the **centroid** of the combined shape. The centroid is then used to determine the crisp output of the inference, in a manner identical to the process of defuzzifying the inferred output from a single fuzzy rule, a process that we described in the previous section, and illustrate in Figure 9.6 for our two example fuzzy rules.

This concludes our review of fuzzy logic. Obviously, this discussion has been rather cursory. Readers interested in learning more about the technology will find some excellent sources cited in the Suggested Readings section of this chapter. We shall now show how the combination of fuzzy logic with neural networks can produce systems that are better able to deal with uncertainty in real-world applications.

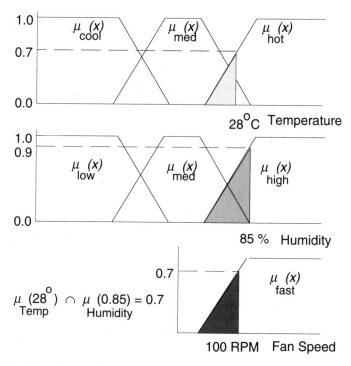

Figure 9.5   This diagram illustrates the process of combining fuzzy assertions, from crisp values. We start by determining the truth in the first assertion in the rule, which, in this case, indicates the current temperature. The belief function indicating temperature is then clipped, or cut off, at the indicated truth value. The process is repeated for the second assertion. We then take the minimum value of the truth indications, which is the application of the logic rule, and use that belief to infer the corresponding belief in the fuzzy output category. The crisp output of the inference is then obtained by determining the value of the output that corresponds to its possibility function at the designated belief value.

9.2   IMPLEMENTATION OF A FUZZY NETWORK

A *fuzzy network* is a neural-processing structure that emulates the fuzzy-logic functions described by Eqs. (9.4 through 9.6). In this section, we shall examine an implementation of a fuzzy network that was originally described by a team of researchers from the National University of Singapore [3]. As we shall show, this implementation is not a neural network in the sense that it adapts to learn the fuzzy operators. Rather, like the neocognitron networks described in Chapter 6, these fuzzy networks are constructed to perform the desired fuzzy-logic functions. However, the fuzzy-network model described in this section provides a foundation for combining the two technologies. For that reason, these networks are worthy of our study.

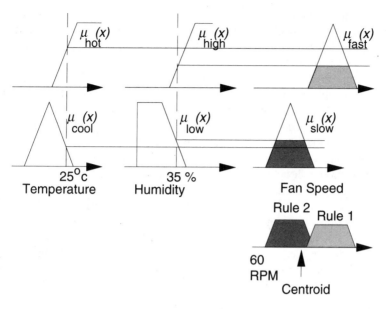

Figure 9.6   This diagram illustrates the process of performing a max-min inference over two fuzzy rules. The top graph illustrates the fuzzy inference performed by Rule 1, while the bottom graph shows the fuzzy inference produced by Rule 2. The centroid of the resulting shape, shown below the two graphs, is then used to determine the crisp output of the inference.

9.2.1   Fuzzy-Signal Interpretation

As with the conventional fuzzy-logic model, the neural implementation assumes that there are n fuzzy sets, denoted as

$$P = P_1, P_2, \ldots, P_i, \ldots, P_n \tag{9.16}$$

and that each set is a subset of the universe of discourse, which we shall refer to as **U.** Further, we shall restrict each of the fuzzy subsets such that they can only exist if, for any given element x of **U,** the corresponding membership functions are known. We shall denote these membership functions as

$$p(x) = p_1(x), p_2(x), \ldots, p_i(x), \ldots, p_n(x) \tag{9.17}$$

where the subscripts establish the association between the fuzzy sets and the membership functions.

To implement the fuzzy-membership rules in a neural-processing structure, we must begin by defining how the information flowing through the network will be interpreted. First, we shall assert that the output signal produced by each processing element in the network is analogous to the value of the appropriate membership function evaluated at a crisp input. In this manner, the input layer of processing elements will hold the values of the fuzzy inputs to the network, and the output produced by the network will be equivalent to the fuzzy combination of the inputs performed by the network.

Because fuzzy-belief functions are continuously variable values in the range from zero to one, we shall have no difficulty preparing the inputs for propagation in the neural-network structure. We shall simply allocate one unit for each truth value to be processed, and apply the fuzzy pattern $\mathbf{p}(x)$ to the input of the network. As with many of the other neural-network models we have studied in this book, we shall use the linear-activation function in each unit on the input layer. The input layer will behave as a fan-out layer, simply holding the set of truth values for propagation through the rest of the network, as in the BPN.

However, the connection weights in the network structure will be used to control the flow of information through the network, and, hence, will provide the basis for implementing the desired fuzzy-logic function. To complement the operation of the connection weights, we shall now define the processing algorithm that will be used by each noninput unit in the network to convert its input stimulation to its corresponding output.

9.2.2   Fuzzy-Signal Propagation

Each processing element in the fuzzy network, like its counterparts in the other neural networks we have studied, operates by combining input signals, then transforming the aggregate input to a corresponding output. In the fuzzy network, the algorithm employed to perform this processing is defined to mimic the evaluation of the fuzzy membership rules described earlier in this chapter.

We start with the first unit on the layer connected directly to the input layer. For each unit on the layer, we then perform the following five-step algorithm:

1. Input signals are reordered, along with their corresponding connection-weight values, such that they are arranged in order of increasing magnitude; that is,

$$\mathbf{p}'(x) = p'_1(x), p'_2(x), \ldots, p'_i(x), \ldots, p'_n(x) \qquad \textbf{(9.18)}$$

$$\mathbf{w}' = w'_1, w'_2, \ldots, w'_i, \ldots, w'_n \qquad \textbf{(9.19)}$$

where each $p'_i(x)$ refers to exactly one of the original $p_i(x)$ membership functions, under the constraint that

$$p'_1(x) \le p'_2(x) \le \ldots \le p'_n(x)$$

Similarly, each w'_i refers to the weight associated with the connection running from the ith input to the current unit.

2. Compute the difference in activation between neighboring pairs of input units, and call the resulting vector $\mathbf{q}$. This computation is defined by

$$q_i = \begin{cases} p_i'(x) & \text{if } i = 1 \\ p_i'(x) - p_{i-1}'(x) & \text{if } i > 1 \end{cases} \tag{9.20}$$

3. Combine the reordered connection weights, $\mathbf{w}'$, to create an aggregate weight for each connection, according to the equation

$$v_i = \sum_{j=i}^{n} w_i' \tag{9.21}$$

for $i = 1, 2, \ldots, n$.

4. Threshold the new connection-weight values to the unit, $\mathbf{v}$, by

$$v_i' = \begin{cases} 1 & \text{if } v_i \geq 1 \\ 0 & \text{otherwise.} \end{cases} \tag{9.22}$$

for $i = 1, 2, \ldots, n$.

5. Compute the output-membership function for the unit by

$$o = \sum_{i=1}^{n} q_i v_i' \tag{9.23}$$

When the processing has been completed on the current layer, continue propagating information through the network by using the newly-determined output values from the current layer as input to the next layer. The process is then repeated until the output layer has been completed. Once the signal-propagation process has been completed, the state of the network indicates the results of all of the fuzzy computations performed from the original inputs.

9.2.3 Fuzzy-Conjunctive Network

We shall now demonstrate the operation of the fuzzy-propagation algorithm for the three fuzzy-logic functions described in Eqs. (9.4 through 9.6). We shall begin with the operation of the fuzzy-conjunctive network, shown in Figure 9.7.

To implement a fuzzy-conjunctive network, we set the connection weights to $1/n$. As we shall now show, setting the weights in this manner has the effect of enabling only the first connection weight, which, according to our signal-propagation algorithm, will gate only the minimum membership value to the unit.

We begin by first performing the reordering of the input pattern and associated weighting values, as described in step 1 of the algorithm. The reordered patterns in this example are, therefore,

$$p'(x) = 0.4, 0.5, 0.8$$

$$w' = 0.33, 0.33, 0.33$$

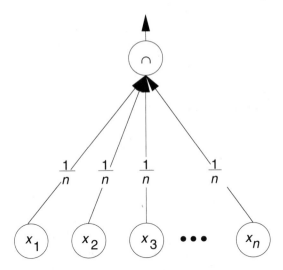

Figure 9.7   This diagram illustrates the architecture of the fuzzy-conjunctive network. The operation of the network is described in the text.

In step 2, we compute the difference in activation between neighboring units. We begin this computation with the first of the reordered activation values, and proceed toward the maximum value. Thus, for this example, the difference vector is computed as

$$\mathbf{q}(x) = 0.4, (0.5{-}0.4), (0.8{-}0.5)$$
$$= 0.4, 0.1, 0.3$$

In step 3, we combine reordered connection-weight values according to Eq. (9.21). Again beginning with the connection to the minimum-value input unit, we compute the combined connection weights by proceeding toward the unit with the maximum membership value.

$$\mathbf{v} = (0.33 + 0.33 + 0.33), (0.33 + 0.33), (0.33)$$
$$= 1.00, 0.67, 0.33$$

Next, we threshold the combined weights according to Eq. (9.22). The thresholded weight vector for this example is, therefore,

$$\mathbf{v}' = 1, 0, 0$$

Finally, we compute the output for the fuzzy-conjunctive unit according to Eq. (9.23). The result is the membership function for the conjunctive combination of the three fuzzy-input measures.

$$o = 0.4(1) + 0.1(0) + 0.2(0)$$
$$= 0.4$$

Evaluating Eq. (9.4) with original fuzzy-membership terms for this example, we find that

$$p_{1 \cap 2 \cap 3}(x) = \min(0.5, 0.4, 0.8)$$
$$= 0.4$$

which confirms the operation of the fuzzy-conjunctive network in this example. Moreover, because we have reordered the original inputs such that the minimum value always occurs first, we can see that any fuzzy network implemented with connection values set to $1/n$ will always perform a fuzzy conjunction, because the minimum value will be the only value allowed to pass.

9.2.4 Fuzzy-Disjunctive Network

The fuzzy-disjunctive network is almost identical to the configuration of the fuzzy-conjunctive network. In fact, the only difference between the two networks is the initial value of the connection weights we set in the network. To implement a fuzzy OR, we must allow the network to compute the maximum of the membership functions applied to the unit. As we shall now show, our fuzzy propagation algorithm allows the network structure to perform this computation directly.

Recall from our previous discussion of the fuzzy-propagation algorithm that each unit has, as its input, the difference vector of input-membership values. Because the original inputs to the network are reordered in increasing-magnitude sequence prior to computing the difference vector, we are, in effect, creating a sequence of values that express the algebraic difference in magnitude between the maximum value and zero.

To illustrate this idea, consider the sequence

$$X = x_1, x_2, \dots, x_n$$

where each value of x_i increases (or stays the same) as the previous value. In computing the difference between adjacent elements, we are creating a sequence of difference values between zero and one, as indicated by

$$X' = (x_1 - 0), (x_2 - x_1), (x_3 - x_2), \dots, (x_n - x_{n-1})$$

If we then algebraically sum the differences, as Eq. (9.21) requires us to do, we obtain the maximum value from the original set. This can be shown by

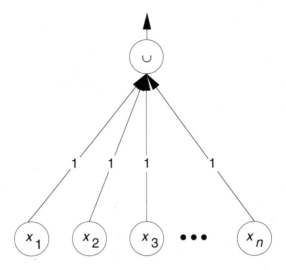

Figure 9.8 This drawing illustrates the architecture of the fuzzy-disjunctive network. The operation of this network is left to the reader as an exercise.

$$Q = \sum_{i=1}^{n} x_i'$$
$$= (x_1 - 0) + (x_2 - x_1) + (x_3 - x_2) + \ldots + (x_n - x_{n-1})$$
$$= x_n - 0$$
$$= x_n$$

Thus, to implement a fuzzy-disjunctive network using our fuzzy-propagation algorithm, all that is required is to ensure that every element of the input is included in the final computation of the membership function for the unit. In order to achieve that goal, we must guarantee that every connection weight has a value that will exceed the threshold value of one after combining weights, as required by Eq. (9.21). The only way that we can guarantee that all combined connection weights exceed the threshold value is to ensure that, initially, the weight value associated with each connection in the fuzzy-disjunctive network is set to one. Thus, the fuzzy-disjunctive network will always take the form indicated in Figure 9.8.

Exercise 9.1: Using the same input values as given for the fuzzy-conjunctive network example in the previous section, work through the fuzzy-propagation algorithm for the fuzzy-disjunctive network. Show all of your intermediate results. ■

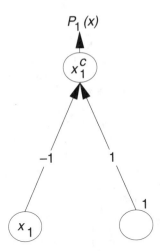

Figure 9.9 This figure illustrates the architecture of the fuzzy-complement network. Notice that the right-most input unit is analogous to the bias unit used in other network structures, in that it always has an output value of one. After performing the fuzzy propagation through this unit, the output produced is equal to the fuzzy complement of the variable input, indicated here as $p_1(x)$.

9.2.5 Fuzzy-Complement Network

The implementation of the fuzzy-complement network assumes that only one fuzzy-membership value is to be converted at any given time. To implement the fuzzy-complement in a neural network structure, we simply construct the network shown in Figure 9.9. Then, according to our fuzzy-propagation algorithm, the computation of the membership function performed by the complement unit is given by

$$o = \sum_{i=1}^{n} q_i v_i'$$
$$= (p_1(x))0 + (1 - p_1(x))1$$
$$= 1 - p_1(x)$$

which is identical to Eq. (9.6), satisfying the fuzzy-complement requirement.

Exercise 9.2: For an arbitrary input to the fuzzy-complement network, called simply $p(x)$, show that the network computes the correct value for the fuzzy complement by stepping through the fuzzy-propagation algorithm. Show all intermediate values computed. ∎

9.2.6   Fuzzy-Network Summary

In this section, we have shown how original authors construct perceptronlike networks that can perform the basic operations of fuzzy logic. In the examples we have presented, we have shown how three of the most fundamental elements of fuzzy logic are implemented in a neural-processing structure. We have also shown how the general signal-propagation algorithm developed for these networks, in conjunction with the connection weights used to construct the network, combine to give the network its behavior, an aspect very similar to traditional neural-network processing. However, these networks are not adaptive, and each must be constructed specifically for its intended application. While this is a somewhat limiting aspect of the architecture, it nevertheless provides a good starting point for understanding how neural networks can be combined with fuzzy logic to perform functions that operate on uncertainty.

Exercise 9.3:   Construct a fuzzy network to perform the following fuzzy computations:

$$o_1 = (h_1 \text{ OR } h_3) \text{ AND } h_4$$

$$o_2 = h_1 \text{ AND } (h_2 \text{ OR } h_3 \text{ OR } h_4)$$

$$h_1 = \text{NOT } p_1(x)$$

$$h_2 = p_1(x) \text{ AND } p_2(x)$$

$$h_3 = p_1(x) \text{ OR } p_2(x)$$

$$h_4 = \text{NOT } p_2(x)$$

Assume that the inputs to the network are $p_i(x)$ and that all other computed values are outputs of some noninput unit. Draw a schematic representation of your network, and show the values associated with each unit and connection in the network. ■

9.3   FUZZY NEURAL INFERENCE

In the previous section, we described a neural architecture capable of performing the basic fuzzy-logic operations. We shall now investigate another neural architecture that performs in ways that are analogous to the fuzzy-inference methods described in Section 9.1. In addition, we shall describe how the original developers of this architecture implement *self-adaptive* methods to create the network from empirical behaviorial examples, in a manner similar to the process used by a BPN as it learns to perform an application.

9.3.1   Fuzzy-Inference Network Architecture

To show how the fuzzy-inference network performs its desired application, let us digress for a moment and quickly review the fuzzy-inference process. Values are obtained for the crisp, independent variables that measure the operation of the fuzzy system. These crisp variables are then *fuzzified* by evaluating a *membership function* that computes the measure of belief in the fuzzy indicator. Once all of the inputs have been fuzzified, the inference system combines the fuzzy indicators in ways described by the fuzzy rules in the system. Each fuzzy rule then produces an output value that indicates the measure of certainty in the inferred value. For all rules that produce outputs that relate to the same measure, the *centroid* of the clipped, fuzzy-membership functions is determined and used to *defuzzify* the output. This process occurs for all outputs generated by the system.

In a paper published in 1992, two researchers at the California Institute of Technology (CalTech) described how a multilayer perceptronlike network could be created to mimic the entire process of fuzzy inference [2]. As shown in Figure 9.10, the network structure is very similar to the architecture of the BPN. The only significant difference between the two is the interconnection strategy used between layers. In the BPN, each unit is completely interconnected between layers, with each connection containing a specific weight that modulates the output signal from the transmitting unit. Conversely, the fuzzy-inference network is connected only between elements that require connections to combine elements for each rule.

An additional difference between the two networks is that the connections in the fuzzy-inference network have no weighting values associated with them.[1] Rather, these connections are implemented simply to transfer information between processing elements without altering that information, much like a conductor transfers electrical signals. As we shall now show, the bulk of the work performed by the fuzzy-inference network occurs in the processing elements.

9.3.2   Fuzzy-Inference Signal Propagation

The network accepts the crisp indicator variables as inputs. The first layer of processing elements performs the fuzzification of these indicators, by evaluating a membership function associated with each unit using the value provided as input to the unit. Specifically, the output of the ith fuzzifier unit is given by

$$o_i^f = f_i(x_i) \tag{9.24}$$

where the superscript is used to denote that the output of the unit is a fuzzified output value. Also, notice that the form of Eq. (9.24) allows each unit to use a different activation function, a fact indicated by the subscript on the function. This processing separation is necessary in order to allow each of the fuzzifying units to evaluate the crisp input according to the specific membership function associated with that unit. Moreover, as each input variable is (usually) classified in terms of different hedges (e.g., *small, medium,* and *big*), the structure of the

---

1. We could, however, cast the connections in the fuzzy-inference network as traditional neural connections with weighting values set to one.

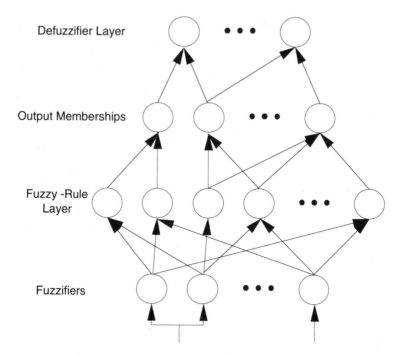

Defuzzifier Layer

Output Memberships

Fuzzy -Rule
Layer

Fuzzifiers

Figure 9.10   This diagram illustrates the architecture of the fuzzy-inference network. The operation of the network is described in the text. *Source: Adapted from* Fuzzy neural–logic system [3]. *Used with permission. Copyright ©1992 IEEE.*

network allows a single input to be fed to different fuzzifier units. Thus, the function $f_i(x_i)$ is the membership function that describes one of the hedges for the given input variable, x_i.

The outputs produced by the fuzzy-membership units are then sent to the next layer of processing elements. These units combine the fuzzy indicators conjunctively, in a manner analogous to combining fuzzy-logic indicators. That is, each unit on the fuzzy-rule layer computes, as its input stimulation, a value given by

$$\text{net}_j^r = \min\{o_i^f\}, \quad \forall i \text{ in } \mathbf{X}_j^r \tag{9.25}$$

where $\mathbf{X}_j^r$ is the connection set associated with the jth fuzzy-rule element. Each fuzzy-rule unit maintains its own connection set, to implement the partial connectivity between layers in this network. Specifically, the connection set associated with each fuzzy-rule unit contains the indices of the fuzzifier units that are connected to this unit. For example, in the network illustrated in Figure 9.10, $\mathbf{X}_2^r$ would be the connection set associated with fuzzy-rule unit 2, containing elements (1,4), while $\mathbf{X}_4^r$ would be the connection set associated with fuzzy-rule unit 4, and will contain the elements (2,3).

The fuzzy-rule units each produce an output signal, which is analogous to the belief in the inferred result. This is simply the conjunctive combination of all the input indicators, which is exactly the input stimulation computed by the unit. Thus, the activation function employed by the units on the fuzzy-rule layer in this network is the same linear-activation function that we have used extensively in other neural-network models. In mathematical terms,

$$o_j^r = \text{net}_j^r \qquad (9.26)$$

The outputs produced by the fuzzy-rule layer are fed selectively into another layer that collects the conclusions produced by all of the rule units that affect a specific output category. Because these units are selectively connected to the rule units, the input computation performed on this layer must reflect that sparse input connectivity. Furthermore, because the total belief in any one assertion can be no higher than the minimum belief in that assertion, we use the same computation that is employed by the fuzzy-rule layer to compute the input stimulation and produce the appropriate output for each of the units on this layer. Specifically,

$$\text{net}_k^c = \min\{o_j^r\}, \quad \forall j \text{ in } \mathbf{X}_k^c \qquad (9.27)$$

$$o_k^c = \text{net}_k^c \qquad (9.28)$$

where, as before, $\mathbf{X}_k^c$ refers to the connection set associated with the kth unit on the conclusion layer.

Finally, we require a layer to combine the fuzzy conclusions and produce a crisp output for each of the fuzzy conclusions, a process that is analogous to computing the geometric shape of the output membership functions and defuzzifying the result. Bart Kosko describes an appropriate method of **fuzzy centroid defuzzification** in Chapter 8 of his seminal work on fuzzy neural systems [5]. The algorithm essentially normalizes the input values and weights them with the geometric centers of the output-membership functions to calculate the crisp output. Specifically,

$$\overline{A} = \frac{\sum_{j=1}^p y_j \mu_A(y_j)}{\sum_{j=1}^p \mu_A(y_j)} \qquad (9.29)$$

where the term $\overline{A}$ is used to indicate the fuzzy centroid, the term y_j is used to indicate the center of the fuzzy-membership function, and the function $\mu_A(y_j)$ describes the membership (or belief measure) of the inferred value in the jth fuzzy subset in the universe of discourse, $Y = \{y_1, y_2, \ldots, y_p\}$. We shall demonstrate an application of Eq. (9.29) in the next section of this chapter.

9.3.3   Learning Fuzzy Rules

In their original paper, Higgins and Goodman [2] describe a method for extracting fuzzy rules from empirical data. Their method is derived from a process of generalizing specific rules obtained directly from the data using an information-theoretic measure to estimate the appropriateness of a rule with respect to a given example set. The measure used to evaluate the fit of each rule is called the **J-measure** and is defined as a function of probabilities by

$$J = p(y) \left\{ p(x|y) \log_2 \left(\frac{p(x|y)}{p(x)} \right) + p(\overline{x}|y) \log_2 \left(\frac{p(\overline{x}|y)}{p(\overline{x})} \right) \right\} \quad \textbf{(9.30)}$$

where x refers to the consequent and y refers to the antecedent in a rule of the form *if y then x*. In the case of a fuzzy system, the antecedent can be thought of as a conjunction of the input variables. Similarly, x can be cast as an output variable.

To use this measure to construct a rule set from empirical data, we begin by developing a set of specific rules, each of the form *if y then x*. The most straightforward method for doing this is to start by writing one such rule for every *exemplar* contained in the data, then generalizing the rules to eliminate redundancies. For example, if our data set is of the form

$$x_1 = y_{11}, y_{12}, y_{13}, \ldots, y_{1n}$$
$$x_2 = y_{21}, y_{22}, y_{23}, \ldots, y_{2n}$$
$$x_3 = y_{31}, y_{32}, y_{33}, \ldots, y_{3n}$$
$$\vdots \qquad\qquad\qquad \vdots$$
$$x_m = y_{m1}, y_{m2}, y_{m3}, \ldots, y_{mn}$$

we can construct m specific rules to describe these relationships. These rules would all take the general form

$$
\begin{array}{ll}
\text{IF} & \text{input}_1 = y_{j1} \\
\text{AND} & \text{input}_2 = y_{j2} \\
\vdots & \vdots \\
\text{AND} & \text{input}_n = y_{jn} \\
\text{THEN} & \text{output} = x_j
\end{array}
$$

Once all such rules have been developed, we can then apply the J-measure, as defined by Eq. (9.30), to each of the specific rules, using the relative frequencies counted in the given discrete sample set to estimate the probabilities. Further, to allow for fuzzy conditions on the variables, we use the fuzzy category with the greatest membership in each input variable. For example, if input$_i$ is more *small* than *medium* or *big*, we should then use the membership function for the *small* fuzzy set instead of y_{ji} when computing the J-measure.

After completing this process, we will have established the nominal measure of each rule. We then generalize each rule slightly, by removing a single-input variable from the antecedent in each rule. If we then repeat the process of computing J-measures using the more-general version of each rule, we obtain a new score for each rule. We can then conclude that the rule with the higher J-measure is a better form of the rule, and eliminate the less-effective form of the rule. If we ever encounter a situation where two rules have the same specific relationship, we eliminate the redundant rule and continue generalizing. This process continues until no more-general rule with a higher J-measure exists. At that point, the remaining rules define the minimal rule set needed to describe the data, and these rules can be codified to predict an output from a new set of input parameters.

9.3.4 Codifying Fuzzy Neural Rules

As we described in Section 9.2, the fuzzy-rule units in the neural-network structure encode the fuzzy rules that we have just derived. In order to implement these rules in our network structure, we must assign functions to each of the units in the network, and establish the connectivity needed to perform the desired processing. The process of constructing the fuzzy-inference network from the derived fuzzy rules, as described here, is analogous to learning in conventional neural-network paradigms.

We begin by inspecting our rules. Every unique fuzzy category used in the minimal-rule set requires an associated unit in the input-membership function layer. Likewise, there will be one fuzzy-rule unit for each rule in the minimal set. Rules that have only one fuzzy variable as input are connected directly to the appropriate input-membership unit. Rules that require conjunctions between antecedent variables are similarly connected to the corresponding membership units. Different rules that have an effect on the same output variable are connected to the same output-membership unit. There will therefore be one output-membership unit for each fuzzy-output category. Finally, all output-membership units are connected to all output-defuzzifier units, to produce the necessary crisp output values.

Once constructed, information is propagated through the network structure using the algorithm described in Section 9.2. The outputs produced by the network are interpreted as indicators of the inferences made by the fuzzy rules encoded in the network structure, thus satisfying our objectives for the network.

9.3.5 Fuzzy Neural-Inference Results

Higgins and Goodman reported using the fuzzy-inference system described in this section for two different applications, one a rather trivial function-approximation problem and the other a more complicated control application. The function-approximation experiment was conducted to demonstrate the ability of the system to learn a two-dimensional pyramid function. In Figure 9.11,

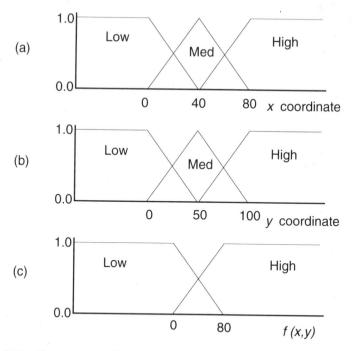

Figure 9.11   These diagrams illustrate the membership functions used to construct the function-approximation fuzzy inference network. (a) The membership function for the *x*-coordinate system. (b) The membership function for the *y*-coordinate system. (c) The membership function showing the desired response for the function $f(x, y)$. *Source: Adapted from* Fuzzy neural-logic system [3]. *Used with permission. Copyright ©1992 IEEE.*

we reproduce the membership functions used in that experiment, while in Figure 9.12 we illustrate the comparison between the optimal response of the system and the learned response.

The control application described by Higgins and Goodman was constructed to control the acceleration of a radio-controlled toy vehicle, to keep the speed of the car constant. To simplify the experiment, the car was set to run in a circle on a flat surface, with no obstacles to avoid.

Figure 9.13 illustrates the membership functions used to construct the speed controller for the radio-controlled vehicle. The data describing the application was acquired by monitoring the velocity and acceleration of the car, and the corresponding output from a conventional control system that was used to start the vehicle and maintain the speed for a short time. The rules derived from the data using the technique described in this section are shown in Table 9.1.

In Figure 9.14, we illustrate the graph of the control response for the radio-controlled speed-control application. It should be apparent from this graph that the fuzzy-inference network did an adequate job of controlling the radio-

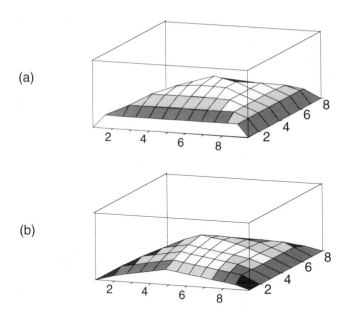

Figure 9.12 These plots illustrate (a) the desired response from the function-approximation system and (b) the actual response from the fuzzy-inference network. *Source: Adapted from* Fuzzy neural-logic system [3]. *Used with permission. Copyright ©1992 IEEE.*

controlled car, even though the speed error tended to oscillate. The original authors attribute this error to the limited training data that were used to develop the rules. Because only one training run was used to capture the training data from the conventional controller, the amount of data that described the controller's response to acceleration was less than desired. Higgins and Goodman contend that the problem could be overcome by collecting substantially more data, and repeating the exercise to more completely cover the control space.

9.4 FUZZY CONTROL OF BPN LEARNING

We have studied how neural networks can be made to emulate fuzzy-logic operations, with the goal of implementing systems that will benefit from the integration of the two technologies. In this section, we shall investigate a different approach to combining the technologies. Essentially, we shall show how a fuzzy controller can be used to dynamically alter the learning rate in a BPN during training. The benefit to this approach is that the fuzzy-logic controller can be generally applied to any BPN application, thus removing the burden of heuristically selecting the learning rate for the application from the developer.

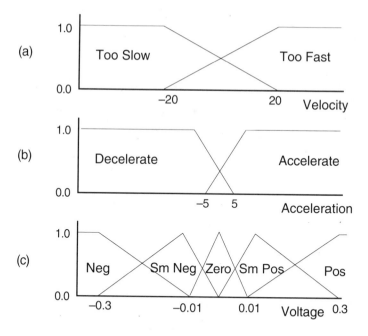

Figure 9.13   These diagrams illustrate the membership functions used to encode the fuzzy rules in the radio-controlled control application. (a) The membership function for velocity. (b) The membership function for acceleration of the car. (c) The output-membership function for the control of the motor voltage on the radio-controlled vehicle. *Source: Adapted from* Learning fuzzy rule–based neuralnetworks for function approximation [2]. *Used with permission. Copyright ©1992 IEEE.*

IF	v = too slow			THEN	out = sm pos
IF	v = too slow	AND	a = decel	THEN	out = sm pos
IF	v = too fast	AND	a = accel	THEN	out = sm neg
IF	v = too fast	AND	a = decel	THEN	out = sm neg
IF			a = accel	THEN	out = sm neg
IF			a = decel	THEN	out = sm pos

Table 9.1   The six rules derived from the empirical control data for the radio-controlled vehicle speed-control application.

As described in Chapter 2, the connection weights in the BPN are updated during training, according to the equation

$$w_{xy}(t + 1) = w_{xy}(t) + \eta \delta_x^* o_y + \alpha \Delta w_{xy}(t - 1) \qquad (9.31)$$

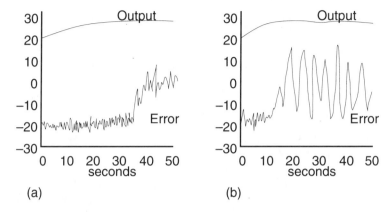

Figure 9.14 These graphs illustrate the performance of the two controllers in the radio-controlled vehicle speed-control application. (a) The response and error of the handcrafted controller used to provide the initial training data for the experiment. (b) The response and error of the fuzzy-inference network on the same application. *Source: Adapted from* Learning fuzzy rule–based neuralnetworks for function approximation [2]. *Used with permission. Copyright ©1992 IEEE.*

where η is a small, real value in the range from zero to one that controls the learning rate in the network, and α performs a similar function for controlling the *momentum* of the change.[2] Inspection of Eq. (9.31) tells us how the value of η influences the learning in the BPN: As η approaches one, the network's ability to converge to a global solution diminishes, as the network oscillates between states that minimize the error for each pattern presentation; conversely, as the value of η approaches zero, the ability of the network to converge increases at the expense of training time, as the number of training passes required to complete the learning process also increase.

Thus, selecting an *ideal* value for the learning-rate parameter is crucial for creating a successful BPN application. Unfortunately, there are no definitive guidelines for determining the proper value for η *a priori*. Bart Kosko [6] and others have suggested that the learning rate ought to vary as training proceeds. However, they offer no clear guidelines for how to select the initial value of η, or for determining the frequency of variation as training occurs.

In an attempt to address these issues, David Hertz and Qing Hu [1], of the University of Miami, developed an architecture that allows the learning rate in a BPN to be varied dynamically, controlling the instantaneous value of η used by the BPN through the use of fuzzy logic. In the remainder of this section, we shall describe the architecture of that system, and show how the original developers

---

2. Momentum, as it is described here, is an optional computation in the BPN paradigm. If used, it serves to keep weight changes on every connection moving in the same general direction from learning pass to learning pass.

evaluated the performance of the *fuzzy-controlled neural network* (FCNN). As we shall discover, this integration of technologies offers a means of minimizing the training times during a typical BPN development, without adversely affecting the ability of the network to learn the application.

9.4.1 Fuzzy-Controller Design

The fuzzy controller developed for this architecture is based on the conventional design of a fuzzy-logic system; that is, the crisp inputs are first fuzzified, inferences are then made to determine the corresponding output, and the result is defuzzified into a crisp control value. In this application, we want to control the *modulation* of η in a standard BPN model. Therefore, we can conclude that the output of the fuzzy controller will be a new value of η for the BPN. The only question left unresolved is: Should the new value of η be globally applied (used by every unit in the network), or should we use a specific value for each unit? Equation (9.31) tells us that η has a direct influence on each connection in the network. Therefore, Hertz and Hu decided to control the learning-rate parameter at each unit in the network structure.

In order to construct such a controller, we must next select input values that are somehow related to the desired output. Unfortunately, in the case of the BPN, it is difficult to say precisely which values ought to be used to determine the appropriate learning-rate value. Intuitively, the *error signal*, given by δ_x in Eq. (9.31), should provide a reasonable indicator of learning rate: A high-magnitude error signal at the unit should indicate a larger corrective action, while a unit with a low-magnitude error should require only a minor correction during each training pass.

Unfortunately, this relationship between error signals and learning rates creates a complication. As we know from our discussion of the BPN in Chapter 2, the determination of the error signal on the output layer is simply

$$\delta_k^o = (d_k^p - o_k^p) f'(\text{net}_k) \tag{9.32}$$

where d_k^p is the desired output from unit k for input pattern p, and o_k^p is the actual output from the unit. The determination of the error signal at any *nonoutput* unit is not as straightforward, however, because we have no *a priori* knowledge of the output that should have been generated by the unit. This is why we recursively backpropagate error signals in the BPN network. Unlike the error signals on the output layer, however, the backpropagated error signals tend to be rather small. For this reason, and others that we shall describe in the next section, Hertz and Hu assert that the learning rate cannot be computed on nonoutput layers in the same manner that it is determined for the output layer.

As shown in Figure 9.15, Hertz and Hu decided to use a fuzzy controller to infer the new learning rate for the output layer of the BPN, then simply use the largest value of η on the output layer as the learning-rate parameter at every

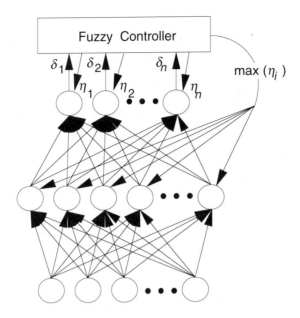

Figure 9.15 This diagram shows the architecture of the FCNN developed to adaptively modulate the learning rate in a BPN structure. Notice that the fuzzy controller is only applied to the output layer in the network. For reasons described in the text, the largest value of η computed by the controller is passed down to every nonoutput unit.

nonoutput unit. The next step in the implementation of this system is the development of the fuzzy rules, which we shall now discuss.

9.4.2 Fuzzy-Rule Development

Hertz and Hu developed seven fuzzy rules to control the determination of the learning rate for a unit, given the error signal at that unit. These rules are illustrated in Table 9.2, and are interpreted as follows:

$$\text{IF } error \text{ is } X \text{ THEN set } \eta_k \text{ To } Y$$

where X is one of the fuzzy subsets in the universe of discourse, denoted as *negative large* (NL), *negative medium* (NM), *negative small* (NS), *zero* (ZE), *positive small* (PS), *positive medium* (PM), and *positive large* (PL). Similarly, Y is one of the fuzzy-output sets, denoted by *zero* (ZE), *small* (S), *medium* (M), and *big* (B).

As shown in Figure 9.16, triangular membership functions for both the input and output fuzzy subsets were selected by Hertz and Hu. The triangular shape was

X	NL	NM	NS	ZE	PS	PM	PL
Y	B	M	S	ZE	S	M	B

Table 9.2   The fuzzy-rule set for controlling the learning-rate parameter in a BPN

selected to simplify the computation of the fuzzy-membership function, given for each subset[3] by

$$
m_A(x) = \begin{cases} 1 & \text{if } x = x_A^c \\ \frac{x_A^+ - x}{(x_A^+ - x_A^c)} & \text{if } x_A^c < x \le x_A^+ \\ \frac{x - x_A^-}{(x_A^c - x_A^-)} & \text{if } x_A^- \le x < x_A^c \\ 0 & \text{otherwise} \end{cases} \tag{9.33}
$$

where the term x_A^- is used to denote the lower bound of the variable x in fuzzy set A, x_A^+ indicates the upper bound of x in A, and x_A^c denotes the center of the membership function, which is determined by

$$
x_A^c = \frac{x_A^+ - x_A^-}{2} + x_A^- \tag{9.34}
$$

9.4.3   An FCNN Example

Using the fuzzy rules and membership functions indicated above, we shall now describe an example to illustrate the operation of the fuzzy controller. For this example, we shall assume that the network we are training has three output units, and that, for the current exemplar, the error values computed at the output of the network are 0.27, 0.53, and −0.47, respectively.

We begin by computing the fuzzy membership of the error terms in the input universe of discourse. The error term δ_1 is a member of the two fuzzy input sets PS and PM. The membership value of δ_1 in each of these two fuzzy sets is computed as

$$
m_{PS}(\delta_1) = \frac{0.35 - 0.27}{(0.35 - 0.20)}
$$

$$
= 0.533
$$

$$
m_{PM}(\delta_1) = \frac{0.27 - 0.25}{(0.40 - 0.25)}
$$

$$
= 0.133.
$$

---

3. Note that Eqs. (9.33 and 9.34) apply only to triangular membership functions, such as those described here.

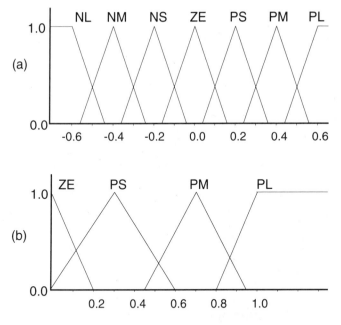

Figure 9.16 These diagrams illustrate the membership functions selected for the fcnn application. (a) The membership functions for the error signal input. (b) The membership functions of the output learning-rate parameter. *Source: Adapted from* Fuzzy controller for backpropagation networks [1]. *Used with permission. Copyright ©1992 Society for Computer Simulation International.*

Similarly, the δ_2 error value produces membership values in PM and PL of $(0.133, 0.533)$, and δ_3 produces membership values NL and NM of $(0.867, 0.467)$.

We then apply Kosko's centroid defuzzification function, defined in Eq. (9.29), to determine the crisp values of the learning rate for the output units in this network. For the first unit, the output value is computed as

$$\bar{r} = \frac{\sum_{j=1}^{n} x_j^c x_j A_j}{\sum_{j=1}^{n} x_j A_j}$$

$$= \frac{(0.3)(0.533)A_1 + (0.7)(0.133)A_2}{(0.533 A_1 + 0.133 A_2)}$$

$$\equiv \frac{0.160 + 0.093}{(0.533 + 0.133)}$$

$$= 0.379$$

where we have simplified the computation by allowing the area of each membership function, indicated by A_j, to be approximated as one. This approximation abides by the model developed by Hertz and Hu, which they assert is adequate for the system, because the learning rate does not have to be very precise.

Similarly, the crisp learning-rate values for output units 2 and 3 are computed as above, producing values of 0.939 and 0.897, respectively. Relating these values back to the original error terms, we see that the fuzzy controller has produced fairly large values for η_k for those units where the error was large, and smaller learning-rate values for those units where the error was fairly small, just as we had planned.

For the hidden layer of units, the learning-rate value we will send down will be the maximum value of η_k from the output layer, in this case 0.939. Note that all of these values are recomputed every time a new exemplar is presented to the network for training, thus allowing the individual units to adaptively control the learning rate needed to encode each pattern.

9.4.4   FCNN Results and Conclusions

The graphs shown in Figure 9.17 illustrate a performance comparison between the FCNN and a standard BPN (without momentum) in learning two associative-memory applications: An autoassociative memory where the BPN is asked to map a pixel character map to itself, and a heteroassociative memory where the BPN is asked to learn the mapping from a pixel character map to the ASCII code associated with the character image. As you can see from these graphs, the results reported by Hertz and Hu indicate that the FCNN learns the training set to the same degree of accuracy as the standard BPN in 36% fewer training epochs, on average.

Another important result of this study was that the FCNN structure is extensible to any application suited to a BPN. Because the initial learning-rate parameters are randomly assigned, instead of predefined, and then controllably modified after every pattern presentation, Hertz and Hu assert that there is no longer any need to "play" with the learning-rate values to get the network to converge. Thus, a working FCNN application can be constructed in much less time than its BPN counterpart.

The integration of fuzzy logic and neural-network technology bodes well for the future, as there are many other fuzzy opportunities for controlling the state of a network. Such opportunities include intelligently *pruning* neurons in a network structure, selectively eliminating certain connections in a network, and even deciding how to determine the proper learning rate at a nonoutput unit. Many of these problems have eluded solution by other means, or have been only partially solved. If other network architectures can be developed along the lines of the FCNN to address these issues, the integration of neural networks and fuzzy logic holds a great deal of promise for future applications.

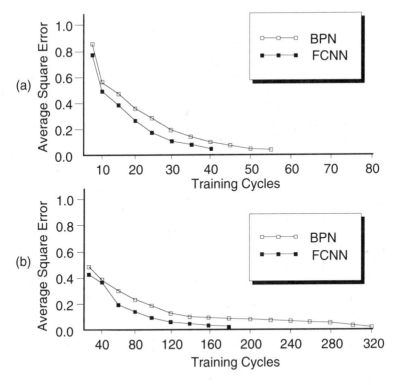

Figure 9.17   The graphs illustrating the performance of the FCNN are shown. (a) This graph compares the operation of the BPN and FCNN on the autoassociative character-to-character image-mapping application. (b) This graph compares the two networks in the heteroassociative-memory character-to-ASCII application. *Source: Adapted from* Fuzzy controller for backpropagation networks [1]. *Used with permission. Copyright ©1992 Society for Computer Simulation International.*

9.5   FUZZY NEURAL-SYSTEM SUMMARY

In this chapter, we have seen how fuzzy logic and neural networks have been combined to form systems that provide a more robust environment for developing real-world applications. The combination of these two technologies is such an exciting area of research that the IEEE has combined its annual conferences on neural networks and fuzzy logic into a single gathering, attracting more participants at this one event than both conferences were able to attract independently. At this writing, there are so many practical applications of the two technologies, and of their integration, that we could have filled another book. Unfortunately, space constraints simply do not allow us to elaborate on these applications. We hope, however, that the (gentle) introduction to neural-network and fuzzy-logic integration we have just completed provides the reader with the incentive to explore the synthesis of these two technologies independently.

SUGGESTED READINGS

Currently, the most complete treatment of neural networks and fuzzy logic is Bart Kosko's seminal work, *Neural Networks and Fuzzy Systems: A Dynamical Systems Approach to Machine Intelligence* [5]. It was written by an engineer, for engineers, and thus provides a fairly rigorous exploration of the two technologies. For a more in-depth analysis of fuzzy logic as it applies to information processing and situation assessment, the most comprehensive work I reviewed prior to writing this chapter was *Fuzzy Sets, Uncertainty, and Information* [4]. Of course, readers interested in obtaining a detailed understanding of the foundations of fuzzy logic are referred to Lofti Zadeh's seminal work, titled simply "Fuzzy Sets," which originally appeared in the journal *Information and Control* [10].

As we indicated earlier in this text, the combination of fuzzy logic and neural networks has only recently achieved a great deal of attention. In this regard, there has been a flurry of excellent technical papers published recently that describe the practical applications of the two technologies. Readers interested in the more practical aspects of the combined technologies will find the papers published in the *Proceedings of the IEEE Fuzzy Logic and Neural Network* conferences the most enlightening. Another good source of practical-application papers can be found in *Neural Information Processing Systems: Natural and Synthetic*, published annually by Morgan-Kaufmann as the edited proceedings of the conference and workshop of the same name.

BIBLIOGRAPHY

1. David B. Hertz and Qing Hu. Fuzzy-neuro controller for backpropagation networks. In *Proceedings of the Simulation Technology and Workshop on Neural Networks Conference,* Houston, TX, pp. 570–574, 1992.

2. C. M. Higgins and R. M. Goodman. Learning fuzzy rule-based neural networks for function approximation. In *Proceedings of the International Joint Conference on Neural Networks,* Baltimore, MD, pp. I(251–256), 1992.

3. L. S. Hsu, H. H. Teh, P. Z. Wang, S. C. Chan, and K. F. Loe. Fuzzy neural-logic system. In *Proceedings of the International Joint Conference on Neural Networks,* Baltimore, MD, pp. I(245–250), 1992.

4. G. J. Klir and T. A. Folger. *Fuzzy Sets, Uncertainty, and Information.* Prentice-Hall, Englewood Cliffs, NJ, 1988.

5. Bart Kosko. *Neural Networks and Fuzzy Systems: A Dynamical Systems Approach to Machine Intelligence.* Prentice-Hall, Englewood Cliffs, NJ, 1992.

6. Bart Kosko and S. Kong. Adaptive Fuzzy Systems for Backing Up a Truck-and-Trailer, in *IEEE Transactions on Neural Networks,* Vol. 3, No. 2, pages 211–223, 1992.

7. N. Rescher. *Many-Valued Logic.* McGraw-Hill, New York, 1969.

8. Steven L. Tanimoto. *The Elements of Artificial Intelligence.* Computer Science Press, Rockville, MD, 1987.

9. Patrick Henry Winston. *Artificial Intelligence,* Third Edition, Addison-Wesley, Reading, MA, 1992.

10. Lofti A. Zadeh. Fuzzy Sets. *Information and Control,* Vol. 8, pp. 335–353, 1965.

ANSWERS TO SELECTED EXERCISES

Chapter 2

2.1 Linear units (on the output layer) tend to train more rapidly than sigmoidal, because the derivative of the linear function does not minimize the amount of change in a saturated unit.

2.2 Sigmoidal units (or at least non-linear units) are needed on the hidden layer of a BPN to allow the network to linearly-separate pattern vectors that are linear combinations of each other.

2.3 As described above, linear units on the hidden layer of a BPN would learn all linear combinations of input pattern vectors. In many applications, exemplars have inputs patterns that, while they are linear combinations of each other, produce distinctly different outputs. To allow for this separation of patterns, a non-linearity (e.g., the sigmoidal logistic function) must be introduced.

2.4 For the parity application, input patterns must be separated into two classes (even and odd parity) based on the number of "ones" contained in the pattern. Thus, input patterns that differ by only a single bit will fall into different categories. The CPN matches input patterns by comparing the input vector to all the weight vectors stored in the connections to the instar layer *in direction only.* Therefore, in order to correctly match an arbitrary input pattern correctly, an instar must be allocated to detect every possible input pattern. If not, it would be possible to misclassify an input, simply because the winning instar was "closest" to the input in Euclidean space. This behavior makes the CPN inappropriate for the parity application.

2.5 The BPN retains no specific *memory* of input patterns. Rather, it encodes the characteristics of a given input which lead to the successful generation of the desired output. After a BPN has learned an exemplar set, training it with new exemplars without reinforcing the previously learned exemplars will cause it to adjust itself to produce only the new exemplars, thus "forgetting" the earlier exemplar set.

Chapter 3

3.1 Let the attributes of the input pattern (x) be: sofa, coffee table, floor lamp, oven, refridgerator (freezer), table, bed, dresser, shelves, desk, book case, work table, and tools. Let the rooms that we want to classify (**y**) be: living room, kitchen, bed room, den, and garage. Using the attribute sequence defined above, one possible encoding for the exemplars for this application is:

$$\mathbf{x}_1 = 1110000000000, \qquad \mathbf{y}_1 = 10000$$

$$\mathbf{x}_2 = 0001110000000, \qquad \mathbf{y}_2 = 01000$$

$$\mathbf{x}_3 = 0000001101000, \qquad \mathbf{y}_3 = 00100$$

$$\mathbf{x}_4 = 0000000000100, \qquad \mathbf{y}_4 = 00010$$

$$\mathbf{x}_5 = 0000000010011, \qquad \mathbf{y}_5 = 00001$$

3.2 Using the same attribute list as above, but allowing for overlap, one possible encoding for the exemplars for this application is:

$$\mathbf{x}_1 = 1110000010000, \qquad \mathbf{y}_1 = 10000$$

$$\mathbf{x}_2 = 0001110000000, \qquad \mathbf{y}_2 = 01000$$

$$\mathbf{x}_3 = 0010001111000, \qquad \mathbf{y}_3 = 00100$$

$$\mathbf{x}_4 = 1010000011110, \qquad \mathbf{y}_4 = 00010$$

$$\mathbf{x}_5 = 0000100010011, \qquad \mathbf{y}_5 = 00001$$

3.3 To scale any component of $\mathbf{x}$ properly, we first squash the given value to the range between 0 and 1 by subtracting the bias from the value, and dividing by the range of values. We then scale the result back to the range between L and U, and add in the new bias value. Mathematically, this process is described by the equation

$$x_i' = \left(\frac{x_i - \min\,(\mathbf{x})}{\max\,(\mathbf{x}) - \min\,(\mathbf{x})} \right) \times (U - L) + L$$

3.4 An ART network could be used, if altered to allow it to generate an output that differs from the memory of the matched input pattern. For an example of this modification, see the tic-tac-toe application described in Section 4.3.

3.5 Solution left to the reader.

3.6 Solution left to the reader.

3.7 The network contains 8,862 connections (207 inputs connected to 42 hidden units, plus 42 hidden units connected to 4 outputs). Each connection requires 2 computations for the feed-forward propagation, and 6 computations for the backward propagation. The 42 units on the hidden layer are all sigmoidal, so each requires 10 computations to determine its output during the forward propagation. We have 8,759 exemplars that must be presented to the network during each epoch, and training requires 100 epochs. The amount of time needed to perform one training cycle on our 1 MFLOP machine is therefore:

$$t_{sec} = \frac{\Big((8862(2) + 8862(6) + 42(10))8759\Big)100}{1,000,000}$$

$$= 62,465 \text{ seconds}$$

$$= 17 \text{ hours, } 21 \text{ minutes}$$

To complete the *hold-one-out* test, we must repeat this process 8,760 times, requiring 17.35 years, with no time off for holidays, weekends, or good behavior.

3.8 Solution left to the reader.

Chapter 4

4.1 The output layer will consist of seven sigmoidal units. The encoding will be one unit for each bit in the ASCII code. For example, the ASCII code for the letter "A" is 41_{16}. The target output pattern for the character "A" input would then be 1000001.

4.2 The CPN would be a good choice for this application, since the output patterns are *accreted*. In this case, each time the given input pattern is presented, the same competitive unit would win the competition. As training progresses, the output vector associated with the winning unit would become the combination of all of the outputs associated with the given input.

4.3 Solution left to the reader.

4.4 The following solution assumes that the second place unit in the competition is the unit associated with the 150° image. It could just as easily be the unit associated with the 90° image.

$$s = 0.5\sin(120°) + 0.5\sin(150°)$$
$$= 0.433 + 0.25$$
$$= 0.683$$
$$c = 0.5\cos(120°) + 0.5\cos(150°)$$
$$= -0.683$$

4.4 Adjust the activation function for the competitive layer such that when a unit wins the competition with an activation of 1.0 (an exact match), only one unit produces an output. If the activation of the winning unit is less than 1.0, use the top two units to interpolate the output as before.

Chapter 5

5.1 The only requirement would be that the candidate indicator must have some (perhaps implicit) relationship to the desired output, in this case, the S&P 500. If, for example, you felt that the skiing conditions at Vale, Colorado indicated whether business people were doing their jobs or were on the slopes relaxing, you might include this indicator in your pattern set since it might indicate the strength of the market. Be warned, however, that the network has no innate understanding of the value of the indicators that you provide, and will therefore attempt to find a correlation between the indicator and the desired output, even if it does not exist.

5.2 Retrain the network periodically with fresh data. You can either combine the new patterns with the old and completely retrain the network, or you could retrain just on the new data. If you choose the latter approach, be certain that the data set is complete enough to provide adequate coverage of the domain, and retrain the network from scratch.

5.3 Solution left to the reader.

Chapter 6

6.1 Solution left to the reader. See Exercise 3.7 as an example.

6.2 Solution left to the reader. See Exercise 2.4 as an example.

Chapter 7

7.1 The compression network was mapping 256 gray-shaded pixels to themselves. Thus, both the input and output patterns were comprised of components that could take on one of 256 different values, a task better suited to linear units than to sigmoidal units.

Chapter 8

8.1

$$F(s) = \frac{s}{s^2 + \omega^2}$$

8.2 The poles and zeros are determined by finding the roots of the equations

$$10^{-5}s^2 + 0.03s + 20 = 0$$
$$10^{-5}s + 0.03 = 0$$

Thus, the pole is at -1000, and the zero is at -3000.

Chapter 9

9.1 For the fuzzy disjunctive network, the weights must all be set to one. After reordering, the input and weights are:

$$p'(x) = 0.4, 0.5, 0.8$$
$$w' = 1.0, 1.0, 1.0$$

We then compute the difference in activation between neighboring units as

$$\mathbf{q}(x) = 0.4, 0.1, 0.3$$

Next, we combine reordered connection weight values.

$$\mathbf{v} = 3, 2, 1$$

After thresholding, $\mathbf{v}'$ becomes

$$\mathbf{v}' = 1, 1, 1$$

Finally, the output membership for the fuzzy disjunctive network is computed as

$$\mathbf{o} = 0.4(1) + 0.1(1) + 0.3(1)$$
$$= 0.8$$

9.2 Solution left to the reader. See Exercise 9.1 as an example.

9.3 Solution left to the reader.

I N D E X

RELATED TITLES FROM ADDISON-WESLEY

Neural Networks
Algorithms, Applications, and Programming Techniques
James A. Freeman and David M. Skapura

Providing useful background for *Building Neural Networks,* this introductory book explains in greater detail the basic concepts and technology underlying common neural network models. Each chapter surveys a successful architecture—Adaline and Madaline, backpropagation, associative memory, simulated annealing, the counterpropagation network, self-organizing maps, adaptive resonance theory, spatiotemporal pattern classification, and the neocognitron. For each architecture, the authors discuss relevant algorithms, applications, and programming techniques. ISBN 0-201-51376-5

Simulating Neural Networks with *Mathematica*
James A. Freeman

This book introduces neural networks, their operation and their application, in the context of *Mathematica,* a mathematical programming language. Readers will learn how to simulate neural network operations using *Mathematica,* and will see how *Mathematica* can be employed to assess neural network behavior and performance. ISBN 0-201-56629-X

On to C   **On to C++**
Patrick Henry Winston   Patrick Henry Winston

A best-selling author has written two books of interest if you already know how to program and want quickly to add C or C++ to your programming-language repertoire. Designed to be brief—about 300 pp each—the books nevertheless contain everything you need to know to get up and running in one or both of these languages. ISBN 0-201-58042-X; ISBN 0-201-58043-8

BUGS in Writing
Lyn Dupré

If you are a scientist, engineer, or other person who writes and who works with computers, Dupré's *BUGS in Writing* will show you how to rid your prose of the most common problems that writers face. With simple principles for lucid writing conveyed by numerous, intriguing, and frequently hilarious examples, *BUGS* may also be the first book on English grammar that you will read for sheer fun. Whether you have a paper, proposal, research study, thesis, software manual, conference talk, business report, or any other document to prepare, if you want to communicate your ideas effectively, first browse through a copy of *BUGS.* ISBN 0-201-60019-6

Up-to-date information about Addison-Wesley books is available from our Internet site, World Wide Web address http://www.aw.com. For Gopher access, type gopher aw.com. You will find these books wherever technical books are sold, or you may call Addison-Wesley at **1-800-822-6339.**